Montreal & Quebec City

4th Edition

COLOURGUIDE

Edited by Susan Hargrove

Formac Publishing Company Limited

Halifax

Contents

Library and Archives Canada Cataloguing in Publication

Montreal & Quebec City colourguide / editor, Susan Hargrove. — 4th ed.

Includes index.
ISBN 10: 0-88780-758-5
ISBN 13: 978-0-88780-758-9

1. Montreal (Quebec)—Guidebooks. 2. Quebec (Quebec)—Guidebooks. I. Hargrove, Susan II. Title: Montreal and Quebec City colourguide.

FC2947.18.M6535 2008   917.14'28045
C2007-907504-5

Formac Publishing Company Limited
5502 Atlantic Street, Halifax, Nova Scotia
B3H 1G4 • www.formac.ca

Distributed in the United States by:
Casemate
2114 Darby Road, 2nd Floor,
Havertown, PA 19083

Distributed in the United Kingdom by:
Portfolio Book Limited
Unit 5, Perivale Industrial Park
Horsenden Lane South, Greenford, UK
UB6 7RL

Printed and bound in China

Formac Publishing Company Limited acknowledges the support of the Cultural Affairs Section, Nova Scotia Department of Tourism and Culture. We acknowledge the financial support of the Government of Canada through the Book Publishing Industry Development Program (BPIDP) for our publishing activities.

Montreal Region

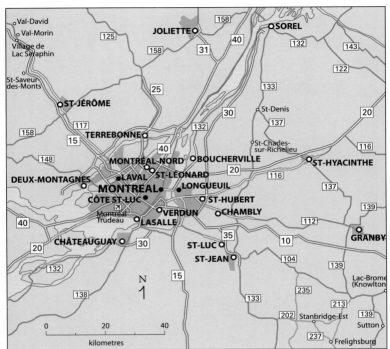

Quebec City Region

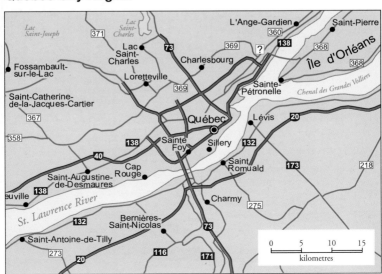

Quebec City Hotels

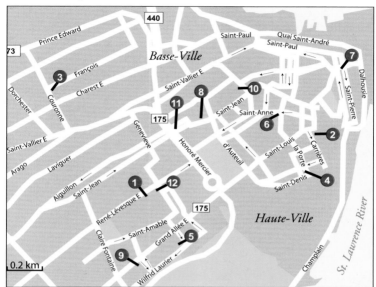

1 Delta Québec
2 Fairmont Château Frontenac
3 Holiday Inn Select Québec City-Downtown
4 Hôtel Château Bellevue
5 Hôtel Château Laurier
6 Hôtel Clarendon

7 Hôtel Dominion 1912
8 Hôtel du Capitole
9 Hôtel Loews Le Concorde
10 Hôtel Manoir Victoria
11 Hôtel Palace Royale
12 Québec Hilton

Locator Map

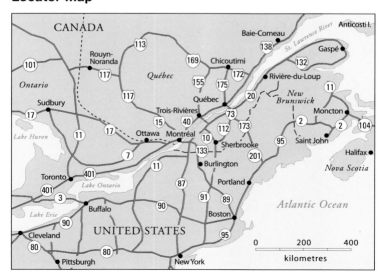

Neighborhoods of Montreal

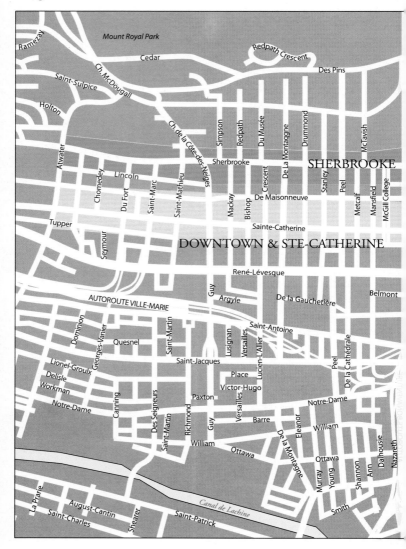

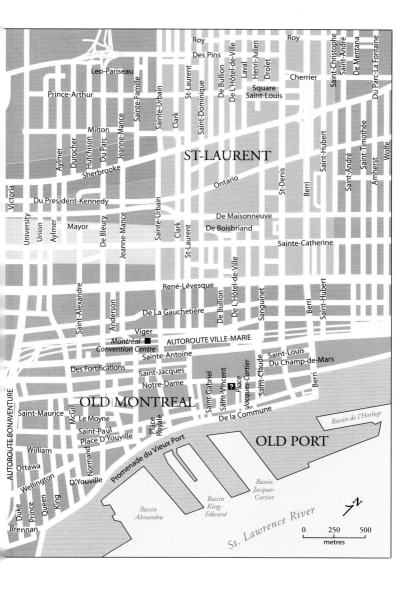

Montreal Hotels

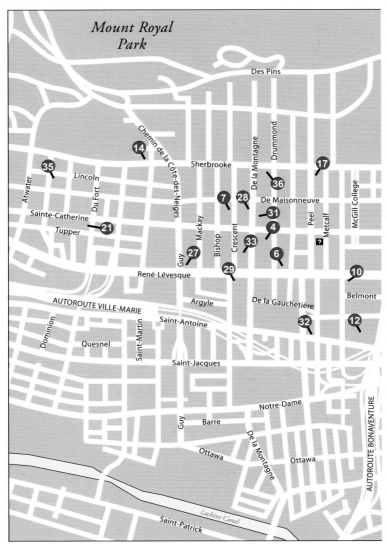

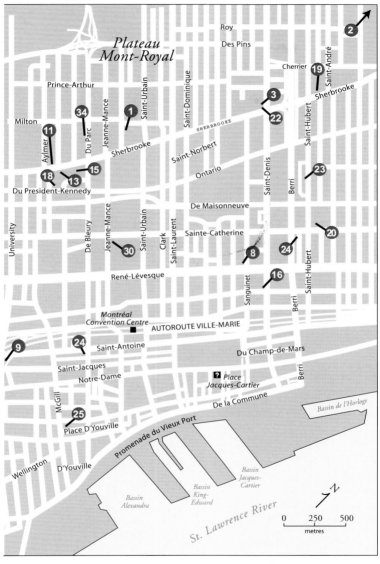

Welcome to Montreal and Quebec City!

From cobblestone streets to neon-lit strips, there are endless possibilities to explore in the province of Quebec's two largest cities. This guide has been written to help you get the most out of your stay in and around Montreal and the provincial capital, Quebec City.

The introductory chapter provides an overview of each city as well as a historical introduction to the province of Quebec. The maps in the preliminary section of the book provide a general view of each city and its major road arteries, while more detailed downtown and specific area maps give key locations such as hotels. In addition, a neighbourhoods map for Montreal shows the districts covered by separate chapters later in the book. When using the maps take note, both cities have an east-west axis. A streetname with O. indicates 'ouest'—French for west.

The guide is divided into two major sections: Montreal and Quebec City, which cover the best each city has to offer and its distinct areas.

The final section of the guide contains select listings with practical information on everything you'll

want to do or find in either Montreal or Quebec City: accommodations, dining, night life, museums and galleries, attractions, festivals and events, shopping and galleries—along with special travel services and tips.

This book is an independent guide. Its editor and its contributors have made their recommendations and suggestions based solely on what they believe to be the best, most interesting and most appealing sites and attractions. No payments or contributions of any kind are solicited or accepted by the creators or the publishers of this guide.

In a city as lively as Montreal—and even in a solid bastion of francophone culture such as Quebec City—things change quickly. The safest thing to do with information you're relying on in this book is to confirm it with a brief phone call. If your experience doesn't match what you read here—or if you think we've missed one of either city's best features—please let us know. Write us at the address on the Contents page (page 3).

Original Contributors:

JAMES BASSIL is a Montreal-based writer and editor.

PHIL CARPENTER is a freelance photojournalist working out of Montreal. His photos have appeared in the National Post and the Montreal Gazette.

SOVITA CHANDER is a historical researcher and freelance writer. Her Quebec City home affords her much grist for both avocations.

BRAM EISENTHAL is an award-winning travel writer and a film unit publicist with more than 60 credits on movies and TV series. He lives in the Montreal suburb of Côte St-Luc.

SEAN FARRELL is a Montreal journalist specializing in sports and travel.

PIERRE HOME-DOUGLAS is a Montreal writer and editor who contributes travel stories and opinion pieces to newspapers and magazines.

THÉODORE LAGLOIRE is a professional photographer working out of Quebec City.

JIM McRAE is a partner in a Montreal communications firm who freelances as a journalist and book editor to local newspapers and trade magazines.

ANASTASIA MICHAILIDIS is a television journalist who grew up in Montreal's Greek community.

SARAH MORGAN is a Montreal-born television producer and writer.

SARAH LOUISE MUSGRAVE is a Montreal food critic and writes a weekly restaurant column for the *Gazette* as well as contributing regularly to other publications.

LORRAINE O'DONNELL is a Quebec City based historian with a long-standing interest in shopping. Her doctoral dissertation, currently underway, looks at the history of women at the Eaton's department store.

MARY ANN SIMPKINS is a travel writer who contributed to the Ottawa Colourguide. After living in Quebec City for six years, she's now back to enjoying life in Ottawa.

Formerly Canada's most sought-after late-morning to mid-afternoon life consultant, PAUL J. SPENCE now concentrates his efforts exclusively on nightlife. He lives in Montreal.

When not teaching children with intellectual disabilities, SARAH WATERS explores the nooks and

crannies of her home city.

PAUL WATERS works as a travel journalist for the city's English daily, the *Montreal Gazette*.

MATTHEW WOODLEY is the Arts Editor at the *Montreal Mirror*, the city's premier English cultural weekly.

Contributing Writers to the Fourth edition:

Student and researcher, JEN BARBATO fills her spare time making decadent desserts and studying for a career in Nutritional Science.

SUSAN HARGROVE, is a professional Montreal writer, editor and publisher with over 25 year's experience. Her English degrees are from Concordia University and she continues to study for sheer pleasure.

LYNN MELANSON is a Montreal writer and an experienced technical communicator.

KRISTINA MÅNSSON is a partner in Simply4 Communication + Design, and both an experienced writer and editor but saves most of her love for visual design.

CATHY TSOLAKOS is a Montreal writer and marketing manager. She is also an avid and keen shopper.

KARNJIT LEHAL is a partner in Simply4 Communication + Design and has a background both in writing, editing, marketing and enjoying all that Montreal has to offer.

MONIQUE POLAK teaches English literature at Marianopolis College in Montreal. In her spare time, she cultivates a widely varied career as a freelance journalist and dines out as often as possible.

LINDA GYUAI is an experienced journalist of repute and now the Civics Affairs Reporter for the *Montreal Gazette*, Montreal's leading English daily.

PATRICK DONOVAN is a heritage conservationist, history lecturer, writer, world-traveller and musician. He recently moved back to his native Quebec City.

TOM WELHAM is a college and university English lecturer, world-traveller and outdoor enthusiast. He moved to Quebec City from England in 1997, searching for broader horizons.

Introducing Montreal and Quebec City

Christ Church Cathedral

Rue St-Denis

Steeped in nearly 400 years of history, Quebec City and Montreal are Canada's two most storied cities. These two urban sisters—capital and metropolis—grew up 200 kilometres apart on the banks of the mighty St. Lawrence River. The hefty river sustained them, aiding the flow of commerce, the spread of religious ideals and offering substantial defensive advantages. Together, Quebec City and Montreal formed the heart of New France, an enormous empire that once extended

Quebec City

from Hudson's Bay in the north to Louisiana, U.S.A. in the south.

In the 16th century, these territories were part of an early democracy: the Five Nations, a longstanding union of native tribes that expanded to become the Six Nations in the 18th century. When Jacques Cartier first arrived at what is now Quebec City in 1535, then called Stadacona, he hoped to find a passage to Asia. He pressed on and soon reached the village of Hochelaga on what is now the island of Montreal, but rapids stopped him from going farther and many of his men died over the winter. The kingdom of France was soon drawn into its wars of religion, putting an end to North American exploration for nearly seven decades.

Petit Champlain

The name Quebec comes from an Algonquin word meaning "where the river narrows," and this narrowing caught the attention of Samuel de Champlain when he sailed upriver in 1608. The site could be defended against Dutch and English rivals with just a few cannons. At the foot of the great cliff that is now crowned by the towers and turrets of the Château Frontenac Hotel, the city was born. Champlain never managed to attract quite as many settlers as he'd dreamed of; French farmers had found reasonable prosperity back home. But fur traders and merchants gravitated to the new city, and it became quite wealthy—wealthy enough that the English wouldn't forget about it. And wealthy enough for merchants to build fine stone homes and churches on the banks of the St. Lawrence.

Eventually, Quebec City's governors, military and clergy abandoned the cramped quarters along the river

Place d'Armes in Quebec City

in Basse Ville for the lofty heights atop Cap Diamant, considering them easier to defend. The elevation didn't offer any advantage, however, when General James Wolfe's army surprised the French in 1759 by scaling the cliffs and taking the city.

Montreal's beginnings were also stimulated by the flow of commerce, but religion steered the new community even more than it had Quebec City. In 1639, Jerome LeRoyer had visions of a religious settlement on the Island of Montreal. He recruited Paul de Chomedey, Sieur de Maisonneuve, who landed on the island in May 1642 with a dream of converting the natives and creating a new Catholic society in the wilderness. Chomedey planted a cross at the summit of Mont Royal, a symbol of his faith that endures (albeit not in its original incarnation) to this day.

Chomedey's missionary ambitions didn't amount to much, however. Commercial incentives soon eclipsed spiritual intentions. Even the name of the settlement—Ville-Marie, in honour of Christ's mother—survives only as the name of an expressway and a skyscraper.

The French regime ended in 1763 with the Seven Years' War, and the Treaty of Paris transferred New France to Britain. English, Irish and Scottish settlers, hungry for commercial conquest, spilled into the new territories, and both cities thrived. In 1775, American troops attempted, and failed, to capture Quebec City, testament to its growing strength. But Montreal was the main beneficiary of the region's new-found wealth. By the 1830s, its population had surpassed Quebec City's. By the mid-19th century, millionaire barons with Scottish names, Protestant values and grand mansions on the slopes of Mont Royal controlled 70 percent of the wealth in Canada.

Layer upon layer of history has settled over these two cities to create a culture that is anything but dull.

Sun Life Building

Commerce and conquest, linguistic and cultural

tensions, religious fervour and conflict, prosperity and poverty, have created two cities that manage to retain their individual character despite the ever-encroaching influences of North American melting-pot and globalization. Both cities are rich in culture and entertainment. On any given evening, crowds gather in a host of galleries and performance venues—spaces often as creative as the works they house—to toast the art scene's latest debuts and seasoned greats. And there is much to celebrate. The two cities boast a world-renowned theatre scene, with Quebec City's Robert Lepage winning the Europe Theatre Prize of 2007. Montreal's symphony orchestra is one of the best on the continent. The circus arts, rooted in the busking scenes of both cities, have undergone a renaissance in recent years, and the arrival of La Tohu, a "circus city" complex that houses training and performance spaces for Cirque du Soleil and the National Circus School, cements Montreal's title as capital of the circus arts. Equally exciting are the choreographic leaps of Montreal's renowned dance companies, namely Les Ballets Jazz de Montréal, Les Grands Ballets Canadiens and La La La Human Steps.

Montreal at Night

Both Montreal and Quebec City have superb restaurants, lively nightclubs and endlessly enticing shops. French Canada, because of its long linguistic separation, has developed its own vast pop culture (movies, rock stars, soap operas, folk singers) that is virtually unknown outside of Quebec, spawning exceptions such as Céline Dion.

Montreal is the metropolis—a jumble of cultures where seldom a day goes by without a reason to celebrate something. From the days of Prohibition, when the city was a mecca for sin-seeking Americans, to Expo 67, when the whole world came to town, Montreal's reputation for good times is long established and still growing. These days, the gay village is one of the largest in North America, and the city hosts some of the hottest circuit parties around. In the summer, rarely a week goes by without a street or two being closed off to cars for one or another of the

Night skyline, Montreal

city's many festivals, and crowds battle heat waves at the Sunday "Tam-Tams" (spontaneous gatherings of drummers) at the foot of the Sir George-Etienne Cartier monument on Mont Royal. In the winter, not even an ice storm will stop locals from heading out for a pint of microbrew.

The two cities are very different. It's possible to live in Montreal without speaking a word of French, although your experience will be richer if you do. Quebec City, on the other hand, is more solidly French, and as the capital, it's the centre of government. It is staid and assured, without Montreal's insomniac edge. Both cities, however, have far too much energy to let the nearly six months of icy weather get in the way. Montreal's winter festival celebrates gourmet dining and classical concerts; Quebec City's focuses on traditional parades, ice palaces and canoe races across the half-frozen St. Lawrence. And both cities are magnificently illuminated when the snow is deep and the nights are long.

The following chapters offer plenty of ideas for how best to explore each city, whether your aim is to sip sundowners on a terrasse, go antiquing on a Sunday, sample the finest market cuisine, enjoy experimental theatre, explore digital and technological arts or dance until daybreak. But how is it best to travel between the two? A boat would be the ultimate option—romantic, adventurous and historically appropriate. But for most, this would be impractical. That leaves road and rail.

The main highway between Quebec City and Montreal is the Autoroute Jean-Lesage—or Highway 20. It's about a three-hour drive. The scenery along the main north shore road—Highway 40—is much more pleasing and the history far more interesting. If you get bored with the four lanes, you can always get off and follow the old route, or Chemin du Roy, along the river.

Trois-Rivières is worth stopping for. The city may seem dingy and industrial to those who sweep through on the highway, but it's actually older than Montreal, and there are some 17th- and 18th-century gems along the historic section that skirts the river.

Train service between the two cities is frequent and efficient. The train follows essentially the same route as that truck-bearing Highway 20, so the scenery on the trip isn't particularly breathtaking. You might as well sleep, and arrive well rested.

Whether you're lacing up your winter boots or slathering on sunscreen, enjoy your adventures in Montreal and Quebec City.

Montreal's Best

Montreal's Top Attractions

Paul Waters

Updates by Lynn Melanson

View of downtown from Mont Royal

Where should I start? That's what you'll be asking yourself when you realize just how much there is to do and see in Montreal. And where should you start? At the top, of course, on the mountain that gave the city its name, Mont Royal.

Mont Royal

It might seem a bit presumptuous to call Mont Royal a mountain; at 233 metres (764 feet) it's hardly any threat to the Rockies. Yet to Montrealers, Mont Royal is their mountain: an ever-present backdrop to the city that nestles at its feet, a green oasis enjoyed year round by Montrealers young and old.

When Jacques Cartier sailed up the St. Lawrence in 1535, it was the Indian village of Hochelaga that nestled at the mountain's feet. Led to the top of the mountain by the natives, Cartier surveyed the surroundings and, in honour of his patron King François I of France, named the mountain Mont Royal. Cartier had no interest in creating a colony, so almost a hundred years

Basilique
Notre-Dame

would pass before Europeans returned to the foot of the mountain. In 1642, Paul de Chomedey, sieur de Maisonneuve, established a colony on what is now Place Royale in Old Montreal. Dedicating the new settlement to the Virgin Mary, he named it Ville-Marie. Over the years, Ville-Marie came to be known more and more by the name of the mountain that overshadowed it. By the 18th century, Mont Réal, introduced by a French or Italian mapmaker, had evolved to become the growing settlement's unofficial name: Montreal.

When Montrealers look up to the mountain, they invariably look for the cross, the 31.4 m (103 ft)-high structure that crowns the mountain. The current steel cross was erected in 1924, and in 1992 a fibre-optics lighting system replaced conventional light bulbs, allowing the cross to be illuminated in different colours depending on the occasion.

As the city developed, so did interest in creating a park on the mountain. The first architect of Mont Royal Park was Frederick Law Olmsted, who also designed New York's Central Park. Olmsted laced the 101 hectares (250 acres) of meadows and hardwood forests with a series of footpaths, so that people could discover and enjoy the natural beauty of the mountain. Since opening in 1876, Beaver Lake and two lookouts have been added to the park.

From the lookout on the Voie Camillien-Houde, you can survey the eastern part of Montreal. You can't miss the Olympic Stadium and the Biodôme, and to the left of it, across Sherbrooke Street and under all that greenery, are the Montreal Botanical Gardens and the Insectarium (see Nature & Natural History). Look to the right of the Stadium and you'll see the Pont Jacques-Cartier (Jacques Cartier Bridge). Follow the bridge as it crosses the St. Lawrence River and you'll see Île Sainte-Hélène and Île Notre-Dame, the former site of Expo 67, now the site of Parc Jean-Drapeau. In addition to its gardens, beaches, and picnic areas, the park is home to the Biosphere, the Circuit Gilles-Villeneuve racetrack, the Olympic Rowing Basin and the Montreal Casino.

From the western lookout, you can take in a panoramic view of downtown Montreal, the St. Lawrence River and the south shore and spot landmarks of Old Montreal, including Basilique Notre-Dame.

Basilique Notre-Dame de Montréal
When Pope John-Paul II came to Montreal, April 21,

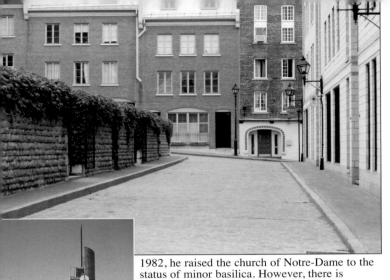

Top: Old Montreal
Above: Musée
d'Archéologie
Pointe-à-Callière

Sailing past the
casino

1982, he raised the church of Notre-Dame to the status of minor basilica. However, there is nothing minor about the Basilique Notre-Dame. Funerals for former Prime Minister Pierre Trudeau and Montréal Canadiens hockey great Maurice Richard were held there. Famed chanteuse Céline Dion was married there and her son was baptized there. The late Luciano Pavarotti once gave a Christmas concert there that became one of his most famous appearances. And the basilica's vast blue ceiling, sprinkled with thousands of gold-leaf stars, graces postcards, posters, calendars and placemats.

The magnificent building could accommodate almost every Catholic in the city when it opened in 1829. It was designed by James O'Donnell, an American who renounced his Protestant faith and converted to Catholicism just before he died, so that he could be buried in the crypt of "his" church. The pulpit and high altar were designed by Victor Bourgeau, and O'Donnell's vaulted stone cave was filled with dozens of paintings, pine and walnut carvings, ornate panelling, fanciful pillars and stained-glass windows from Limoges. The reredos features a larger-than-life-sized depiction of the crucifixion surrounded by four life-sized scenes of sacrifice from the Old Testament—all carved in wood by local artisans. The pulpit, with its curving staircase, and the baptistery, with murals by Ozias Leduc, are works of art. Hearing the Casavant organ in this jewel box is a delight to the senses. Behind the main altar is the Chapelle du Sacré-Coeur, the most popular wedding chapel in Montreal. In 1978 much of its Spanish-style Gothic revival interior was destroyed in a deliberately set fire. Architects rescued what they could and added a modern roof with a huge skylight as well as a Plexiglas altar designed by Charles Daudelin, with an enormous bronze sculpture rising above it. Daily tours are offered in English and French, and in the evenings, a multimedia sound-and-light show illuminates the founding of Montreal and the creation of this architectural masterpiece located in the heart of Old

Montreal or Vieux-Montreal.

Vieux-Montreal

Vieux-Montreal's narrow cobblestone streets are the site of centuries of Montreal history, and an area that, since it was revitalized in the late 1960s, is noted for its joie-de-vivre. Summer finds Vieux-Montreal packed full of locals and tourists alike enjoying the many cafés, clubs, boutiques and art galleries. Vieux-Montreal is also home to Centaur Theatre, Montreal's leading English-language theatre company.

Casino de Montréal

If you want to see where Montreal began, head for the Pointe-à-Callière Museum. In the basement of the museum, you can see archaeological excavations that have brought to light remnents of Indian, French, British, as well as more contemporary occupations of the site.

Wander along meandering Rue St. Paul and you're on the oldest street in Montreal. Lined with buildings that date before 1850, Rue St. Paul was once a hub of commercial activity in the old city. This street ends at Rue de la Commune, a street that doesn't follow a straight line — not because it parallels the river, but because the buildings that line it were built on top of the stone walls that once enclosed the city. Head east along de la Commune and you'll eventually arrive at the Bonsecours Market. This example of the Classical Revival style opened in 1847, but the market garden stalls have long since given way to boutiques and temporary exhibits. Next to the market, you'll find the Notre-Dame-de-Bon-Secours Chapel. For over 350 years, a chapel has stood on this site. The first stone chapel was erected in 1675, the results of the efforts of Marguerite Bourgeoys. In the basement of the Marguerite-Bourgeoys Museum, which is next to the chapel, you can see the traces of earlier Amerindian camps that predate the founding of Montreal. Head west from the chapel and you'll come to Place Jacques-Cartier. Today, Place Jacques-Cartier is the centrepiece of the old city, surrounded with outdoor cafés and a good place to pick up treasures created by

Soldiers at the Stewart Museum

local artisans. Just around the corner is Chateau Ramezay, built in 1705 for Governor de Ramezay, which houses Montreal's oldest museum. For something a little more contemporary, take a look at Rue Saint-Jacques. If you have a feeling of deja vue, you may be right. At the beginning of the 20th century, St. James Street, as it was originally known, was home to

many of Montreal's head offices. Times have changed and today this Wall Street look-alike is often used by film crews to recreate the New York of bygone days.

And of course, if you wander though Vieux-Montreal toward the river and you'll eventually find yourself in the Old Port or Vieux-Port.

Vieux-Port

During the 19th and 20th centuries, intensive port and commercial activity led to the emergence of Montreal as a major port and international city. In 1960, port facilities were moved east of the city, and the 47.3-hectares (117-acres) of the original Port of Montreal, which stretch along 2.7 kilometres of the St. Lawrence River waterfront, were eventually developed into a centre for tourism and recreation.

The four quays, or piers, of the Vieux-Port jut out from the landscaped park that parallels Rue de la Commune. At the western end of the Vieux-Port you'll find the first of the Lachine Canal locks and International Flora, a delight for gardeners looking for new ideas and inspirations. At the eastern end, on the Quai de l'Horloge, you can check the time on the Clock Tower, built in 1922 to commemorate the men of the Merchant Fleet who were lost during World War I; the clock still keeps time, and another bird's-eye view of the city can be had from the tower's observatory. Between International Flora and the Clock Tower, there is lots to do and see on the Quays. Getting there could be half the fun.

While you could walk the length of the Vieux-Port, other means of transportation are available. La Balade, a little train on wheels, runs along the Promenade des

Quais between the Clock Tower and International Flora. Bicycles are available for rent, or, if you're a group of four, you might want to try a quadricycle, a four-wheeled pedal-powered vehicle that looks a little like a Model T. The ultimate fun, though, might be in renting a Segway—don't worry, demos and training are provided. Now that you've settled on

transportation, where do you want to go?

Want to marvel at how the other half lives? Just take a look at some of the luxury yachts that moor alongside the Quai Jacques-Cartier. Want to know more about recent Canadian innovations and inventions? Head for the Montreal Science Centre, with its IMAX theatre, located on the Quai King-Edward. Want to get hopelessly lost and have fun doing it? Then it's off to the Shed 16 Labyrinth on the Quai Jacques-Cartier. Or if you want to just sit and enjoy the ambience, you can relax at one of the many terrasses and cafés to be found throughout the Vieux-Port.

Of course, what would a port be without water fun and transportation? Several cruise lines provide day and evening tours of the Montreal harbour, and for the more adventurous, there's jet boating through the Lachine Rapids. If you have time, there's also the ultra-modern, 300-passenger catamaran that plies the waters between Montreal and Quebec City. The shortest "cruise" of them all, a 20-minute hop across the St. Lawrence, will take you to Montreal's jewel in the middle of the river: Parc Jean-Drapeau.

Parc Jean-Drapeau

Parc Jean-Drapeau sprawls across the two small islands, Île Sainte-Hélène and Île Notre-Dame. Île Sainte-Hélène was enlarged with and Île Notre-Dame was created from stone rubble excavated for the construction of the Montreal Métro system. Jean Drapeau, in whose honour the park is named, was the larger-than-life mayor who brought Expo 67 and then the 1976 Olympics to Montreal.

Parc Jean-Drapeau has the city's only natural beach, with a cleverly disguised filtration system, a rowing basin, a vast floral display called Floralies and a couple of hundred acres of trees and walkways. Grand Prix drivers compete here every summer, and pyrotechnicians from a dozen countries spend summer weekends trying to outdo each other during the Montreal International Fireworks Competition.

And of course, being part of Montreal, the park has history. The fort on Île Sainte-Hélène was built to fend off an American attack that never came. It now houses the Stewart Museum (see Museums). The grounds of the fort are used as a drilling ground for the Olde 78th Fraser Highlanders and the Compagnie Franche de la Marine and sometimes the sound of

Examining at the Insectarium

muskets drowns out the shrieks from nearby La Ronde.

The La Ronde amusement park, located on the eastern end of Ile Sainte-Hélène, is one of the most successful reminders of Expo 67. The park's 45-metre-high Ferris wheel still sports the Expo symbol. For the ride of your life, try Goliath, the highest and fastest roller coaster in Canada, custom-designed for La Ronde. There are plenty of other tamer rides, not to mention the restaurants and arcade amusements in the park.

Another remenant of Expo still in use is the geodesic dome designed by Buckminster Fuller to house the United States pavilion. This skeletal structure now houses the Biosphère. Interactive exhibits within the Biosphère are designed to foster a better understanding of major environmental issues related to water, air, climate change, sustainable development and responsible consumption.

The old French pavilion now tinkles with the sounds of 3,200 slot machines. Since 1993, it has been home to the Casino de Montréal, a success story with more than 18,000 visitors a day. In addition to the slot machines, the Casino offers 115 gaming tables, a keno lounge, a Royal Ascot electronic racetrack, four restaurants, four bars, a cabaret-style dinner theatre and lots of automatic bank machines. If you're looking for fine dining and great views of the Montreal skyline, the Casino's Nuances restaurant was named "2007 Restaurant of the Year" by the prestigious Guide Debeur.

Oratoire Saint-Joseph du Mont-Royal

Back on the northern side of Mont Royal is another of the city's top attractions, the Oratoire Saint-Joseph du Mont-Royal. Thousands of pilgrims visit it every year; many still climb the outside stairs on their knees, seeking favours and cures from both St. Joseph and Blessed Frère André Bessette, the humble Christian brother who was responsible for the building of the oratory. The building actually houses two churches: the nondescript little crypt church on the ground floor and the immense but sombre oratory church beneath the copper dome. The latter is the home church of the Petits Chanteurs du Mont-Royal, the finest boys' choir in the city. Surrounded by gardens and trees, the complex also includes a museum dedicated to Frère André, a cafeteria, a souvenir shop and a hostel for pilgrims.

Montreal's Underground City

This vast, nearly 32-kilometre (20-mile) network of underground corridors links 60 commercial buildings, shopping centres, cinemas, hotels and 10 Métro stops making it possible to practically live underground. The Underground City offers lots of shopping, interesting art in the Métro stations and a truly unique way to get about the city.

Heritage & Architecture

Jim McRae

Updates by Lynn Melanson

Hôtel de Ville

Montreal is a city of many gifts. It brims with cultural diversity, flourishes with art and fashion and serves up fine dining and entertainment in banquet-like proportions. And all this is celebrated in an urban setting decorated with some of the richest architecture on the continent. Since its founding in 1642, Montreal has grown from a frontier settlement of New France to a cosmopolitan city in the new millennium.

Fragments of 17th- and 18th-Century New France

While it is commonly believed that Old Montreal is full of buildings that date from the French Regime, there are only a handful of gems from that epoch still standing (not including L'Église de la Visitation de la Bienheureuse Vierge Marie, which is located in the north end of the city). These structures are, however, historical jewels, some over three centuries old.

The Séminaire de Saint-Sulpice, built in 1685, is one such gem. Located beside Basilique Notre-Dame, it is the oldest building in Montreal, constructed to house Sulpician priests. The seminary features several medieval characteristics: cradle-vaults in the foundation, corner towers with staircases and building practices common to artisan tradesmen of the period. The low storeys and small windows are signatures of French Regime architecture. The central door is

Château de Ramezay

engraved with the date 1740, the year when the portico was added to the seminary.

Several blocks to the southwest, the Grey Nuns' general hospital at Rue St-Pierre and Place d'Youville was built in 1693 as the second hospital in the city. Its name honours the congregation of the Sisters of Charity, also known as the Grey Nuns, founded by Marguerite d'Youville around 1750. The hospital was destroyed by fire in 1765 and the walls that were left undamaged were used in the rebuilding. It was later partially demolished to be replaced by an imposing greystone warehouse.

Roughly a kilometre's walk from the old hospital, the Château de Ramezay on Rue Notre-Dame E. stands as a well-preserved monument of the French Regime. The residence was constructed for the governor of Montreal, Claude de Ramezay, and work on it began in 1705. The Château is a blend of urban row house and detached rural home, a trend in Montreal-area dwellings of that time. It was converted into a museum in 1895. The house is a fine example of 18th-century architecture and named after Pierre du Calvet, a Frenchman and republican partisan during the American Revolution, who became a resident of Montreal. It now houses a charming little inn and one of the city's fine French restaurants.

Maison du Calvet

Victorian Influence, 1837–1914

Victorian architecture is an influence, not a single style. And in Montreal, rich Scottish and British industrialists would wield considerable influence over the city's buildings for seven decades—well past the reign of Queen Victoria. The nouveau riche of this New World borrowed from classical traditions, putting their own elaborate stamps on the business addresses where they plotted their economic conquests. Some say that Basilique Notre-Dame, although constructed prior to the reign of the famed British monarch, heralded the era of Victorian architecture in Montreal. Built in 1829, Notre-Dame is the neo-Gothic creation of Irish-

American architect James O'Donnell. He used decorative components of the Gothic style to produce a monument resembling the celebrated cathedrals of Europe: a majestic façade, elaborate portico and soaring bell towers.

Opposite Notre-Dame at Place d'Armes is the Banque de Montréal building, perhaps the richest example of Victorian architecture in the city. It was designed by Englishman John Wells and dates to 1847. Although a major expansion at the turn of the century left only the façade as part of the original construction, it alone is considered a magnificent architectural achievement. Its detailed and expert stonework, often compared with that of the Bank of the United States in Philadelphia, evoked the power of Montreal's commercial elite. A short distance to the southeast, William Footner's Marché Bonsecours on Rue St-Paul is an example of the level of extravagance associated with the Victorians. Costing a staggering $70,000 when completed in 1842, Bonsecours Market features cast-iron Doric columns in its portico, while an imposing dome rises above its roof line. Located on the harbour, the three-storey-high, 152-metre-long building was a beacon for the era, sending a message of the city's commercial success to those arriving by river. Bonsecours once served as parliament and town hall. Today, cultural events and exhibitions are frequently held here. Montreal's current city hall, or Hôtel de Ville, is also a Victorian structure. Designed by architect H. Maurice Perrault, it is an example of the French Second Empire style. Built between 1872 and 1878, it fell to fire in 1922. The remaining walls were used

Basilique Notre-Dame

Banque de Montréal

Marché Bonsecours

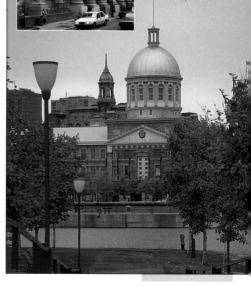

Ravenscrag

in its reconstruction and a tall mansard roof was introduced.

The Square Mile

While the mercantile elite of the Victorian era were branding their edifices with labels of commercial success, they were also building domestic monuments to themselves in an area known as the Square Mile, later dubbed the Golden Square Mile. This neighbourhood was bordered by Rue Sherbrooke to the south, the slope of Mont Royal to the north, Chemin de la Côte-des-Neiges to the west and Rue de Bleury to the east. Its residents controlled 70 percent of Canada's wealth at the turn of the 20th century. These magnates owned some of the most extravagant private homes ever constructed on the continent.

Unfortunately, many of these urban palaces were razed in the late 1960s and early 1970s during a time of careless city planning. Among the few examples that remain are Ravenscrag (now the Allan Pavilion Memorial Institute of the Hôpital Royal Victoria on Avenue des Pins), home to Sir Hugh Allan, railway baron and the richest of Montreal's elite. The sprawling house features a mixture of architectural styles but borrows mostly from the Italian Renaissance. From its location on the southern flank of Mont Royal, it represented the pinnacle of personal success for the rest of the growing metropolis to see.

While not as ostentatious as Allan's mountainside monument, Trafalgar House, located on Avenue Trafalgar on Mont Royal's southwest side, is a fine example of a wealthy Victorian domicile. Built in 1848, it was designed by John George Howard, an English draftsman and engineer who had immigrated to Toronto. He incorporated Gothic and Tudor features into the design of the house. Its red-brick façade and stone-framed windows and doors display considerable craftsmanship and contribute to an overall look of solidity. The former Engineers' Club is another example of an opulent Victorian residence. Located at Place du Frère André (formerly Beaver Hall Square), just north of Boulevard René-Lévesque, the mansion was completed around 1860. It is said to be designed by William T. Thomas, one of the most accomplished architects of the period, and the mastermind behind Église St-George, the Anglican church at Square Dorchester. The residence has the flavour of an Italian Renaissance mansion.

Residential Architecture

If the homes of the Victorian era's elite were an expression of the individual through elaborate decoration and outward displays of wealth, the row houses of the working class of Montreal were the opposite: nondescript structures designed to huddle the masses close to the industries that kept the Square Mile golden.

Multifamily vertical housing, one or two flats above a main-floor flat, first appeared in Montreal between 1850 and 1860 in Pointe St-Charles. These buildings were erected to house Irish immigrants who worked on the Victorian Bridge or shops of The Grand Trunk Railway. Streets such as Sébastopol, Charon and Le Ber are lined with these dwellings. Recently, Montreal architect Michael Fish renovated 12 of these structures on Sébastopol. The condos he refitted are the oldest extant multiple dwellings in

Église St-George

Montreal. Wooden frame in construction, they are finished with red brick and extend right to the sidewalk, with no balcony. The roof is flat, mansard or has a steep, sloping side with dormers looking out onto the street. Any decoration on the façade usually occurs at the roof line, incorporating the dormers and simple cornices.

Although the working-class homes closer to the city centre exhibit more architectural flair than those in the Pointe, they are still models of simplicity. Apart from some examples of upscale, stone-faced British-style row houses on Avenue Laval and Carré St-Louis, they

Vertical housing

are typically like those on nearby Rue Hutchison— two storeys high with greystone façades and picturesque architectural motifs. This style became common throughout the city. Grey limestone quarried on the island of Montreal is also a common façade in the solidly built apartment blocks on St-Hubert and St-Denis between Ste-Catherine and Sherbrooke.

In the more densely populated areas of Verdun, Rosemont and Plateau Mont-Royal, the row houses feature two or three levels of flats finished in brick. These flat-roofed homes have porches, balconies and outside staircases in front and back. This type of dwelling became typical housing for the city's working class, and, because it is more prevalent than any other building type in the city, it represents a de facto Montreal architectural style.

When duplexes and triplexes were springing up all over the city to handle the influx of rural migrants and immigrants, builders began to standardize their techniques and to use prefabricated building materials, such as the outside staircase. Montreal's distinctive outside staircases were seen as a space- and cost-saving feature: having the stairs on the outside meant more living space inside and required less fuel to heat an area that would only be used for entering and exiting the unit. Curved versions are used where homes have little frontage.

Church Architecture

Mark Twain once said that you couldn't throw a brick in Montreal without breaking a church window. And although there is no hard evidence to prove that the American literary icon ever put his theory to the test during his visit in 1881, several important churches dominated the core of the city at the time, their spires and domes competing for space on the skyline. Notre-Dame, located at Place d'Armes, was principal among these historic houses of worship with its chapel having been part of the main fort in 1642 and the present building dating from 1829. Basilique St-Patrick on

Basilique St-Patrick

Boulevard René-Lévesque, completed in 1847, also punctuated the landscape as did Cathédrale Christ Church, built in 1859, near Carré Phillips. The Cathédrale Marie-Reine-du-Monde (originally named St-Jacques) is a scaled-down version of St. Peter's Basilica in Rome, and was the project of Montreal's second archbishop, Ignace Bourquet. It was in the heart of the Anglo-Protestant district and was over halfway built by 1881, when Twain visited Montreal. While many of the churches mentioned were a stone's throw from the Windsor Hotel, where he made his quip, farther afield stood the only church that dated back to the French Regime. Located at Sault-au-Récollet, west of Papineau on Boulevard Gouin, Église de la Visitation was begun in 1749 and was ready for Mass by 1751. Charles Guilbault, a parishioner, supplied the rough masonry of the main building, which also features classical arched windows. In the early 1850s, the prolific Montreal

Christ Church Cathedral at Ste-Catherine and University

architect John Ostell added a new front in a severe English neo-Baroque style. The interior is equally rewarding, as master sculptors such as Philippe Liébert, Louis-Amable Quévillon and David Fleury-David lent their skills to various aspects of the church over time. The tabernacle of the main altar was completed in 1792, the altars between 1802 and 1806 and the vault and much of the present interior between 1816 and 1831.

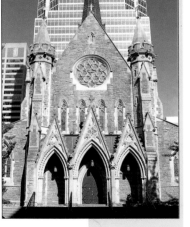

Skyscrapers Then and Now

Although church steeples and bell towers defined Montreal's skyline from its earliest days, the city's first office towers began to challenge them near the end of the 19th century. It was elevators and the use of iron and steel framing that allowed architects to push buildings higher than the standard of five or six storeys.

Oddly enough, the city's first "skyscraper," or gratte-ciel, featured neither of these innovations. Still, the New York Life Insurance Co. building at Place

BNP and
Laurentian Bank

1000 Rue de la
Gauchetière,
Marie-Reine-du-
Monde, Sun Life

d'Armes, completed in 1888, was the city's first eight-storey office building. The Banque Royal Bank, reaching 23 storeys, was completed in 1928. Located on Rue St-Jacques, not far from the renowned church, the bank's exquisite ground floor was a symbol of Montreal's mercantile elite. Another example of the increasing wealth of the city was the Sun Life building on the east side of Square Dorchester. Built in three stages between 1914 and 1931, it was the largest building in the British Empire when completed. Its steel framing is wrapped in Stanstead granite, and Corinthian columns line its ground floor.

The era of the modern-day Montreal skyscraper began in the early 1960s and involved the efforts of several world-renowned architects. Place Ville-Marie, an I.M. Pei creation, was conceived in the late 1950s but not fully completed until 1966; the tower dates from 1962. Its cruciform design makes it one of the most recognizable structures in Montreal.

Slightly to the east at Square Victoria, Luigi Moretti and Pier L. Nervi put their finishing touches on La Tour de la Bourse in 1964. It was the first earthquake-proof building ever constructed and, at 47 storeys, was the tallest concrete structure in the world at the time. Slightly to the west of the city core, the black-metal and tinted-glass office towers of Westmount Square, unveiled in 1965, are considered masterpieces of Ludwig Mies van der Rohe, the former director of the Bauhaus School.

In recent years, other significant towers have staked their claim in the celebrated skyline. The quiet elegance of the 205-metre-high 1000 Rue de la Gauchetière is one example, the 47 storeys of glass and granite at 1250 Boulevard René-Lévesque is another.

The glass and steel of the downtown skyscrapers may punctuate Montreal's modern skyline, but in no way do they supersede the structures that are cast in their shadows. The city has been under construction for over 350 years and its architecture is rich and diverse. It reflects the influences of its founding fathers and incorporates the styles, and often the personal tastes, of those who followed. Just as few cities in North America can match Montreal's history, few can match, in age and diversity, its architectural heritage.

Museums

Sarah Morgan

Updates by Lynn Melanson

Artifacts on display at the Musée McCord

It would be hard to find a North American metropolis with more history than Montreal. The city's roots reach back to the middle of the 17th century, and it's virtually impossible to dig up a sewer or repair a street without turning up some artifact from Montreal's past. There was a time in the 1950s and 1960s when history was viewed as something you knocked down or pushed aside to make room for another skyscraper or freeway. But Montrealers have learned to revere—even revel in—their rich heritage. You can see that pride in the cobbled streets of Old Montreal,

Kahnawake Mohawks in 1869

Iroquois beadwork

the Victorian row houses of the McGill University ghetto and the comfortable Second Empire homes built by the francophone elite in the Quartier Latin. You can also see it in the city's museums, where every effort is made to bring the past to life and render it vivid and relevant for modern visitors. Some museums are tiny. The Banque de Montréal, for example, has squeezed a modest but interesting little display on early banking practices into one room on the ground floor of its head office at Place d'Armes. Some focus on the contributions of one person; others, like the Musée McCord and the Musée d'Archéologie Pointe-à-Callière, take a much broader view.

The Broad View

The broad view is probably a good way to start any exploration of the city's history, and it would be hard to find any museum broader than the Musée McCord d'Histoire Canadienne, just across Rue Sherbrooke from the McGill University campus. The heart of its collection is a glorious hodgepodge of artifacts collected by a lawyer named David Ross McCord (1844–1930). He was an inveterate pack rat with a passion for anything that had to do with life in Canada—books, photographs, jewellery, furniture, clothing, guns, old documents, paintings, toys, porcelain. And he gave all this to McGill University so it could open a museum of social history. Some of the best exhibits are the collections of First Nations and Inuit artifacts. These items aren't limited to the ubiquitous west coast and Arctic art but include tools and weapons and intricately decorated clothing. The museum also has one of the best photographic archives in Canada, with more than 70,000 pictures. Some of the most interesting images come from the studio of William Notman, a photographic pioneer who captured life in Victorian Montreal. Notman's work includes a lot of exterior pictures: families tobogganing, soldiers marching and members (several hundred of them) of the posh Montreal Amateur Athletic Association posing in snowshoe regalia on the slopes of Mont Royal. The

Musée d'Archéologie Pointe-à-Callière

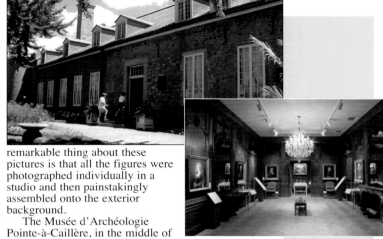

Château Ramezay

remarkable thing about these pictures is that all the figures were photographed individually in a studio and then painstakingly assembled onto the exterior background.

The Musée d'Archéologie Pointe-à-Caillère, in the middle of Old Montreal, probes a little deeper — literally — into the city's history. It's housed in a startlingly modern building on the waterfront that looks rather like a concrete ship. It's quite a tall building, but the guts of the museum are in the basement, where archaeologists have dug their way through several layers of settlement down to the remnants of the city's earliest days. You can wend your way down to the banks of a long-filled-in river where early settlers used to trade with the local First Nations bands, visit the oldest Catholic cemetery on the island and examine the foundations of an 18th-century waterfront tavern. A tunnel connects the museum to the Vieille Douane (Old Customs House) at Place Royale, a fine old building with a huge gift shop.

The Musée du Château Ramezay on Rue Notre-Dame E. is one of the few reminders the city has of the French Regime. This mansion was built in 1702 by Claude de Ramezay, Montreal's 11th governor, and its interior reflects the grace and tastes of the early 18th-century elite. The most magnificent room is the Nantes Salon, which is decorated with intricately carved panelling by the French architect Germain Boffrand. The uniforms, documents and furniture on the main floor reflect the life of New France's ruling classes, while several rooms in the cellars depict the more ordinary doings of humbler colonists. But the museum's collection is fairly eclectic. One of its most prized possessions, for example, is a bright red automobile that was produced at the turn of the 20th century by the De Dion–Bouton company.

At first glance, the exhibits in the Centre d'Histoire de Montreal, a 19th-century firehouse, seem to cover much the same ground as those at the Château Ramezay and the Musée d'Archéologie Pointe-à-Caillère. That's a misleading impression, however, as the focus here is fixed firmly on everyday life. Some of the most effective parts of the museum are the exhibits on city life in the 1930s and 1940s. You can sit in a period living room and listen to a play-by-play of

37

Centre d'Histoire
de Montréal

a Canadiens hockey game or step into a phone booth and eavesdrop while a young factory worker tries to make a date with the shop clerk he adores.

A Tale of Two Women

One of the unique things about Montreal history is the large and acclaimed part that women have played in it. Two women in particular were absolutely vital to the city's development: Jeanne Mance, who co-founded the original settlement of Ville-Marie with Paul de Chomedey, Sieur de Maisonneuve, and Marguerite Bourgeoys, the colony's first schoolteacher and now a canonized saint. Both women were feisty, devout and determined; they left behind concrete reminders of their presence: Jeanne Mance's Hôtel-Dieu de Montréal hospital still serves the city's sick, and the religious order that Marguerite Bourgeoys founded still runs schools and colleges across Canada. Several museums offer insights into the lives of these remarkable and indomitable women.

Maison Saint-Gabriel on Place Dublin is an isolated little fragment of New France lost among the apartment buildings of working-class Pointe St-Charles. It was a farm when the formidable Marguerite Bourgeoys bought it in 1668 as a residence for the religious order she had founded in 1655. The house, rebuilt in 1698 after a fire, is a fine example of 17th-century architecture, with thick stone walls and a steeply pitched roof built on an intricate frame of heavy timber.

Marguerite Bourgeoys and her tireless sisters worked the farm and ran a school on the property for First Nations and colonial children. They also housed and trained the filles du roi (the king's daughters), orphaned young women sent to New France by Louis XIV to be the wives and mothers of his new colony. The house's chapel, kitchen, dormitory and drawing rooms are full of artifacts from 17th, 18th and 19th centuries, including a writing desk the saint actually used. There's a smaller museum dedicated to Marguerite Bourgeoys and her mission in North America attached to the chapel of Notre-Dame-de-Bon-Secours in Old Montreal. It too is worth a visit.

Musée des Hospitalières is located near the McGill University campus on Avenue des Pins O. Jeanne Mance was as pious as her friend Marguerite Bourgeoys and even more important to the establishment of a colony on the island of Montreal. But she never joined or founded a religious order, so she left behind no band of sisters to promulgate her memory. She did, however, bring the Religieuses

Hospitalières de Saint-Joseph to Montreal in the mid-1600s to run Hôtel-Dieu, the hospital she'd founded. And while the sisters no longer run the hospital, they still maintain this small but charming museum that reflects Jeanne Mance's zealous spirit. Books, documents and artifacts from the early days are on display, and there is a sometimes-chilling exhibit on the history of medicine and nursing.

Great Personalities
Montreal's history is filled with colourful characters—strongman Louis Cyr, hockey player Maurice (Rocket) Richard, artist Marc-Aurèle Fortin and Mayor Camillien Houde, who spent time in an internment camp for his opposition to conscription during World War II. Every one of them would be worthy of a museum, but only a few have permanent exhibitions in their honour.

The Maison Sir George-Étienne Cartier historic site on Rue Notre-Dame E. is the most elaborate museum dedicated to a single individual. George-Étienne Cartier (1814–73) was largely responsible for persuading French Canada to join the new Canadian confederation in 1867, arguing that a federal system would give French Canadians the powers necessary to protect their language, religion and culture. The national historic site comprises two adjoining greystone houses the Cartier family owned on the eastern edge of Old Montreal. One is dedicated to Cartier's career as a lawyer, politician and railway builder. An exhibit within gives visitors the opportunity to sit at a round table with plaster models of the Fathers of Confederation and listen in either French or English to a very good summary of the founding of Canada. The second house, on the other side of a covered carriageway, focuses on the Cartiers' domestic life and the functioning of an upper-middle-class family in the mid-19th century. Visitors wander through formal rooms full of fussy, overstuffed furniture, listening to snatches of conversation from "servants" gossiping about the lives of their master and mistress.

Maison Sir George-Étienne Cartier, exterior and interior

The Musée du Bienheureux Frère André, tucked away in the Oratoire Saint-Joseph du Mont-Royal, is a little museum dedicated to the diminutive man who

started the whole project—Brother André Bessette. Models, photographs and documents chronicle his early life, and a shrine containing his embalmed heart is testimony to the reverence in which he is still held. The office

Oratoire Saint-Joseph de Mont Royal

where Frère André worked, the room where he slept and the hospital room where he died have been reconstructed and preserved. Not a bad monument for a man who was born into abject poverty and never held a job more important than that of porter in a classical college.

Le Monde de Maurice (Rocket) Richard isn't really a museum at all, just a room tucked way in the Aréna Maurice-Richard. The Rocket was one of the most exciting hockey players who ever lived and the exhibits reverently trace the great man's life and career.

La Compagnie Franche de la Marine

Deservedly, Marc-Aurèle Fortin is the only Quebec artist with his own museum—the Musée Marc-Aurèle Fortin. The man virtually invented Quebec landscape painting and pioneered the painting of images on a black background. No one has painted grander trees than Fortin.

At play in the Old Fort

Military Adventures

The Old Fort on Île Ste-Hélène was built in 1825 to protect Montreal from an American attack that never came. Its red stone walls enclose a grassy parade square that is used today by members of the Olde 78th Fraser Highlanders and the Compagnie Franche de la Marine, re-creations of two 18th-century military formations that fought each other over the future of New France. The fort also houses the Musée Stewart, a small but excellent historical museum with an interesting collection of 17th- and 18th-century maps, firearms and navigational

instruments. The costumed guides give an accurate, unsentimental and yet quite humorous account of the first encounters between Europeans and Native North Americans.

Trade and Commerce

A cyclist can coast comfortably into Montreal's industrial past by following the bike path along the Canal de Lachine from the Old Port to Lac St-Louis. The canal, built to enable shipping to avoid the treacherous Rapides de Lachine, was supplanted by the St. Lawrence Seaway in

North façade from entrance gate, CCA

the 1950s and has become a kind of long, thin and very popular park. Near the end of the trail in the lakeside suburb of Lachine is the Canal de Lachine Centre d'Interprétation, which houses an interesting display on the building and operation of the canal. Further along the Lachine waterfront is an old stone warehouse with a cumbersome name: Lieu Historique National du Commerce-de-la-Fourrure-à-Lachine (Fur Trade in Lachine National Historic Site). Constructed in 1802 as a trading depot, today the building offers displays on the trade that created Montreal's wealth. Because of its position west of the trade-blocking rapids, Lachine became a prosperous town. One of its oldest houses, built in 1670 by merchants Jacques Le Ber and Charles LeMoyne, is now the Musée de Lachine, with historical exhibits and an art gallery.

Stones and Laughter

Not all city museums are dedicated to Montreal's history. There are art museums (see Galleries), museums that focus on nature (see Nature & Natural History) and some museums that are just difficult to categorize.

The Centre Canadien d'Architecture (CCA) is a place for serious scholars. Its library has more than 165,000 volumes on various

Bookstore at the CCA

aspects of architecture, and the centre's collection of plans, drawings, models and photographs is the most important of its kind in the world. It also has six well-lit exhibition rooms for rotating exhibits that range from the academic to the whimsical. Recent shows have focused on dollhouses, miniature villages and American lawn culture. All this is housed in an

Shaughnessy
House Tea Room
at the CCA

austere, modern building that embraces a grand old mansion built in 1874 for the family of the president of the Canadian Pacific Railway, Sir Thomas Shaughnessy. The house is open to visitors and has a remarkable art nouveau conservatory with an intricately decorated ceiling. The CCA's most playful exhibit, however, is outside—the architecture designed by artist Melvin Charney. It's stuck in an unlikely spot, between two highway ramps across busy Boulevard René-Lévesque and separated from the museum itself, but its whimsical bits and pieces of architecture perched in unlikely places is a delight.

The Musée Juste Pour Rire opened in 1993 as an outgrowth of the city's Just for Laughs Comedy Festival, and it seems appropriate somehow that one of the world's few museums dedicated to laughter is housed in an old brewery. The museum uses film clips and old movie sets to explore the history of comedy.

Musée Juste Pour Rire

Galleries

Matthew Woodley

Updates by Kristina Mansson

Art abounds in Montreal, from works by classical masters to experiments by cutting-edge contemporary artists and everything in between. With all there is to see, even if you're planning on indulging in just a few art spaces, it's a good idea to pick up a Montreal Museums Pass. The $35 package gives three consecutive days of access to 30 of the city's art, archaeology and science hot spots. As an added bonus, the pass also permits access to public transport for an extra $10, including the Métro, an arty landmark in its own right, as many of its 68 colourful stations bear the mark of a wide variety of artists.

Top: Jean-Noël Desmarais and Benaiah Gibb pavilions.
Middle and bottom: Ceramic display at the Musée des Beaux-Arts.

An essential stop in the city is the Musée des Beaux-Arts de Montréal, the oldest fine arts museum in Canada, with a permanent collection of over 33,000 works and an ever-impressive series of special exhibitions. The museum is housed in two principal buildings across the street from one another on Sherbrooke O.: the Benaiah Gibb Pavilion and the newer Jean-Noël Desmarais Pavilion. Designed by architect Moshe Safdie, the Desmarais building integrates the façade of an early 20th-century apartment block with a variety of modern materials, from glass to steel, creating a balance

L'Étang aux antilles by James Wilson Morrice at the Musée des Beaux-Arts de Montréal

between the area's Gothic churches, Victorian houses and the downtown buildings with which they share the cityscape.

One wing of the Desmarais Pavilion houses many of the museum's special exhibitions. Over the years, these shows have included borrowed masterpieces from the Guggenheim in New York and the Hermitage in St. Petersberg and have encompassed themes focusing on such movements as the French avant-garde and the 1960s. The museum also exhibits works by such celebrated artists as Lichtenstein, Colville, Magritte, Picasso, Riopelle and Monet.

The museum's Canadian section highlights the history and cultural diversity of the country with an eclectic selection of First Nations, colonial and modern works. Traditional carvings from pre-colonial cultures share the space with works that trace the course of European immigration through paintings, sculpture and furniture. Distinctive landscapes by the Group of Seven hang alongside pivotal works by Paul-Émile Borduas, who, along with a group of like-minded artists, spawned the controversial 1940s Automatisme movement and subsequent anti-establishment manifesto, the Refus Global. Works by distinguished Montreal artist Betty Goodwin, whose striking use of the figure as symbol of the human condition, are another highlight.

The museum's European collection spans eras in art from the Middle Ages to present times. There, you can take in 14th-century religious paintings and artifacts, and an extensive collection of Baroque art, featuring French, Italian and Dutch works by masters such as Rembrandt, Emmanuel de Witte and Peter Bruegel the Younger. Nineteenth-century works in the collection have been largely donated by wealthy Montreal families, with a leaning towards the French-realist Barbizon School, including Tissot's famed *October*.

Impressionist and post-Impressionist paintings include works by Renoir, Monet and Cézanne, while a sampling of 20th-century works are on display from artists such as Picasso, Matisse and Dali.

The year 2001 marked the opening of the Liliane and David M. Stewart Pavilion, bringing some 700 objects spanning six centuries to the museum's decorative art collection. This acquisition adds to a display of objects donated by several major connoisseurs that includes English porcelain, antique glass and a collection of 3,000 antique Japanese incense boxes, the largest such assembly in the world. Among the pieces in the Mediterranean archaeology collection are Greek and Roman sculptures, as well as woods that have been discovered in the anaerobic sands of Egypt and Luristan bronzes from the 6th to the 4th-century B.C. The museum also features a massive art library, the oldest in Canada, with a collection of over 200,000 books, auction catalogues, artist files, slides and CD-ROMs. The library is not open to the public, but it does offer a reference service to which requests can be made in writing.

Just a few Métro stops from the Musée des Beaux-Arts is the Musée d'Art Contemporain de Montréal, located on the city's main

Jeune fille au chapeau by Pierre Auguste Renoir at the Musée des Beaux-Arts de Montréal

Ancient Egyptian cat

45

commercial artery, Rue Ste-Catherine. The museum is Montreal's central contemporary art site, which, since 1992, has been part of the Place des Arts, Montreal's central

Musée d'Art Contemporain de Montréal, exterior (above) and interior (below)

performing arts complex and home to the Orchestre Symphonique de Montréal and Les Grands Ballets Canadiens.

The fundamental component of the museum is its vast permanent collection. Some 7,000 works make up the collection, produced by 1,500 artists, 80 percent of whom are still living. An ongoing acquisition of works and related research reflecting ever-changing trends in expression keeps the museum on a progressive edge. This approach stems from the Contemporary Arts Society of Montreal. Founded by John Lyman in 1939, the organization fuelled a newfound interest in contemporary art. Since then, the museum has obtained works by major artists such as Picasso, Lichtenstein and Warhol. Given that the museum's principal goal is to conserve and promote Quebec art, more than half of

its collection originates chez nous, including the largest collection of work by Paul-Émile Borduas in the world.

The Salle Beverly Webster Rolph in the lower level of the museum presents art that branches beyond the visual, including modern dance performances, theatre and conferences with established artists. In many senses, these activities define the museum's character, where alongside traditional media, it's not uncommon to find digital creations and interactive installations. A decidedly un-digital experience can be had by stepping out for a breath of fresh air in the sculpture garden, which is accessible through the temporary exhibition area.

The Centre Canadien d'Architecture (CCA), located on Rue Baile, is a prominent landmark on Montreal's Golden Square Mile. The name refers to a district bounded by four streets that held roughly 70 percent of Canada's wealth at the turn of the 20th century and formed roughly a square mile. The CCA is housed in the 133-year-old Shaughnessy House, one of the few old Montreal mansions open to the public, and in a modern building that was integrated into the house in 1989. Since then, the structure has won numerous international design awards.

Inside the CCA, a collection of works dating from the Renaissance to the present focuses on the art of architecture throughout the world, with a keen eye on the future. Incorporating drawings, models, plans, prints, artifacts and conceptual studies, the CCA exposes the roots of design and presents plenty of fodder for the imagination.

Though it's somewhat off the beaten track, the Liane and Danny Taran Gallery at the Saidye Bronfman Centre for the Arts on Chemin de la Côte Ste-Catherine is a short walk from the Côte Ste-Catherine Métro station and well worth the trip. The gallery has emerged as one of Montreal's finest in presenting innovative works from both emerging and established artists from places local to international. The Saidye, as it is commonly known, serves its mandate in presenting provocative, often playful, work in all media. Contemporary artists showcased over the years have included Betty Goodwin, Jochen Gerz, Susan Rothenberg and John Scott. Complementing the major exhibitions, the gallery presents conferences, screenings, lectures and other special events.

Sculpture installations by Pierre Granche, Musée d'Art Contemporain de Montréal

Inuit art on display at Musée des Beaux-Arts

The Leonard and Bina Ellen Gallery is Concordia University's main art venue, located in the school's urban-integrated campus in the downtown core on Boulevard de Maisonneuve O. The gallery's permanent collection comprises of over 1,700 works, the majority of which are by Canadian artists.

Two large buildings on Rue Ste-Catherine O., a mere five-minute walk west from the Musée d'Art Contemporain, house an eclectic array of smaller

galleries that can be sampled in an afternoon (please note, though, that many of them close during the summer months). The Belgo Building has emerged from a rundown refuge for struggling local artists to one of the city's most important art spaces, with bright, airy lofts branching off long hallways on several levels. It now houses over 30 galleries and artist-run spaces. Optica Gallery has a consistent line-up of provocative contemporary exhibitions, while Galerie René Blouin is home to several renowned artists, including Betty Goodwin. Galerie 303, a non-profit group, is dedicated to the development of and interdisciplinary practices of performance art. It is also a good spot to find a fun show. Another place of interest is La Centrale, one of Canada's oldest artist-run galleries and the only one dedicated to the diffusion of women's art.

In contrast to the galleries in these two more worked-in buildings, Galerie de Bellefeuille, on Avenue Greene, just inside the borough of Westmount, is an excellent place to see realistic figurative paintings as well as sculptures and limited-edition prints, in an elegant setting. Then there is VOX's recently opened space on Boulevard St-Laurent, mixed in with the lingering clubs of the former red-light district and the theatres and performances in an area that the city of Montreal is actively converting into an arts district. VOX, which has retained the mirrored ceilings of the former tenants, is responsible for founding the large biennial Mois de la Photo festival and home to some of the best contemporary photo exhibitions in town. Up the street, Zeke's Gallery curates its exhibitions on the grounds that they must be an artist's first solo show, resulting in a hit-or-miss rotation, yet one that's often worth the risk.

Back in the Old Port, Quartier Éphémère in the Darling Foundry, located on Rue Ottawa, supports up-and-coming artists by providing them with space in old abandoned buildings, including its own: a bright and serene warehouse that opened in 2002. Old Montreal is full of such spaces, as well as many commercial galleries that cater to all areas of interest and taste. With such choice, wonderful art experiences are bound to be had just strolling about the cobblestone streets, peeking through windows and leaving your discoveries to fate.

Photography on display along Avenue McGill-College

Nature & Natural History

Anastasia Michailidis

Updates by Lynn Melanson

St. Lawrence marine ecosystem in the Biodôme

There are the obvious ways to slip away from the bright lights and excitement of the big city. You can hike up Mont Royal, for example, or take the Métro to Île Ste-Hélène for a picnic. But there are other, more exotic ways to get a taste of the wild in Montreal. One of the best is the Biodôme.

Biodôme

From the outside, Montreal's most popular natural-science museum resembles a bicycle helmet. This isn't as odd as it sounds. It was originally built as a stadium for the 1976 Olympic Games track-cycling races. Its transformation into an ecological museum that re-creates four different ecosystems found in the Americas is remarkable. The animals and most of the plants are real, but their habitat— the cliffs, caves, rocks and even some of the enormous trees—is made of concrete. The rocks conceal most of the water and heating systems that keep the ecosystems functioning, and the enormous concrete trees emit warm, moist air to maintain the proper humidity.

Biodôme

49

Tropical forest and
Laurentian beaver
in the Biodôme

The Biodôme attracts a million visitors a year, many of them winter-weary Montrealers who are drawn to the museum's tropical forest, where the temperature never dips below 25 degrees Celsius and the air is heavy with the scent of vegetation. Dozens of animals creep, crawl and scurry amid all that vegetation, most of them quite freely, but the more ferocious (the anaconda, piranha and poison-arrow frogs) are safely behind glass. Many of the residents of the tropical forest belong to endangered species, including the hyacinth macaw, the world's largest species of parrot, and the golden lion tamarin, a cute little primate that is now scarce in its native Brazil. Through its involvement in the global Species Survival Plan, the Biodôme breeds endangered animals in captivity with the ultimate goal of reintroducing them into the wild.

Spring comes slightly earlier in the Biodôme's Laurentian forest than it does in its natural counterpart north of Montreal. But, like the real thing, this exhibit changes with the seasons. Plants become dormant towards the end of the summer, the leaves on the live hardwood trees turn red and yellow and fall in the autumn, and leaves and blossoms reappear and the cycle begins anew in the spring. Among the inhabitants of this ecosystem are dozens of species of fish, along with reptiles, birds and mammals such as beavers, porcupines and lynx.

The main feature of the St. Lawrence marine ecosystem is a glass-walled tank holding 2.5 million litres of sea water produced by the Biodôme itself. As you stroll by, you can spot 20 different species of fish,

St. Lawrence
marine ecosystem
in the Biodôme

including cod, halibut and salmon. Eventually, the pathway leads to a saltwater marsh and past a rocky shore basin filled with starfish, sea anemones and crabs.

The subpolar regions of the Arctic and Antarctica are both represented at the Biodôme's polar ecosystem. You'll find puffins at the subarctic exhibit, while the subantarctic exhibit features those ever-lovable penguins. Don't worry about getting cold; you can watch the antics of the birds from a glassed-in corridor that protects you from these frosty climates.

Another recommended stop is the Naturalia Discovery Room. Find it by following the green frog tracks. This is an exploration and discovery room where touching is encouraged. You can inspect a whale bone, stroke an otter pelt or examine a feather under a microscope. The nature guides on duty organize special games and demonstrations for children.

You can enjoy the Biodôme's ecosystems at your own pace. An easy-to-follow pathway leads you through the different environments. Information panels are posted along the way, and nature guides are on patrol to answer your questions. And if travelling from the humid heat of the tropical forest to the cool air of the Laurentian forest makes you hungry, there's a restaurant on site. There's also a souvenir shop where you'll find neat stuff like bat houses and bug-catching kits.

Polar World penguins at the Biodôme

Reception garden at Jardin Botanique

Jardin Botanique de Montréal

If you visit the Jardin Botanique de Montréal during the summer, you're likely to come across at least one wedding party posing for photographs in one of the 30 outdoor gardens. There are many stunning locations within the botanical garden's 185 acres. One of the most popular is the refined Japanese garden. Here, every plant and rock has been carefully placed to create a meditative atmosphere. An elegant pavilion at the entrance houses a tea room where the Japanese tea ritual is often enacted. The Jardin Botanique de Montréal is also the site of the largest Chinese garden outside of Asia, as well as a pond garden, an alpine garden and a superb rose garden filled with the perfume of 10,000 bushes. A singular achievement is the First Nations garden inaugurated in 2001, and inspired by Amerindian and Inuit cultures. It highlights native use of plants and trees, from growing corn, squash and beans, to gathering berries and medicinal plants, to building homes and canoes. A pavilion houses a permanent exhibition that includes a slide show on contemporary

Above: Chinese garden at the Jardin Botanique de Montréal
Below: The magic of lanterns in the Chinese garden every fall

native lifestyles and a gift shop selling native art and handicrafts.

Above: Wigwam frame
Below: First Nation displays

If you want ideas for your own perennial garden, this is the place to come. And if you've wondered what cooking herbs and medicinal plants look like before they're dried and stuffed into a jar, there's a collection of healthy, live specimens. There's also a garden of plants to avoid. No matter how good a diagram may be, it's much easier to identify poison ivy in the wild if you've already seen the live plant.

Construction of the Jardin began in the early years of the Great Depression, funded partly by federal and provincial make-work project grants. Directed and inspired by its founder, Frère Marie-Victorin, it has grown to become one of the world's leading horticultural centres. There are 21,000 species on display. A sightseeing train can help you cover the grounds quickly, or you can stroll at your own pace along one of the many nature trails.

Each fall, from early September through till the end of October, the Chinese garden stays open until 9 p.m. to host La Magie des Lanternes, or the Magic of Lanterns. Thousands of silk lanterns handcrafted in Shanghai twinkle as night falls, transforming the garden into an illuminated sanctuary. It is a truly spectacular sight to behold.

When snow covers the outdoor gardens in the winter, the trails are taken over by cross-country skiers, but if you'd rather pretend you're in the desert or the tropics, you can amble through 10 connected greenhouses and admire the orchids, cacti and banana plants. The main greenhouse stages special annual events, such as a pumpkin-decorating contest at Halloween as well as Christmas and Easter shows.

In the Chlorophyll Room children learn about plant life, and for adults there are horticultural clinics throughout the year. One of the most popular clinics is the mushroom-identification session that takes place in the fall.

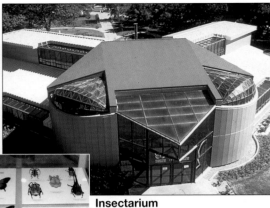

Above and below:
Insectarium
exterior and
exhibits

Insectarium

Montreal's Insectarium started with
one man's personal fascination with
bugs. For many years Georges
Brossard travelled the world
collecting insects of every size, shape
and colour. He identified and mounted thousands of
specimens, but his spectacular collection was hidden like
a buried treasure in his basement. Fortunately, he
managed to persuade the city of Montreal to build a
museum to house it, and now anyone can see and learn
about the creatures that some people have described as
our rivals for control of the Earth.

Even if you've spent most of your life thinking that
insects are repulsive, your loathing will turn to intrigue
when you see their amazing variety. There are insects
that look like green leaves, dry leaves, sticks or thorns,
and insects that reflect every colour of the rainbow.
The colours and patterns on the wings of the butterflies
and moths are stunningly beautiful. Many varieties of
beetles have such brilliant metallic bodies that people
make jewellery out of them, and you'll be astonished
at how big some of them get.

Not all the insects are dead and mounted. The
Insectarium has several live exhibits. Stroll through a
room where butterflies fly freely from flower to flower,
watch bees come and go through a glass-cased hive to
the Jardin Botanique outside, or observe ants at work
in a wall-length ant farm.

From time to time the Insectarium
becomes a restaurant of sorts, serving up
delectable dishes such as biscuits made
of ground-up beetles and chocolate-
covered grasshoppers. Believe it or not,
this event attracts 20,000 insect
gourmets. Yes, people do try the samples
and although most prefer their insect
tidbits in a disguised form, many happily
crunch right into a cricket or gobble up a
mouthful of larvae. This event is
organized only occasionally, but if you
are really tempted to have a taste you can
buy a cookbook specializing in insect
cuisine at the Insectarium's boutique.
With recipes in hand, you'll be ready to

cook up a feast anytime,
any place....

Biosphère

Did you know that less than
one percent of all the water
on Earth is fresh and
available for use by living
organisms? And did you
know that the water formed
3.8 billion years ago is the
same water that exists today
and will exist in the future?
The water that made up a
tear in Cleopatra's eye could
be part of that apple you are about to bite into.

Interactive exhibits
at the Biosphère

Everything you could possibly want to know about
water you can learn at the Biosphère, an interactive
museum dedicated to our most precious resource. The
Biosphère is on Île Ste-Hélène, in the St. Lawrence
River. The location is fitting because the St. Lawrence
is one of the great rivers of the world, flowing out of
the Great Lakes, which themselves make up one-fifth
of the world's supply of fresh water. The Biosphère's
exhibition halls are designed to entertain and educate.
Discovery Hall focuses on how essential water is on
earth. Most of the fascinating facts about water are
stored in interactive terminals. They are easy to
operate, with touch-screen technology. For younger
children there is a giant globe and many large-scale
models that will better hold their interest.

The Water Delights exhibit lets you experience
water as a source of pleasure and a medium for
recreation. Take a virtual trip down a ski hill, squirt at
targets with a water pistol and compose your own
water music. Finally, treat your feet to a refreshing dip

Finding out how
water works at the
Biosphère

in a pool of water. There are stacks of pastel towels available for drying off.

As a member of the EcoWatch Network for conservation, the Biosphère encourages environmental awareness through education. Its EcoAction Hall is a reference centre with access to computer databases and a library with more than 2,000 books, documents and videos about water. By the time you have completed your tour you will understand the cyclical nature of water: water evaporates into the sky, falls back to earth, penetrates plants and animals, flows through streams, is piped in and out of our homes, and returns to the water cycle. When it comes into contact with pollutants it picks them up and carries them along. Because we all share the water that is on this planet, the way each of us uses it affects the people who will come into contact with it down the line, and because that line draws a circle, the people affected along the circle could be ourselves.

The Biosphère is worth a visit for the simple admiration of the sphere itself. Buckminster Fuller's enormous geodesic dome was built for the United States pavilion at Expo 67. A fire destroyed its acrylic skin in 1976 but left the impressive skeleton that surrounds the museum. The Visions Hall at the very top of the Biosphère and the outdoor observation deck provide a magnificent view of Montreal and the St. Lawrence River.

Biosphère

Shopping

Emma McKay

Updates by Cathy Tsolalos

Faubourg merchant
displaying Tibetan
textiles

Montreal is one of North America's premier shopping
destinations with next year's trends to turn-of-the-
century treasures sure to assuage every retail craving.
Although the main retail streets are all relatively close
to one another, shoppers might want to set aside more
than just one day to see it all. Many spend a whole day
in Old Montreal alone, which is filled with art galleries
and antique shops as well as the ubiquitous souvenir
shops filled with cheap trinkets made in faraway
places. But chances are that the perfect souvenir is
waiting elsewhere in the city.

There may be a memento hiding in Antique Alley
on Rue Notre-Dame O. Two long stretches between
Avenue Atwater and Rue Guy boast a string of stores
that stock antiques and collectibles. Or perhaps a
treasure lies nestled in the Golden Square Mile
downtown, where the bankers and railway barons who
built Montreal in the 19th and early 20th centuries
lived. Those who live for designer labels will want to
peruse Rue Peel, being sure to stop in at the Cours
Mont-Royal mall. The same crowd that frequents these
boutiques also patronizes nearby Avenue Greene in
Westmount, which features more exclusive
establishments. The wares on Sherbrooke and Greene
are complemented by offerings uptown on Avenue
Laurier. The stretch between Boulevard St-Laurent and
Chemin de la Côte-Ste-Catherine is home to many
unique and generally upscale shops.

The
Bay

To sample the city's latest styles, St-Laurent and St-Denis are the streets to visit. Hard-core bargain hunters should trek out to the garment district in the Rue Chabanel area at the northern end of St-Laurent. Showrooms with wholesale prices are often open to the public on Saturdays only, selling samples and extras.

Simons

Remember that most stores are open from 10 a.m. to 6 p.m. on Monday through Wednesday, 10 a.m. to 9 p.m. on Thursday and Friday, 10 a.m. to 5 p.m. on Saturday, and noon to 5 p.m. on Sunday. If you're a foreign visitor, remember to save your receipts because you can claim a refund on the 7 percent Goods and Services Tax when you leave the country. The GST is levied on just about all goods except basic groceries.

And if you're here in the dead of winter when it's below -15 Celsius, don't worry, you can still shop until you drop with our 35km of underground shopping, restaurants and services between different malls—all connected underground—Eaton Centre, Place Ville Marie, Les Cours Montréal et les Ails de la mode.

Clothing

Montreal is known for its jaw-dropping style, and chances are that you'll be driven to refresh your own wardrobe to better blend in with the locals. From thrift-shop threads to designer digs, it's all here.

Rue St-Denis boasts many specialty shops like the Boutique Médiévale Excalibor, which stocks an array of one-of-a-kind period dresses (and outfits many a medieval bride) as well as an arresting collection of decorative swords, knives and jewellery. Another interesting niche for seafaring folk to explore is Depart

Fripperie
St-Laurent

en Mer, which stocks the kind of clothing needed for sailing trips, as well as unique gifts and decorations for diehard mariners.

Those who love vintage clothes but don't want to rummage around in dusty bins for them will want to check out some of Montreal's famous fripperies. Requin Chagrin on St-Denis is one such place, as is Montreal Fripe on Avenue du Mont-Royal and Friperie St-Laurent on St-Laurent at Avenue Duluth. On St-Laurent below Sherbrooke, Eva B. carries a mélange of vintage clothes, creations by local designers and an assortment of shoes and accessories. Natural-fabric fanatics might want to visit Je L'ai, a boutique filled with all things hemp, located on Duluth, not far from St-Laurent.

Bedo offers a local clothing line ranging from basics to fun and funkier pieces at quite reasonable prices. Bedo can be found on St-Denis, another on Ste-Catherine and an outlet at the corner of St-Laurent and St-Joseph.

The tried-and-true chains, such as Mexx, Gap, Roots and Le Château, can be found on St-Denis close to Rue Rachel as well as on Ste-Catherine in the downtown core.

The stretch of St-Laurent between Sherbrooke and Avenue des Pins offers a range of boutiques to suit eclectic tastes. Soho Mtl is worth a look for its selection of shoes and fashionable clothing for men and women. Space FB is a local institution,

Shopping on Ste-Catherine

filled with hot tracksuits and simple but flattering T-shirts in brilliant colours and soft, clingy fabrics. For breathtaking and utterly unique style, U&I can't be beat.

West of St-Laurent on Rue Prince Arthur, a few higher-end boutiques have opened their doors in recent years. One of these, IMA, carries designs by David Bitton, best known for his more widely accessible Buffalo clothing line that specializes in denim.

It's worthwhile to save some time for Ste-Catherine where the shop windows are filled with colour year-round. The street has enjoyed a revitalization of sorts in recent years, evident in the abundance of new boutiques and buildings that stretch from Rue University westward to Atwater. Make sure to stop at Simons for a wide variety of men's and women's clothing.

A little farther down the road, BCBG carries that special something to spruce up every wardrobe, be it evening wear or office attire. Olam, with locations on both St-Denis and Ste-Catherine, is filled with vibrant pieces that will take clients from the beach to the bar and beyond. New additions on St. Catherine include Banana Republic, Zara, Lucky Jeans, Adidas, Puma, Lululemon and Mango.

For accessories, visit Rudsak, for leather bags, jackets and belts for both men and women.

Montreal is home to the hippest of chains: such as Urban Outfitters, a massive shop filled with all kinds of novel and funky paraphernalia. Montreal's shops include unique items by local designers. Young hip-hop heads flock to shops such as City Styles and Off

the Hook, both of which overlook Ste-Catherine from second-floor vantage points. Those in the know will also visit FLY, which carries a wide selection of urban attire from established labels as well as up-and-coming Montreal-based designers.

Shoes

Whether it's Cinderella slippers or pavement pounders, there's no shortage of selection in this town. The typical chains, such as Aldo, Transit, Simard, Brown's and Footlocker, are well represented with shops along St-Denis and Ste-Catherine. But there is an increasing number of smaller specialty shops that carry footwear the rest of the world isn't wearing yet. One good place to start is at Scarpa.

For sensible shoes try Sena, at the corner of Rachel and St-Denis, for brands such as Ecco, Birkenstock and Rockport. For running shoes try

Boutique Courir on St-Denis, which carries all kinds of clothing and gear for running and other outdoor activities. For sneakers that put the "fun" in "functional," check out La Godasse, with locations on St-Denis and St-Laurent.

For dressier shoes, try UN Iceland on Ste-Catherine or, if money is no object, stop in at Mona Moore on Sherbrooke.

Jewellery

There's much that glitters in Montreal. Start at Birks, a Montreal institution. Birks deals in fine jewellery and also has a wonderful selection of silverware and china.

A short distance farther east on Ste-Catherine, there are a number of small but excellent jewellers that deal primarily in gold but sell a wide selection of other trinkets. For something a little more specialized, visit AmberLux in the Promenades de la Cathédrale for amber jewelry all shapes and sizes

For something a little more low-key, stroll through Carré Phillips, nestled in the shadow of the Birks building. Weather permitting, it's filled with artisans and entrepreneurs selling a range of items, from handmade, one-of-a-kind treasures to imported costume jewellery.

Top: UN Iceland boots
Above Left: Boutique Courir
Above right: Mona Moore shoes

Art

Art is in the eye of the beholder, so it's hard to recommend any one gallery in Montreal. Shoppers who are willing to do a little exploring will certainly find one to suit their tastes. The two best areas for this quest are Rue St-Paul in Old Montreal and Rue Sherbrooke O. downtown, between Rue de la Montagne and Rue Guy. Both are lined with numerous galleries that are wonderful places to browse. Many galleries feature the canvasses and prints of established artists from Canada and abroad. Representative of the spectrum are Galerie Laroches and Galerie Parchemine in Old Montreal and Galerie Walter Klinkhoff on Sherbrooke.

Galerie le Chariot, at Place Jacques-Cartier, bills itself as the largest collection of Inuit art in Canada, with

Musée des Beaux Arts

Galerie Walter Klinkhoff

an exquisite collection of soapstone and whalebone carvings from the country's northern communities. Take a look at what this gallery has to offer before buying a cheap imitation in a souvenir shop.

In the summer months artists display their wares at the corner of McGill-College and Ste-Catherine and on parts of St-Paul in Old Montreal. There are reasonably priced watercolours and sketches of the city to take home as souvenirs.

The Musée des Beaux-Arts de Montréal has a fantastic gift shop. The selection is always changing to reflect the exhibits on display at the museum and includes posters, reproductions, art books and much more.

Antiques

Excursions along Antique Alley on Rue Notre-Dame O. are always good for surprises. "Antiquing" is a popular Sunday afternoon pastime for Montrealers, so it may be wise to visit in the middle of the week to avoid the crowds. Noteworthy shops in the alley include Antiques Hubert, Spazio and Grand Central.

Le Village des Antiquaries concentrates several dealers under one roof. Some deal in old jewellery, others in furniture, still others in vintage clothing.

Milord sells elegant European furniture, mirrors and the like. Shifting gears, the Salvation Army's giant thrift store is like a year-round garage sale. A smattering of other antique stores can be found around town, notably in Old Montreal and on Avenue Greene in the borough of Westmount.

Collectibles

Memorial buffs and collectors will find a few shops in Montreal to feed their obsessions.

Sports collectors won't want to miss Antiques Lucie Favreau on Rue Notre-Dame O., which specializes in sports memorabilia. Even those who aren't buying will enjoy taking a look at the amazing items in stock. It's like visiting a sports hall of fame.

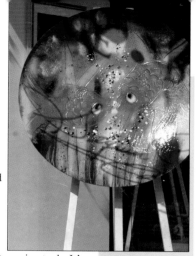

Gallery on Sherbrooke

A few steps away is Retro-ville, a paradise for lovers of all things vintage. For sale are old magazines, toys, neon signs, Coca-Cola collectibles and much, much more. Pause Retro is a similar sort of nostalgia store on Rue St-Denis, with an emphasis on sports cards.

Books

Montreal is a bibliophile's paradise. Amazingly, quite a few independent bookstores have survived—and even thrive—in this city. The western part of Ste-Catherine has developed into a tidy little book district with a number of small used-book shops. Notable are Vortex, which carries literary works. It's easy to lose track of the time while browsing through the selection of books

Gift Shop at the Musée des Beaux-Arts

and music at Cheap Thrills, located just southwest of McGill University. In the McGill ghetto, a few blocks east of the main campus, visit The Word, a tiny shop that carries used textbooks at the beginning of each semester but stocks a wide selection of other works too.

For new books, try Paragraphe, at the corner of McGill-College and Sherbrooke. And there's no shortage of specialty stores. Babar Books in Westmount specializes in children's literature in both English and French. Ulysses travel bookstore stocks guidebooks and maps. Bibliophile on Chemin Queen Mary specializes in Judaica, and the Diocesan Book Room in the Promenades de la Cathédrale mall specializes in Christian books. Ethnic

Vortex Books

Origins, across from the Lionel-Groulx Métro station, specializes in books from the African and African-American diaspora.

The biggest bookstore in the city is Chapters' flagship store for Montreal on Rue Ste-Catherine O. The store sells books on just about every topic imaginable. Indigo Books in the Place Montréal Trust stocks a wide variety of books and sells a range of delightful objects for the home in addition to cards, stationery and other paper items.

If you have managed to learn a few French words while visiting Montreal and would like to pick up a few books in French, visit Renaud-Bray—they also have fun stationary items, office items or home décor pieces.

Housewares

There's no place like home—and with the range of housewares available in Montreal, home bodies can create an abode like no other. In the past couple of years, a mini furniture district has come into being along Boulevard St-Laurent, just south of Avenue du Mont-Royal. The shops display goods straight from the latest home décor magazines, as well as vintage gems and all the basics needed to outfit a stylish home.

There's also an assortment of shops that cater to domestic needs, from bathrooms to patios, along Rue St-Denis. Morphée carries stylish furniture and a great selection of smaller accessories. The pieces at Atmosphère bridge the gap between furniture and art, worth a look, even if redecoration isn't in your immediate plans. A little farther down St-Denis, Côté Sud has lots of enticing items for the home, from novel gifts to must-have classics.

Furniture at Atmosphère

To stock up on all things Provence, try Senteurs de Provence for tablecloths, ceramics, soaps, even bolts of fabric.

Try Zone, with three locations—one on Sherbrooke in Westmount, another on St. Denis and another in Côte-des-Neiges. Each store is filled with stylish wares and gifts. To give your surroundings a slightly younger, funky feel, browse through Urban Outfitters, also on Ste-Catherine.

Stroll through China-town,

on the northern border of Old Montreal, for great prices on tableware from teapots to rice cookers, plates to chopsticks.

Furniture at Atmosphère

Electronics

For gadgets and electronics galore, Boulevard St-Laurent between Avenue du Président-Kennedy and Rue Sherbrooke is the place to visit. There are

generally grey-market items, semi-legally imported from the United States or other countries. Great deals can be had for those who know what they're buying, but ask about warranties, and be prepared to haggle.

Those who prefer to read prices on tags will like nearby Audiotronic or Dumoulin La Place. Both offer a similar range of consumer electronics at decent prices, and both also stock camera equipment. Audiotronic has another shop on Ste-Catherine near the behemoth Future Shop, a Canadian chain that sells relatively low-priced computer equipment, home electronics, CDs and DVDs.

Music

Montreal may march to the beat of a different drum, but music lovers can find just about any rhythm they desire in the city's multiple music stores. The biggest and loudest is HMV's main store on the corner of Peel and Ste-Catherine which also sells DVDs.

One of HMV's closest competitors is Archambault, with two locations farther east along Ste-Catherine: one in the Les Ailes de la Mode complex, and the other at the corner of Rue Berri. Besides CDs, Archambault locations carry a large collection of sheet music and songbooks.

Gates of Chinatown

Montreal's cultural mosaic is well represented in the musical selection available at smaller record shops, several of which also stock a wide range of used vinyl. Check out Pop Shop on St-Laurent for CDs and vinyl that reflect Montreal's cosmopolitan character, Primitive on St-Denis, which also has a terrific selection of CDs and vinyl, or Inbeat for the latest in house music.

Cameras

Camera buffs will want to visit Simon Cameras. They have all the latest camera technology as well as an excellent selection of used equipment.

Another great source for camera equipment is Image Point on Ste-Catherine. Visitors who need to have something fixed or just want more film can stop by Place Victoria Cameras near Old Montreal—it

carries all the essentials and the
service can't be beat.

Games & Toys
This city boasts a fantastic array of
toys for children of all ages. Stop
by Le Valet d'Cœur on St-Denis for
its awesome selection of games as
well as its collection of gadgets and
playthings. And it's not just for kids
— in stock are board games for
grown-up get-togethers, Tarot cards
and novel knick-knacks sure to
amuse and delight. Farther down St-

Oink Oink

Denis is FrancJeu, full of art supplies, toys and games
for children. Stop by the shop to pick up a copy of the
calendar of free Saturday-morning workshops—kids
can take their projects home with them.

A refreshing alternative to the world of mass-
produced plastic toys can be found on Avenue Duluth,
at a charming little shop called La Grande Ourse. The
beautiful handmade wooden toys here are designed to
engage young minds and to endure the test of time.
And on Avenue Greene in Westmount, Oink Oink has a
great selection of top-quality toys.

Odds & Ends
Many of the shops that make shopping in Montreal
such a unique experience
don't fit into any
conventional categories—all
the more reason to visit
them. One such shop is
Kamikaze Curiosités on St-
Denis, which purveys
fanciful socks and
accessories.

Farther up on St-Denis is Rubans, Boutons, a store
that sells only buttons and ribbons. These items aren't
on your shopping list? No matter—the overwhelming
selection is a wonder to browse, and few shoppers
leave empty-handed.

Those who fold for fancy paper products will want
to visit L'Essence du Papier. This charming
St-Denis boutique has a lovely selection of
stationeries and cards. Another paper store to
visit is the Japanese Paper Store on Avenue
St-Viateur, which sells delightful handmade
paper products and offers a number of
workshops on making paper, kites, lanterns
and other imaginative creations.

Montreal's Co-op La Maison Verte on
Sherbrooke Street in Notre Dame de Graces is
the first environmental co-op initiative in Canada
containing a shop filled with environmentally
safe household products and a fair-trade café-
shop. Offering locally made, natural and
ecological products and clothing, customers have

Mélange Magique

the satisfaction of knowing that their purchase will make a positive impact on real people's lives.

For frequent travellers, Jet-Setter on Avenue Laurier has every sort of travel gadget anyone could possibly need, along with more traditional items such as suitcases, backpacks and outdoor wear. Another shop for travellers is Tilley Endurables, also on Laurier. Tilley sells sensible travel clothing but is best known for its hats.

Maybe it's the French influence, but more than a few shops in Montreal carry toys for adults. One of these, La Capoterie on St-Denis, specializes in condoms. This isn't a sex shop with gag gifts but rather a place for playful couples to have fun shopping for contraceptives.

Another shop to visit is Mélange Magique, which offers something for every New Age need. And no matter what the time of year, it's always holiday time at Noël Éternel, a shop that only sells Christmas goodies.

As you stroll by all the galleries heading West on St. Paul street, stop in at Espace Pepin, corner of St. Paul and St. Pierre. Lysanne Pepin, owner and artist creates portraits and a house collection of clothing. Espace Pepin has been transformed into an apartment-like concept where customers can walk around a home, carefully furnished with individual touches from Canada's design community.

A definite fun odds & ends/funky store is Mortimer Snodgrass (near the Centaur Theatre). It is a shop that has a wide variety of items you will not find in any other store and you will find almost something for everyone here.

Finally, what visit to Montreal would be complete without a trip to the home of its hockey heroes, the Canadiens? The Bell Centre souvenir shop has jerseys, photos and other items to satisfy the sports fan.

Festivals & Events

Bram Eisenthal

Updates by Kristina Mansson

No city in North America is better at throwing a party than Montreal. It's a tradition that goes back to Expo 67, the world's fair that marked Canada's 100th birthday. Celebration continues to be a Montreal theme to the present day. Every summer is filled with festivals from late June until Labour Day.

The granddaddy of all these celebrations is the Festival des Films du Monde, or World Film Festival (WFF). This celluloid showcase presents a plethora of films from more than 70 countries. It's one of the only competitive festivals in North America accredited by the International Federation of Film Producers Associations. Held the final week of August through to Labour Day, the WFF screens some 400 films; a dozen or so are screened under the stars. The city is rapidly becoming one of the main film-production locales in North America. In recent years stars such as Brad Pitt, Denzel Washington, Angelina Jolie, Ben Kingsley, Mira Sorvino, Ewan McGregor, George Clooney and Quebec's own Donald Sutherland have come to the city to work and to play. During the film festival you can usually increase your odds of spotting a star by hanging around Boulevard St-Laurent after the show.

Outdoor festival sites have serious clout—the streets around the Place des Arts complex are

Above and below:
Festival
International de
Jazz de Montréal

Top: Performance at Festival International de Jazz
Above: Just for Laughs Comedy Festival

closed to vehicle traffic for much of the summer as one celebration flows into another. The first major event of the festival season is the Festival International de Jazz de Montréal, which fills the first two weeks of July with concerts and jam sessions. The jazz fest attracts performers such as Manhattan Transfer, Chick Corea, Count Basie, Dave Van Ronk, France's Orchestre National de Barbes and Canada's hottest singer-pianist, Diana Krall. Virtually every big-name jazz entertainer and band has appeared here since the festival's debut—including many legends. In addition to ticketed events, there are many free outdoor concerts.

The Just for Laughs Comedy Festival began as a humble two-night French-language show that attracted little attention, and it laboured for the first couple of years in the shadow of the jazz festival. But its founders—Gilbert Rozon and Andy Nulman—have turned it into the most important festival of its kind in the world. Just for Laughs fills two weeks in July with more than 1,300 shows and performances, indoors and out. Many of the performers are household names—people like Jerry Seinfeld, Tim Allen, Roseanne Barr, Drew Carey, Howie Mandel, Rowan (Mr. Bean) Atkinson, Sandra Bernhard, and the late Marcel Marceau and George Burns—but this is also where many new comics get their first real recognition. Comedians like Mike McDonald and Bowser and Blue, for example, make a point of appearing as often as they can. It's wise to book early if you're thinking of attending, especially the French and English Gala performances and the most popular events.

While these three festivals attract most summer tourists to Montreal, there are a slew of smaller events year-round that add to the charm and excitement of this city that never sleeps, where joie de vivre brings people back year after year.

Almost 50,000 people seeking a mid-June event whose motto is "no artistic direction, no minimum standards and no limits" attended 2003's Festival St-Ambroise Fringe de Montréal (Montreal Fringe Festival), a theatrical celebration of differences and, often, lunacy, as some of the more unusual acts you have ever encountered play the city's venues. Acts range from comedy to dance, drama and musical performances. http://www.Montrealfringe.ca/

The event that opens the summer season is arguably the most beautiful to gaze at: the L'International des Feux Loto-Quebec, or the Montréal International Fireworks Competition. Incendiary masters from around the world light up the night skies over Montreal

every weekend between mid-June and the end of July, with some midweek displays thrown in. These spectacles have become so popular that the best viewpoint, the Pont Jacques-Cartier (Jacques Cartier Bridge), is clogged with spectators and often closed to traffic from mid-evening to midnight.

If hot-air ballooning is your passion, investigate the Festival des Montgolfières de Gatineau, held at nearby St-Jean-sur-Richelieu (half an hour south by car, over the Pont Champlain). Enthusiasts from around the world assemble to fly their contraptions and fill the skies with yet more beauty for all to behold. This festival is held at the end of August.

Montreal International Fireworks Competition

For something a little more traditional, try the Festival de la Gibelotte de Sorel-Tracy in Sorel, a 90-minute drive downriver from Montreal. Gibelotte is a robust stew made with barbotte, a fatty, flaky species of catfish that lives in the waters around the Îles de Sorel. Every July, the cooks of the town serve it up with bread and locally brewed beer in one of the finest and most cheerful street festivals in the province. Beer lovers can also attend Montreal's Mondial de la Bière, a five-day outdoor extravaganza that attracts some 25,000 brew fans. It's held in early- to mid-June at the Windsor Station and Courtyard in downtown Montreal and provides an opportunity to sample beer from breweries such as McAuslan's (St. Ambroise), Unibroue and Les Brasseurs du Nord (the Boréale line).

The Holocaust Education Series, held mid-October to mid-November has a strong impact on its visitors. Free activities held citywide include lectures by world-class speakers, panel discussions, films and a variety of exhibitions. All events are free of charge.

The Présence Autochtone, or First Peoples' Festival, is a 12-day exploration of film, dance, crafts, music and workshops that ends by marking the summer solstice on National Aboriginal Solidarity Day, June 21.

Les Francofolies de Montréal

Outdoor urban events proliferate during the summer. Two of the best are the Tour de l'Île de Montréal and Les FrancoFolies de Montréal. The first is the world's largest gathering of cyclists, attracting some 30,000 riders for a 50-kilometre route through the city in early June. The tour generally marks the end of the Féria du Vélo de Montréal (Montreal Bike Fest), which includes a children's tour and a night tour held the preceding week. Les FrancoFolies is equally impressive, bringing some 1,000 musicians, composers, authors and performers into the open air at Place des Arts. Rock, pop, hip-hop, jazz, funk and Latin music are just some of the rhythms you'll hear in late July and early August—en français, of course.

Other film festivals throughout the year include the Festival du Nouveau Cinéma de Montréal, held during

Tour de l'Île de Montréal

the fall to avoid scheduling clashes with the major competitor. This festival focuses on emerging trends and developments in cinema and digital media. Cinemania celebrates French films with English subtitles. The festival has become quite respectable after several years and is worth a visit if you're in Montreal in November. Teitelbaum is showing more and more premières, often with the stars and directors in attendance.

FanTasia, Montreal's Fantasia Film Festival. Started in 1996 primarily as a vehicle for Asian action and fantasy films and rapidly became a celebration of international horror, sci-fi and fantasy. Screenings are generally sold out; many premières feature the directors. This month-long festival begins in the middle of July.

Montreal is also known as the city of festivals which occur just about every month of the year. A selection follows.

La Fête des Neiges de Montréal is held in the dead of winter so make sure you dress appropriately to take advantage of all the events and enjoy them. It is held at the end of January to the beginning of February for three weekends in a row with tube-sliding, snow sculptures, an outdoor discothèque and many more outdoor winter events. http://www.fetedesneiges.com/en/

The Hydro-Québec Celebration of Light presents, on the illuminated Festival site, free outdoor concerts and activities with themes emphasizing light, fire and pyrotechnics. Festival goers are invited to come warm up their winter evenings, alone or with family or friends. Gathered around bonfires, sipping wine or hot chocolate, crowds can watch the antics of strolling street entertainers and performers, gaze at the spellbinding light displays, as well as dance to the beat of the free outdoor sound and light shows, against a backdrop of majestic fireworks. The High Lights Festival takes place at the end of February to the beginning of March http://www.Montrealenlumiere.com

The Blue Metropolis Montréal International Literary Festival is run by the Blue Metropolis Foundation, a Montreal-based non-profit organization dedicated to bringing people from different cultures together to share the pleasure of reading and writing. It organizes innovative activities that give diverse audiences direct access to various modes of literary expression of the highest calibre. The Foundation organizes three sets of activities: Literacy and the Literary, Educational programs and Blue Metropolis Montréal International Literary Festival. It is held at the end of April. http://www.blue-met-bleu.com.

Montreal Chamber Music Festival is dedicated to promoting chamber music in all its diverse forms through collaborations with other artistic disciplines. Performances in historic sites by renowned international artists and rising stars emphasize Montreal's cultural richness and diversity. It runs from

the beginning of May until the first of June.
www.festivalMontreal.org

Although Montreal Museums Day is not a festival, but it is a great way to see Montreal's museums all in on day. In 2007, twenty-seven museums participated and 108,000 people joined in on the event. Shuttle service is available and the event is normally on a Sunday at the end of May.
www.museeMontreal.org/site/museumday.htm

Mutek, the Electronik Music and Digital Creativity Festival, brings over one hundred artists, many of whom arrive from the world's corners for these five days of astonishing showcases that will surely prove unique and sophisticated. Each of these talented explorers brings to the festival their own brand of electronic music and digital creativity; together they create a program at once eclectic and stimulating. It runs for five days between the end of May and the beginning of June. http://www.mutek.ca

Suoni per il popolo is an unofficial music festival featuring diverse genres of music, such as bent rock, noise, avant-garde folk, free jazz, urban beats, experimental electronics and contemporary composition. The shows run throughout the month of June at two different venues and even includes a free family picnic day.
http://www.casadelpopolo.com/suoni/about.htm

Montreal's Grand Prix weekend turns the whole city into a big party. During the weekend, cars are banned from two main blocks in the heart of the city, Crescent and Peel. Crescent street bars are packed with people; the street is lined with Formula One cars, various booths and a stage for live bands at one end of the block. Peel Street, when it is blocked off, is lined with Ferraris. A little farther North-East, on St. Laurent above Sherbrooke Street, is also blocked off for serious partying and various events all weekend long.
www.grandprix.ca

Old Montreal's Early Music Festival, Montreal Baroque, offers a unique opportunity to hear music of the 17th- and 18th-centuries, performed by Canadian and international celebrities. Snaking through the narrow streets of the old city to the sound of a hundred flutes at the festival's Grand Parade, relaxing at a garden concert, catching a choral concert in a chapel, or simply enjoying a street performance, this festival gives a new cultural identity to Old Montreal. International tourists alike are

Dragon boat racing

attracted to Early Music. End of June.

The Montreal International Reggae Festival started as a small not-for-profit event and has now grown to attract over 24,000 people. The cohesion of internationally acclaimed artists, ethnic arts and crafts, various cultural cuisines, a designated kid's area, a Bob Marley free stage, main stage attractions, multimedia attractions and many other activities give attendees reasons to stay for the day's events and the evening's nightlife. http://www.Montrealreggaefestival.com

Dragon boat racing has been practiced in China by around 20 million people. But over the past 25 years it has spread beyond Asia to Europe, North America, Australia and Africa, to become an international sport with a huge following. Today it is among the fastest growing water sport and remains the largest team sport, with over 60 million participants in over 50 countries. The biggest Dragon Boat Festival racing events outside of Asia are in Canada. Vancouver, Toronto and Montreal each host races featuring more than 180 twenty-five-person crews. These races take place over two days in mid-to-late June or July to correspond with the Chinese fifth day of the fifth month custom. http://www.Montrealdragonboat.com

Pop Montréal is committed to providing opportunities for independent musicians, promoters, fans, and creative minds of all types to participate in what is a world class international event. They have been able to curate an event for unknown artists and forgotten legends that they feel deserve a unique platform. You will see the occasional superstar and breakthrough act, but most of all Pop Montréal is where you will see the headliners of the future play to their first excited crowds in intimate venues. Pop is where you will see 90-year-old crooners jamming with 20-year-old wunderkinds. The event occurs over five days at the end of September to the beginning of October. http://www.popMontreal.com

The Osheaga Music and Arts Festival is a two-day outdoor rock festival focused on cutting-edge talent from ground-breaking indie-rock to thumping relaxed reggae grooves; experimental orchestral pop to turntable mastery. It also incorporates innovative visual arts, gastronomic delights from several continents and after parties taking place in the downtown core. Beginning of September. http://www.osheaga.com

The festival Rencontres internationales du documentaire is place for meetings, debate and reflection on politics, the environment and society's felt concerns. And a place to discover documentary film, along with its authors and the writings that imbue it. Held in November. www.ridm.qc.ca

Dining

Monique Polak

Montreal is a great city for food. You'll notice that life here revolves around eating: Shopping for food—picking out just the right shallots, going from one specialty shop to the next in pursuit of cheese, baguettes, coffee and wine, talking and of course going out to eat. Montreal has a great selection of food in different price ranges. Historically, Montreal has been known for its French cuisine. Today there are still plenty of French restaurants, though many of them have been influenced by the latest trends in Thai and California cooking. The many immigrants to Montreal have also brought their own unique flavours to the city, such as delicious Greek, Italian, Chinese, Indian, Vietnamese and Caribbean food.

Terrace diners in old Montreal

Breakfast at Beauty's

Brunch

Sunday brunch is a Montreal tradition. And in summer, when the weather's good, every day is Sunday.

Expect a line that heads out the front door and onto nearby rue St-Urbain if you turn up at Beauty's later than 10 a.m. on a weekend. Located at the foot of Mont Royal on Avenue du Mont-Royal O., Beauty's has been a hit with Montrealers since it opened in 1942. Everything here is sold à la carte, so expect to pay extra for your freshly squeezed orange juice. The most popular item on the menu is the Beauty's Special, a bagel sandwich filled with cream cheese, lox, tomato and onion. If you're too hungry to survive the line, it'll take you less than five minutes to walk to Pizza des Pîns on Avenue du Parc. The food is similar

Chez Cora
Déjeuners

and just as good, but you won't be able to say you had breakfast at Beauty's.

Though sophisticated Montreal diners disapprove of food chains, one that specializes in breakfasts has been drawing crowds. With more than a dozen locations on the island of Montreal, Chez Cora Déjeuners offers a variety of hearty breakfasts, most of them served with an artful—and abundant—arrangement of fresh fruit. Downtown, there's a Chez Cora on Rue Stanley. Everything sounds so good on the colourful menu that it'll be difficult to choose, but you might try the French toast made with zucchini bread.

Or you can go for something completely different: dim sum breakfast. "Dim sum means 'touch your heart,'" says Chuck Kwan, owner of Maison Kam Fung, one of the most popular dim sum spots in town. Consider it a good sign that most of the diners here are Chinese. This huge restaurant overlooks Chinatown. Dim sum is available here seven days a week from 7 a.m. until 3 p.m. Waiters go by with stainless-steel carts carrying a variety of exotic delicacies. Each item costs between $2.25 and $6. The steamed shrimp or pork dumplings and the deep-fried crab balls are delicious. For dessert, try the sesame seed balls or the mango pudding—or both.

If you prefer to sleep in a little longer, Café Santropol on St-Urbain opens at noon. In summer, try to get a spot in the garden, an urban paradise complete with small pond, chimes and birdfeeders. The specialty here is huge, healthy sandwiches made with thick slabs of pumpernickel bread. The Midnight Spread is filled with cream cheese and peanut butter, the Killer Tomato with cream cheese and sun-dried tomatoes. The combinations might sound odd, but they taste delicious.

Café Santropol

Quick Eats

At some Montreal landmarks you can order take-out as well as eat on the premises. Forget your diet and order your smoked meat medium when you go to Schwartz's delicatessen on Boulevard St-Laurent. Built in 1930, this old-fashioned deli has long, plain tables at which customers literally rub elbows. To pass for a local, order a cherry Coke and pickles on the side. Arahova Souvlaki is probably Montreal's best-known souvlaki joint. The original Arahova, located on Avenue St-Viateur O. in Montreal's Mile-End district, has been around since 1972. Several others have opened in

Schwartz's

recent years, one on Rue Queen Mary in Snowdon. A combo plate with a lamb souvlaki pita, salad and fries goes for $11.95. What makes Arahova souvlaki so good? "The secret is our tzatziki sauce. It's yogurt-based, with garlic, cucumber and salt," says Nector Koutroumanis, whose father began the business. Drive slowly on Avenue Victoria in the Côte-des-Neiges district or you might just miss the Caribbean Curry House. Try the roti—curried meat and potatoes served in a chapati, or Indian flatbread. If you're feeling brave, go for the jerk chicken. You'll need a rum-based calypso punch—or two—to wash it down. Luckily, a calypso punch here costs only $4.95—and it's the best-tasting one this side of Jamaica. A slightly different twist on roti can be found at the Jardin du Cari on St-Viateur. Here, the home-style Guyanese food made to order and hot sauce is to die for.

Arahova Souvlaki

For a taste of Jerusalem, head to Pizza Pita for the finest falafel in town. Located on Boulevard Décarie, this kosher restaurant is equally popular with hip Montreal vegetarians and Orthodox Jews. The falafel sandwiches are made fresh daily with chickpeas, garlic, coriander and spices. They're served on pita bread with tahini, a sauce made from ground sesame seeds. Charisa, a hot sauce, is optional. Other specialties here include homemade soups, vegetarian pizza, shawarma sandwiches and spicy french fries. Say hello to Chaim and Zvi Spiegelman, the friendly brothers who own the restaurant.

Ever had a PoBoy? That's a pulled pork sandwich with a slice of Swiss cheese, barbecue sauce and french fries inside. You can get one at Bofinger, a Texas-style smokehouse on Rue Sherbrooke O. in Notre-Dame-de-Grace, a leafy neighbourhood in the city's west end. Other specialties include the half chicken, which sells for $9.99 and comes with two side dishes. There are five barbecue sauces to choose from. The décor here is casual, customers place their orders at the cash. When your food's ready, one of the staff

Restaurant Daou

will holler your name. In warm weather, chow down at one of the picnic tables outside.

Family Fare
It's a bit of a trek, but Restaurant Daou on Rue Faillon in Montreal's northeast is worth it. This family-owned Lebanese restaurant has been around since 1975. The atmosphere is informal, with long tables set close together. Begin with the fattouch salad—morsels of cucumber, parsley, tomato, onion and toasted pita in a dressing of olive oil and lemon. Proceed directly to the marinated breast of chicken. If you have a craving for Indian food, try La Maison du Cari (not to be confused with the previously mentioned Caribbean Curry House). Located downtown on Rue Bishop in what might be described as a hole in the wall, this restaurant serves food that is authentic and spicy. Try the onion bhaji or samosas—phyllo triangles stuffed with vegetables and meat—as an appetizer. The butter shrimp and butter chicken are the most popular main dishes. Served with aromatic basmati rice, the shrimp and chicken will transport you directly to India. The nan bread here is also first class. Wash the whole thing down with a British beer.

Another good bet for lovers of Indian food is Ganges Restaurant on Rue Sherbrooke O. Regulars swear by the butter chicken, the shai rezala—a sweet-and-sour beef dish—and the shrimp tikka masala, charcoal-broiled shrimps served in a ginger-garlic sauce. Also on the Indian theme, the lunch buffet at Bombay Palace on Rue Bishop. is great for better-than-average favourites.

If you're in the mood for grilled chicken, head directly to Restaurant Agora on Rue Somerled in Notre-Dame-de-Grace. This simple, down-to-earth restaurant opened in 2004 and has been drawing crowds ever since. They come for the Greek-style chicken—seasoned with spices and herbs and cooked on an open flame—the Greek salad and the oven-baked lima beans. A full chicken costs $16.95 and feeds a family of four.

BYOB
BYOBs, or bring-your-own-bottle establishments, abound in Montreal. They help keep dinner prices down, making fine dining accessible to the budget-conscious. And because Quebec liquor stores carry an excellent selection of French wines (some from lesser-known regions such the Loire Valley and Languedoc), you can treat yourself to a nice bottle of wine. Consider it a good investment.

Bring a bottle of Chianti to La Trattoria on Notre-Dame Street West, a five-minute drive east of the Atwater Market. This restaurant could easily be in

Trattoria interior

Italy. Choose from 10 kinds of pizza, including one made with fresh tomato sauce, Italian sausage and mozzarella cheese. Pasta dishes are equally authentic. Another specialty is conigllio trattoria—rabbit cooked in its own juices— served with baked potatoes.

One BYOB that everyone keeps raving about is La Colombe on Avenue Duluth. Because it only seats 36 people, you'll need to phone ahead for a reservation, especially on a weekend. The specialty at this elegant yet cozy restaurant is French cuisine. Chef Moustafa Rougaibi's menu changes weekly. The $40 table d'hôte includes soup, appetizer, main dish, dessert and coffee. The venison, the veal chops and the bison are highly recommended. Leave room for the fondant au chocolat, a chocolate cake served with a dark chocolate sauce.

Restaurant Le P'tit Plateau on Rue Marie-Anne E. near Rue St-Denis is another popular BYOB. Here, too, you'll need to reserve at least a week in advance for a weekend rendezvous. The table d'hôte that

La Colombe

includes soup or salad, main course and coffee, tea or tisane is available for $28 to $34. The restaurant is owned by Alain Loivel, a young Bordeaux-born chef and his wife, Geneviève Desnoyers. Loivel's specialties include confit de canard, jarret d'agneau confit and cassoulet Toulousain. Doesn't everything sound delicious en Français? Loivel's duck is cooked in its own fat in the traditional style of southwestern France; his lamb is cooked in its own juices and is served with spring vegetables, and his cassoulet—another French classic—is made with white kidney beans, pork and sausage and is topped with duck confit. In case you can't get a reservation, consider ordering in your dinner: all of the food on the menu is available for take-out.

Four-Star Dining

If you are in the mood to splurge there are plenty of four-star restaurants in Montreal just waiting for you.

Toqué! has been attracting a lot of attention since it first opened in the mid-1990s. In 2004, the restaurant moved from Rue St-Denis to a new location at Place Jean-Paul-Riopelle in Old Montreal. Chef Normand Laprise continues to be known for his innovative market cuisine. His menu changes constantly and relies heavily on local produce. The word toqué is Québécois slang and means "stubborn"—but in a good way.

Toqué!

According to Laprise's business partner, Christine Lamarche, that's exactly how the couple feels about food: "The emphasis here is on food. Almost all of the vegetables we use are organic." Delicacies include leg of Basses Laurentides suckling pig with a curry glaze, served with maple syrup-roasted carrots. For dessert, Lamarche recommends the crispy raspberry, creamy yogurt and raspberry sorbet. Expect dinner for two to cost $170 before wine, taxes and tip.

Another vedette on Montreal's four-star dining scene is Joe Beef. This restaurant, which opened in 2004, is where well-heeled Montrealers go to see and be seen. It's located on Rue Notre-Dame, just west of the Atwater Market, and co-owned by innovative chefs David McMillan and Frederic Morin. Despite the mention of beef in the restaurant's name (it's named after a now defunct Old Montreal tavern), the specialty here is fish and seafood. McMillan recommends the fresh oysters by the dozen and the spaghetti with lobster. There are only 28 seats, so phone well ahead to reserve. Dinner for two before wine, taxes and tip costs about $140.

Another good choice is Ariel Bar à Vin Cuisine Locale, located downtown on Rue Drummond. There are three dining rooms from which to choose; each room is decorated with paintings by well-known contemporary Quebec artists. The garden room, a covered atrium with a fountain, is particularly delightful. One room is a private salon. Here, too, the menu is constantly changing, but signature dishes include the crispy kataifi-wrapped shrimp, served with a lobster mayonnaise and a curry oil drizzle; and the veal schnitzel, a veal scallop pounded thin and served Cordon Bleu-style, filled with Gruyère cheese and prosciutto. For dessert try the fine cocoa pavé with bourbon vanilla ice cream and candied kumquats. Dinner for two will set you back about $80 before wine, taxes and tip.

Les Caprices de Nicolas

Brunoise, on Rue St-André near Parc Lafontaine is another fine dining favourite. This elegant and intimate restaurant seats only 50 people, so phone ahead for a reservation—especially on a weekend. Brunoise is owned by two young chefs, Zach Suhl and Michel Ross. Their goal, says Suhl, is to offer an upscale dining experience at a reasonable price.

The table d'hôte, a four-course meal which changes

seasonally, costs $48. One out-of-this-world appetizer is the marinated salmon with cocoa oil and avocado. An equally delectable main dish is the roasted scallops served with caramelized onions and an olive oil and lime emulsion. The cheese plate is a lovely way to prolong your meal—and don't leave without trying the panacotta with basil syrup and fresh passion-fruit pulp.

Brunoise

In February 2007, Suhl and Ross opened Brasserie Brunoise on Rue de la Montagne downtown. This restaurant offers a more casual dining experience than the original Brunoise and is open for lunch. "The specialty at Brasserie Brunoise is French comfort food, bistro-style," said Suhl. Specialties include steak frites (at $24, the priciest item on the menu), calf's liver, and of course, French onion soup.

On the more established side, Montrealers have been coming to Chez La Mère Michel on Rue Guy for over 30 years. Specialties of the house include barquette Alsacienne and lobster served out of the shell with a garlic-flower sauce. The fish (try the Arctic char) is brought in fresh each day. Caribou and bison appear as seasonal dishes. The wine list is large and reasonably priced; dinner for two will see you adding $100 or so to the cost of your bottle.

Another longtime favourite is L'Express on Rue St-Denis. Paris meets Montreal in this lively bistro, where little has changed since it first opened in 1980. The black and white tile floors and mirrored walls give it a French feel; same goes for the wonderful baguette and jar of cornichons the waiter brings over when you sit down. Try the poached salmon served on potato purée with chervil, or the grilled onglet—hanger steak—served with shallot butter and French fries. Dinner for two before wine, taxes and tip costs about $60.

Milos

Where do Cate Blanchett, Paul Newman and Bette Midler hang out when they visit Montreal? At Milos Restaurant, an upscale version of the traditional Greek psarotaverna located just north of Mont Royal on Avenue du Parc. Start with an appetizer of crab cakes—they're served with a light mustard sauce. Grilled octopus is another specialty, but most customers order fish by the pound. They choose it themselves from what looks like an open market at the back of the dining room. Imported from as far away as

The Beaver Club

Tunisia and Greece, your fish is grilled whole and is then deboned before being served up on a platter. Dinner for two starts at about $120 before wine, taxes and tip.

One of Montreal's hottest new restaurants is Taverna Zante, which was opened in March 2007 by three former Milos employees. These guys know what they're doing. The partners set up shop on the trendiest block of Boulevard St. Laurent near Rue Sherbrooke; the décor manages to be sleek and inviting at the same time; and the fish couldn't be fresher. One house specialty is the grilled Mediterranean bass. Two of the restaurant's owners wait tables; the third prepares the fish. Leave room for the loukoumades – Greek honey balls. Dinner for two before wine, taxes and tip will run about $80.

A hands-down favourite with local foodies is Le Club de Chasse et Pêche. Tucked away on a little street in Old Montreal, this place doesn't even have a sign with the restaurant's name on it. But it's well-worth searching for. Two dining rooms seat 80 people. The atmosphere is old-fashioned clubby with contemporary details. "Our food is bold, accurate and intense. We work as much as possible with local ingredients," said co-owner Hubert Marsolais. Regulars love chef Claude Pelletier's crunchy sweetbreads, served with crab, artichoke and field tomatoes. Dinner for two before wine, taxes and tips costs about $100.

Located off the main lobby of the Hôtel Le Reine-Élizabeth, The Beaver Club is a Montreal dining institution. First opened in 1958, the restaurant has its roots in the 18th-century fur trade. The walls are done in brick and oak panelling; there's an open rotisserie by the restaurant's back wall. Specialties include the lobster blanquette and Quebec foie-gras. Dinner for two runs about $150 before wine, taxes and tip.

Lastly, if you feel like a short excursion, Au Tournant de la Rivière is just reward for those who can find it, on Rue Salaberry in Carignan. (Take Autoroute Décarie south to Highway 10 East, turn west at Exit 22 and then immediately take the right turn for Sherbrooke, then make a left on Boulevard Brunelle—the restaurant is at Brunelle and Salaberry in a converted barn behind a farmhouse.) The atmosphere is luxurious and the service first rate. Chef Jacques Robert gives conventional dishes the kind of treatment that makes them exceptional, but they can be prohibitively priced. If you decide to splurge, go all the way with the crème brûlée with maple syrup.

Restaurant Globe

Night Life

Paul Spence

Updates by Karnjit Lehal

Winnie's and Thursday's on Rue Crescent

Montreal's nightlife begins far before night falls. Suppertime is a very European eightish here, and by then, most residents have already been socializing over food and drink for some time during the daily cinq-à-sept. What's a cinq-à-sept, you ask? Why, it's a brilliant doubling of happy hour, and it literally translates to "five-to-seven." On Avenue du Mont-Royal at Edgar Hypertaverne for example, one can enjoy a pint of fantastic local brew while nibbling on a platter of wonderful cheeses from all over the world or head over to the trendy Bily Kun's with ostrich heads sticking out of the walls, microbrews, DJs and live jazz on Thursday evenings.

A great place to start an evening on the town is the heart of the club scene for Montreal's English-speaking crowd. Between Rue Ste-Catherine O. and Boulevard René-Lévesque are the well-known party streets of Peel, de la Montagne, Crescent, Bishop and MacKay. The imposing old stone buildings now house dance bars, discos and pubs and cater to both visitors and locals alike.

Rue Crescent is the epicentre of downtown nightlife, where many of Montreal's most established bars sling suds and grub every night of the week. Thursday's is a good choice for relaxation in an old-style pub environment with a Montreal classic—bagels with cream cheese and lox.

In 1967, Sir Winston Churchill Pub opened its doors on Crescent, and in almost forty years it has lost none of its charm. Crescent is also home to Vocalz, a popular karaoke bar where both amateur and

professional singers belt out the classics.

Also on Crescent is Newtown, owned by Formula One racer and local celebrity, Jacques Villeneuve. This nightspot was converted from two adjoining town houses and now has all that you need for a night out—a rooftop terrace, lounge, restaurant and club—all on four floors of one building.

Just below St. Catherine are university crowds drinking fresh, full-flavoured beers brewed on the premises at Brutopia. It consists of three bars on three floors served up with live music on most nights.

Still on Crescent is laid-back Hurley's Irish Pub and in the neighbourhood on Bishop Street are McKibbon's and O'Reagan's all which offer a genuine pub atmosphere. Imported beers, wood panelling and live

Celtic music lend a rustic feeling to these popular joints. McLean's pub just over on Peel Street offers friendly service and selection of imported and domestic beers.

Don't want to miss a moment of the "big" game (be it soccer, baseball, hockey or cricket)? The Dominion Pub on Metcalf is the place to be. This friendly neighbourhood pub offers a big-screen TV and a host of tasty dishes. The adventurous spirit might be inclined to try the house specialty: pig knuckles with sauerkraut!

Just down the road on Rue MacKay is Upstairs Jazz Bar and Grill, a spot for great jazz and classy eats every night. For more great music, head up to the House of Jazz (formerly known as Biddles) on Rue Aylmer for a classic trio: jazz, booze and ribs.

Over on Rue de la Montagne is Hotel de la Montagne, a nice quiet place to go for drinks and if you bring your bathing suit, you can go swimming on the rooftop! Not far down the street is Club 1234 with three rooms and renowned DJs at the turntables.

Segafredo's reputation is built on its own brand of espresso is the first Canadian franchise located Ste. Catherine Street, west of Peel Street. Segarfredo is a bistro/lounge/coffee shop melded into one with breakfast and lunch menus available at reasonable prices and a live DJ Thursdays.

Fiddlers at McKibbin's Irish Pub

If walking is impossible (those enjoying Montreal's nightlife are often impeded by "club foot," a.k.a. high heels), hop in a cab and direct the driver to the corner of St-Laurent and Sherbrooke, where, for a significant stretch, St-Laurent welcomes the beautiful and the chic. Hip restaurants Shed Café, Sofia, MED, Globe Supper Club, Time Café and Buonanotte are where the famous wine and dine.

There are various clubs on the strip that have open rooftop terraces in the summer such as B-side, The Main Bar and Terrace—the newest club on the block—and Club Tokyo, one of Montreal's favourite party places over the years.

Farther up on St. Laurent Street close to Duluth are the classic watering holes such as Bifteck and Frappé both with pool tables and foosball and cater to the university crowd. For great live music and no pretension, stop by Barfly, which features live bands almost every night. On Sundays it also hosts excellent open country jams.

For theme bars try the Go Go Lounge for classic 1960s and 1970s music. For more dancing, the Blue Dog and Blizzarts offer a host of musical styles (electronica, reggae, old school, etc.) and if you're up that far on St. Laurent, be sure to check out Laika which attracts some good DJs, as well as Le Reservoir which is a very relaxed bar.

Another area that buzzes at night is St-Laurent's sister street to the east, the noticeably more Francophone St-Denis. It's home to some of Montreal's best patios, including the massive backyard party found nightly at Le Saint-Sulpice (just below Rue Ontario), the great live venue L'Escogriffe and Le Monkey (two storeys of fun). Quai des Brûmes offers live music from all genres.

O'Regans Bar

Though historically quiet after dinnertime, Old Montreal has made a comeback on the nightlife scene. The owners of Holder have brought their winning formula for a successful French bistro to the corner of Rue St-Paul and Rue McGill, and next door, Bistro Boris has great food as well as a patio that's always hopping on the weekend. On Saint-Jacques Street West, Tribe Hyper Club always has a line up, but when you get in the music pumps through your veins.

Celebrities such as Paris Hilton, the Wayans brothers, Rihanna and Akon have walked through these doors. Not too much farther West on the corner of Place d'Armes and Saint-Jacques O is Place d'Armes Hotel & Suites, Suite 701, a gourmet lounge, urban chic, with an upscale clientele.

A little off the main hot club areas is Club 737 (corner of Réne-

Tending bar on Crescent

Lévesque and University). This is the best rooftop to see the Montreal skyline at night.

Rue Ste-Catherine runs all the way from its residential Anglophone origins in the west to the more Francophone east, extending deep into the gay village. For drag shows and wild theme nights, the Cabaret Mado is a must, while just down the street is the giant Bourbon complex, housing such favourite gay hangouts and discos as Le Drugstore, Club Mississippi, La Track and Bar Cajun. Other haunts in the area are Unity II and Sky Pub & Club.

Some of the city's best after-hours clubs are also in the area. Stereo, Le Parking, Circus and Millennium all keep the party going until 10 a.m. and feature some of the world's best DJs on a regular basis.

For late night eateries, there is a 24-hour casse-croûte (burgers, fries and poutine) in the Plateau Mont-Royal neighbourhood, there's Rapido on Avenue du Mont-Royal, Chez Claudette on Rue Laurier (try the famous Michigan Burger) and LaFleurs (until 4 a.m.) located in different areas within Montreal. If you're the plateau, check out the LaFleurs on St. Denis. And if a poutine is judged by the size of its curds, don't miss Frites Dorée which serves up the best poutine in Montreal until 4 a.m. If you're closer to Crescent Street try out Boustan for some delicious Lebanese food, and if you don't know what to choose—order the shish taouk pita and garlic potatoes.

If you want to know about shows in and around Montreal or which DJ is in town, pick up the Montreal Mirror, it's a free local paper with a listing of the week's events.

Downtown Montreal by night

Montreal
by Area

Old Montreal

Sean Farrell

Updates by Karnjit Lehal

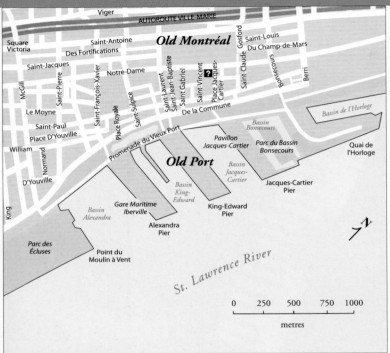

18th-century market

Montreal's first settlers had dreams of establishing a new civilization founded on Christian principles when they straggled ashore in 1642. They christened their collection of rude dwellings Ville-Marie in honour of Christ's mother and set out to convert the natives. The name is all that is left of that old settlement, but there is still plenty of history in Vieux-Montreal, or Old Montreal, the little chunk of land that stretches along the waterfront from Rue McGill in the west to Rue St-Denis in the east. This was the heart of the city's commercial and political life for most of the 19th century. Today it thrives in its new role as the city's centre of tourism. You can rattle along the cobbled streets in a horse-drawn calèche or rumble along them on a tour bus, although the district's easy to get to by Métro, Montreal's subway system. There are three stops in the area—Square-

Victoria, Place d'Armes or Champ-de-Mars. No matter which stop you get off at, the area is small enough to be explored on foot. Most of the history you'll see is 19th century, but there's a generous scattering of 18th-century gems, and some of the buildings rest on 17th-century foundations.

Place Jacques-Cartier

Place Jacques-Cartier, near the Champ-de-Mars Métro station, is a good place to start for two reasons: first, there's a tourist office on the northwest corner of the square where you can pick up a copy of a booklet that outlines a self-guided walking tour; second, Place Jacques-Cartier is one of the prettiest and liveliest squares in the whole city. It stretches from Rue de la Commune on the riverfront north to Rue Notre-Dame, and its whole length is lined with restaurants and snack bars with terraces that open onto the square. In summer, jugglers, fire-eaters and musicians amuse the crowds and the whole area is bright with flowers. The column at the north end of the square bears a statue not of Jacques Cartier, as you might expect, but of Admiral Horatio Nelson. It was erected in 1809 to celebrate Nelson's victory over the French fleet at Trafalgar.

French seafaring does get its due at Place Vauquelin, on the other side of Notre-Dame. This little square and its fountain are named for the French admiral who defended Louisbourg. Just beyond Place Vauquelin, a

Hôtel de Ville

flight of stone steps leads down to Champ-de-Mars, a handsome green space that is used occasionally for public gatherings.

Archaeologists have excavated the foundations of the walls that used to surround the old city.

Captains of commerce fled Old Montreal long ago, but the district is still the heart of civic and legal activity. The extravagant Second Empire building on the east side of Place Vauquelin, for example, is city hall, and the balcony above the main door is where Charles de Gaulle made his infamous "Vive le Québec libre!" speech in 1967. If you look west along Notre-Dame you will see three courthouses—two on the north side of the street and one on the south side. They are the old courthouse, newer courthouse and the newest courthouse. Only the last is still active as the Palais de Justice, and you should have no trouble picking it out: it's the big modern slab that doesn't belong.

Far handsomer is the Château Ramezay, right across from city hall. It was built in 1705 as a residence for the city's governor and looks a little like a Norman castle. It houses a museum with an extensive collection of art, furniture and documents dating from the 18th- and 19th-

Château de Ramezay

centuries. A five-minute stroll east along Notre-Dame to Rue Berri brings you to two grand old buildings that used to be train stations. The Dalhousie station on the southeast corner of Berri and Notre-Dame linked Montreal to Vancouver, while the Viger station on St-Antoine at Berri served points to the east. Walk south on Berri, stopping to visit the lovingly restored home of Sir George-Étienne Cartier, the man who led Quebec into Confederation in 1867. When you get to Rue St-Paul, turn right and walk west to the Notre-Dame-de-Bon-Secours chapel at the foot of Rue Bonsecours. The huge statue of the Virgin Mary on the roof faces the river with its arms outstretched in welcome. Sailors regularly visited this little church to give thanks for a safe crossing. The beautifully restored interior is decorated with lamps in the form of model boats, which were left as gifts by grateful mariners.

Across St-Paul at the corner of Bonsecours is one of the finest examples of 18th-century architecture in Montreal: the greystone Maison du Calvet built in 1725. Pierre du Calvet was a merchant and ardent admirer of the American Revolution, and Benjamin Franklin was a regular visitor. The long, low building with the tin-roofed dome next to the chapel is the Marché Bonsecours. The market has had a number of incarnations over the years, serving at various times as a concert hall and even as city hall. The Marché Bonsecours had new life breathed into it when it was restored to its original purpose as a marketplace for the city's 350th anniversary celebration in 1992.

Notre-Dame-de-Bon-Secours Chapel

A short stroll west and you're back at the southern end of Place Jacques-Cartier. Walk another 50 metres or so and turn right on Rue St-Vincent, a narrow lane jammed with artists and artisans peddling their wares. When you get back to St-Paul, take a careful look at the buildings on the south side of the street. Merchants once coveted these places. They could take in their goods directly from the docks along Rue de la Commune behind their shops and sell them to the customers they received on the fashionable St-Paul side.

Waterfront Rue de la Commune, from Berri to the Canal de Lachine, connects Old Montreal with the Old Port. Many of the buildings on de la Commune still display the names of the businesses once housed there with what is left of old signs painted on the brick or stone walls. A few blocks to the west along de la Commune sits Pointe-à-Callière, the site where Paul de Chomedey, sieur de Maisonneuve, and his brave followers landed in 1642. The triangular building with the lookout tower is an archaeological museum built over an excavation of the site. Visitors can actually wander among the various layers of development, from the 17th century to the Victorian age. The museum is linked underground with the Vieille Douane (Old Customs House), which boasts one of the finest museum gift shops in the city.

Waterfront Rue de la Commune

The Centre d'Histoire de Montréal,

Pointe-à-Callière

just a few blocks away in the heart of Place d'Youville, is worth seeking out for a better appreciation of the city's past. Renovated and housed in a beautifully restored fire station, the museum displays objects and models from its collection of over 1,500 artifacts. The ground-floor exhibit takes you through five episodes from the past to tell the story of Montreal from its founding to the present day, while the second-floor exhibit shows what life was like for individuals in the city during the 20th century.

If you walk north along Rue St-Pierre, you'll come to some imposing stone ruins. This is all that's left of one of Montreal's first hospitals, built by the Frères Charon. In 1747 it was taken over by one of the heroines of city history, Sainte-Marguerite d'Youville, founder of the Grey Nuns. Three blocks farther north is Rue St-Jacques, or St. James Street, as it was known when it was the financial capital of Canada. The

Place d'Youville

business barons who worked in the grand old buildings

lining the street from Square Victoria to Place d'Armes controlled three-quarters of the country's wealth. And if you think they were a stodgy lot, take a closer look at the buildings. They're decorated with a fanciful array of stone cherubs, naked goddesses and lots of granite grapes and vines. Some, of course, are simply grand; the Banque Royal monolith at the corner of St-Pierre, for example, was the tallest building in the British Empire when it was completed in 1928.

Just across the street from the Banque Royal is the Centre de Commerce Mondial (World Trade Centre), one of the district's most imaginative developments. It was created by glassing over Ruelle des Fortifications, a fetid, narrow alley that traced the route of the old walls. This renovation resulted in a narrow, six-storey mall linking two rows of decaying buildings that the developers sandblasted into respectability. Throw in a luxury hotel, a link to the Métro and a magnificent black-marble fountain, and presto: a delightful interior space with a food court and a row of boutiques. The graffiti-covered slab of concrete at the east end of the centre is a section of the Berlin Wall, a gift from Berlin on the occasion of Montreal's 350th birthday in 1992.

Paul de Chomedey

A block east of the Centre de Commerce Mondial is the old city centre, Place d'Armes. The heroic stone figure in the middle of the square is of Paul de Chomedey, Sieur de Maisonneuve. The domed Greek temple behind him is the head office of the Banque de Montréal, whose interior also boast Greek architecture. The redstone building on his left is the city's first skyscraper and the soaring black tower on his right is the headquarters of the Banque Nationale. But it's the magnificent Gothic façade opposite that gets all the attention from tourists. This is Basilique Notre-Dame, possibly the most famous church in Canada. The interior is a vast blue cavern studded with gold-leaf stars and dimly lit by a row of stained-glass windows crafted in Limoges. The reredos, with its life-sized tableaux from the Old Testament, is a display of virtuoso wood carving. The Chapelle du Sacré-Coeur behind the main altar is as large as some churches and more ornate than most. Spend an hour at the basilica before going home. If you're lucky, the Orchestre Symphonique de Montréal will be practising in the sanctuary and you can watch and listen. Or there might be a string quartet playing on the plaza in front. Alternately, you can just sit and meditate and let the colours soak into your soul.

Old Port

Sean Farrell

Updates by Karnjit Lehal

Montreal is an island city in the middle of the St. Lawrence River and is still one of Canada's most important ports. Nowhere is the city's bond to the sea more apparent than at the lively Vieux-Port, or Old Port, along the southern edge of Old Montreal. This strip of docks is no longer the commercial heart of the city—the big container ships and bulk carriers of modern trade load and unload at more modern wharves farther east—but it has become one of the most appreciated parks in Montreal.

Popular all year round, new activities and diversions seem to spring up year after year. While the relatively new Centre des Sciences de Montréal is a fabulous place to explore during any month of the year, most of the Old Port's other attractions are decidedly seasonal. In February, it is the site of the annual Fête des Neiges, and its huge outdoor skating rink is used all winter long.

But the place really blossoms in summer. On warm summer days and late into the evening, the Promenade du Vieux-Port that runs the length of the waterfront from the Canal de Lachine in the west to the Quai de l'Horloge (Clock Pier) in the east is crowded with strollers, inline skaters and cyclists. Whole families glide by in pedal-driven vehicles that look like a cross between a horseless carriage and a surrey with a fringe on top. The less energetic mosey on with rented electric scooters or in little motorized trains that run tours all along the waterfront. This is also where Montreal celebrates Canada Day with concerts and dances that last well into the night.

Old Port at night

Sometimes a cruise ship will be docked at the Gare Maritime Iberville, at the western end of the Old Port just south of Pointe-à-Callière. Cruise passengers are among the best accommodated of Montreal's visitors, living in floating luxury with a view of the river and Île Ste-Hélène. And all this is just an easy walk from the sights of Old Montreal. Visiting warships also use the docks when they pay courtesy calls on the city, as do the tall ships that some countries use as training vessels for their navy cadets.

The best way to get here is by Métro—Montreal's subway system. You may wish to get off at the Square-Victoria station and walk south on Rue McGill to the waterfront. It's a bit of a hike, but it's better than trying to park a car on Rue de la Commune (impossible), unless you're willing to pay for parking in one of the Old Port's lots. If you do go by Métro, a good place to start exploring the Old Port is at its western end, at Parc des Écluses (Locks), in the shadow of the great grain elevators. This spot marks the entrance to the Canal de Lachine, a 19th-century engineering marvel that took ships past the Rapides de Lachine farther west. The St. Lawrence Seaway has rendered it obsolete, but its grassy banks form a kind of long, thin park that ends on the shores of Lac St-Louis. This is where Flora Montreal, horticultural display is set up. Open through early fall, the exhibit filled the park with colourful and meticulously crafted three-dimensional floral works of art.

Habitat '67

The canal's bicycle path is also the source of many of the bikes coasting along the waterfront. Look across the Alexandra basin and you'll see a building that looks a bit like a cliffside pueblo dwelling in the American southwest. It is even the right colour to blend in with the Arizona desert. This is Habitat '67, built for the Expo 67 World's Fair by architect Moshe Safdie as an experiment in modular, moderately priced housing. Its waterfront address makes it a little less modest than Mr. Safdie planned.

Habitat is the most impressive building on Parc de la Cité-du-Harve, a long, thin park that leads to the Pont de la Concorde (Concorde Bridge) and Parc des Îles. If you walk west past the Gare Maritime Iberville on the Quai Alexandra to the Quai King-Edward at the foot of Boulevard St-Laurent, you'll find the home of the Centre des Sciences des Montréal, a building that occupies the entire pier. It is, first and foremost, a hands-on interactive museum with emphasis on audio-visual elements to encourage an exploratory approach to learning about science. The centre also houses its own IMAX theatres. These special-format movies are shot with oversized film and projected on gigantic

IMAX movie theatre

screens. The theatre generally schedules a double-bill for its screenings and alternates these between English and French. The films are guaranteed to assault your senses, making you feel like you're part of the action.

The Quai King-Edward and its eastern neighbour, the Quai Jacques-Cartier,

Pedestrian bridge on Canal de Lachine

frame a marina full of pleasure craft. It's a popular place to people-watch or daydream, especially over some of the bigger yachts or sailboats berthed there. But if you want to do a bit of boating, you don't have to own one of the luxury yachts. The western side of the Quai Jacques-Cartier is lined with opportunities. You can chug along the river on an ersatz paddle-wheeler or do high-speed 360-degree turns on a speed boat. The glass-topped Bateau-Mouche—looking very much like those boats that cruise the Seine in Paris—offers dinner cruises on the river. If you're looking for a day trip and money is no object, you can take a high-speed hydrofoil down the St. Lawrence and spend a few hours in Quebec City before returning to Montreal in the early evening. The best deal, however, is probably the little ferries that take pedestrians and cyclists to Île Ste-Hélène and Longueuil, located on the south shore. One of the more unusual ways to tour the Old Port and Old Montreal is on the Amphi-Bus, which leaves from the Quai Jacques-Cartier. As its name suggests, this odd machine is part boat and part bus. It has both wheels and propellers and offers visitors an amphibious view of the waterfront. The Quai Jacques-Cartier also has a boutique, restaurant and washroom facilities, which makes it a good place for a rest stop.

On the east side of the Quai Jacques-Cartier is the Bassin Bonsecours (Bonsecours Basin), where you can control a radio-operated miniature sailboat or pilot your own paddleboat in the basin. There's a lovely little park in the middle of the basin, a kind of grassy island linked to the mainland by narrow footbridges.

The last pier is the Quai de l'Horloge on the eastern edge of the Old Port. It was once called the Quai Victoria, and it's shaped a little like a crooked thumb with the tip pointing east, down the river. If you want a little more adventure, the labyrinth in Shed 16 is a popular attraction that lets you get lost—and enjoy doing it. And if you need more of an adrenaline rush, check out the Saute-Moutons jet boats in the basin between the thumb and the mainland. Saute-

Bonsecours Bassin

Moutons—literally "jumping sheep"—is the French term for running the rapids, and these big, flat-bottomed boats will take you upriver for a wet and wild ride in the Rapides de Lachine. There aren't many major cities where you can do this kind of thing without going beyond the city limits. Though not cheap, it'll satisfy your taste for extreme adventure. But be warned: you will get wet.

Walk along the pier to the clock tower that

gives the pier its name. If you want to hear your heart pound, climb its 192 steps for a fantastic view of the waterfront and its surroundings. You don't have to count your steps most of the way up because each stair is numbered, except for the top ones, which form a tight, spiralling staircase opening onto the top deck. There isn't room for more than a few people at a time to stand and enjoy the view, but it's worth the effort to climb all those stairs if you want to get a new and different perspective on Montreal. The tower was built in 1922 to honour the merchant mariners who kept the supply lines open to Europe during World War I.

Quai de l'Horloge

The pier itself is the prettiest on the waterfront and now features a child's playground, where grateful parents can let their tykes burn some of that boundless energy. The little park at its western end is set aside for kite-fliers, and the benches and rock gardens at the eastern end under the clock are popular with the crowds who come out on weekends to watch the International Fireworks Competition.

Other Old Port Events

One of youngest festivals at the old port is the annual Reggae Festival in July, which started in 2004 as a non-profit festival. In 2006, they strategically aligned themselves with the Latin social scene inviting Latin artists to perform at the Festival.

The Grand Masquerade is a Halloween celebration in Old Montreal with four days of indoor and outdoor events for the whole family.

Tango Libre happens every Friday evening in the month of August. A live orchestra plays while you can dance the tango under the stars in Place des Vestige.

Every Sunday, Salsafolie occurs from June to September, at the stage at the end of King Edward Quay where Montrealers enjoy a weekly Latin party. Salsafolie gets you moving with shows, infectious rhythms, dance lessons and various other activities.

International Expo Art Festival Montréal began in August of 2006 and features over 600 visual artworks.

Paddling the Lachine Rapids

It attracts artists, collectors, painters, photographers, sculptors, digital artists and many others.

Cirque du Soleil was founded in 1984 by two Quebec street performers and has become an international marvel. Cirque du Soleil's headquarters resides in Montreal and shows usually sell out. If you haven't been and they are in town, be sure to go!

Downtown & Ste-Catherine

Pierre Home-Douglas

Updates by Linda Gyulai

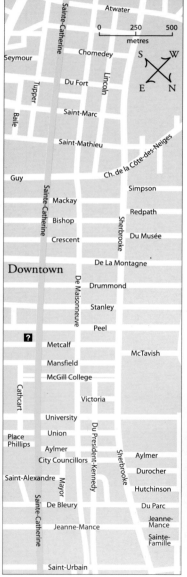

Every great city has its main street where locals and visitors throng to shop, stroll, people-watch and tap into the spirit of the town. London has its Oxford Street, New York its Fifth Avenue, Toronto its Yonge Street. In Montreal it's Rue Ste-Catherine, a gritty, jaunty strip of flash and dash that cuts a 15-kilometre swath right through the metropolis, from the affluent enclave of Westmount in the west to the factories and row housing of the working-class east end. In between lies a world of upscale boutiques, grand old department stores, seedy striptease joints, quirky shops and restaurants of every ethnic type imaginable. And at just about any hour of the day or night you'll find Montrealers milling about, heading off to a rendezvous at a nearby bar, stopping for a café au lait, checking out the latest fashion trends or just, well, living. Rue Sherbrooke, a couple of blocks to the north, may offer more refinement, more old-world gentility, but if you want to feel the real pulse of the town, head for Ste-Catherine and take a walk. At its western end, Ste-Catherine begins where it merges with

Ste-Catherine

Boulevard de Maisonneuve, a few hundred metres east of the Vendôme Métro station. But for most Montrealers the route kicks into high gear at Avenue Atwater, a couple of kilometres east. The intersection was once hockey mecca in this hockey-mad town. Here stands what used to be the Montreal Forum, home for more than 70 years to one of the most storied franchises in sports: the Montréal Canadiens. The fabled building closed in 1996, when the team shifted to new digs at what is now called the Bell Centre. Once a thriving shopping and entertainment area, this stretch of Ste-Catherine suffered more than most parts of Montreal when the economy of the city turned sour during the

The Bell Centre

1980s and early 1990s. Locals watched as store after store was either boarded up or torn down. To many observers, the Forum's closing seemed the final nail in the area's coffin.

But then, Lazarus-like, the street started to make a comeback. New shops emerged, and other stores, like Garnitures Dressmaker, endured despite the economic roller-coaster ride. This shop has been at the same address since the late 1950s, sewing up a storm and dispensing craft supplies And then word came that the Forum was destined to become an entertainment centre. Renamed the Forum Pepsi, it opened in 2001 and features 22 cinemas under the AMC banner. It also houses Jillian's, a triplex that boasts arcade games, a bowling alley, a night club and a restaurant. And for hockey fans, the Forum Pepsi's owners added a nice touch for weary shoppers: a collection of original Forum seats from the red section. Sit down for a minute or two and imagine all the Stanley Cup–winning teams that were witnessed by former occupants of these seats.

If you happen to have missed breakfast, take a side

Moe's

The Faubourg

trip one block north on Rue Lambert-Closse to Casse-Croûte du Coin. Regulars still call it Moe's, after its original owner. When the Forum was in full swing across the street, you would often see visiting hockey players eating huge breakfasts on game day such as Wayne Gretzky and Mario Lemieux.

Over the years, the strip from Avenue Atwater to Rue Guy has evolved into a magnet for Montreal book lovers. Some call it Bookstore Row. In addition to Mélange Magique, Quebec's largest English-language occult and metaphysical bookstore, you'll find shops like the used bookstore Westcott Books. There are also a couple of magazine shops that can satisfy just about any taste. Mediaphile, for example, offers hundreds of magazines to hungry readers and will allow you to order from a list of 10,000 titles.

Part of the regeneration of this stretch of Ste-Catherine during the last decade or so can be found in the Faubourg. The block-long building features a good collection of ethnic take-out foods from a dozen nations, running the gamut from Szechuan to sushi. People who like Thai food swear by Cuisine Bangkok, located in both the food court upstairs and a restaurant setting down the street. At Bagel Place, you can watch bakers pulling piping-hot bagels out of a wood-burning oven. Locals stop by the Faubourg on Sunday morning for their paper and a cup of cappuccino from Starbucks or Second Cup and sit by the windows that face out onto Ste-Catherine. Light streams in from the skylights far above the ground floor. On the way out

La Maison du Bagel

you can pick up a tasty cinnamon bun at Saint-Cinnamon or a baguette from Pagnelli's Boulangerie-Bistro.

There's also evidence of new life at the intersection of Guy and Ste-Catherine, where the impressive new Fine Arts and Engineering building of Concordia University is open. This environmentally-sensitive building is a beautiful collaboration of science and art with five three-storey stacked atria, interconnecting spiral stairs, a magnificent glass mural by Nicolas Baier on the exterior, a Holly King mural at the Metro-level entrance, and natural light to support sustainability. Together with new shops beginning to spring up in this

previously desolate neighbourhood, there is a tangible optimism in the air.

Pagnelli's in the Faubourg

A couple of blocks east of Guy, Ste-Catherine intersects with two streets filled with some of Montreal's best-known watering holes. Although many of the under-25 crowd have departed in the last few years for the hip bars on Boulevard St-Laurent, Rue Bishop and Rue Crescent are still hopping, particularly on Friday and Saturday nights. Among the best-known spots are Sir Winston Churchill Pub, reputedly David Letterman's favourite place to meet people in Montreal; Hurley's Irish Pub, which sells more draft Guinness than any other bar in North America; Grumpy's, where you'll often find a good collection of media types and various movers and shakers; and Brutopia, which offers live music and some of the best home-brewed beer in town.

Sir Winston Churchill pub

The block between Rues Crescent and de la Montagne is dominated by Ogilvy, one of the grand dames of Montreal's department stores. Founded in 1866 by James Angus Ogilvy, the store received a much-needed facelift in the 1980s, when the five-floor edifice was converted into a series of upscale boutiques. There have been welcome additions, including the Nicholas Hoare bookstore. And some traditions still endure: every day at noon a kilted bagpiper marches through the main floor playing his pipes, and in December locals line the snowbound sidewalk in front of the store with their children to view the elaborate antique

Christmas scene on display in the Ogilvy windows.

There's more history in this area than even most Montrealers realize. Half a block south on de la Montagne stands a row of mid-19th-century townhouses. Next door to number 1181 is where Confederate President Jefferson Davis lived after the American Civil War. Davis's house was ripped down in the 1950s to make way for an alley (this was at a time when preserving the past carried little weight in Montreal), but the limestone buildings on the right that once adjoined it are identical to the ones in which Davis spent two years before leaving to live out his final years in Mississippi.

Ste-Catherine and Peel

Ahead lies one of the busiest stretches of Ste-Catherine. Montrealers have long considered the intersection with Rue Peel as the absolute dead centre of town. The stores along this stretch are decidedly more upscale than those to the west. Names like Guess, Gap and BCBG display the latest fashions to the crowds strolling by. For a quick snack, pop over to the corner of Rue Mansfield and head upstairs to Basha, a Lebanese restaurant that offers tasty, filling meals such as plates of shish taouk chicken and shawarma beef for around $7. Across the street, the department store for au courant fashions, Simons, occupies the former home of the now-defunct Simpson's chain.

One block farther east, take a look up Avenue McGill-College, the closest thing Montreal has to a Champs-Elysées. This is one of the best views in the city, with the copper-roofed buildings of McGill University at the top of the street, behind the curved entrance of the Roddick Gates, and Mont Royal in the background. At Christmastime, McGill-College is lit up with innumerable small red and white lights.

Roddick Gates

A couple of blocks east you'll see another casualty of the recent shift in shopping habits of Montrealers—and Canadians as well. The imposing edifice at the corner of Ste-Catherine and Rue University was once home to Montreal's largest department store, Eaton's. The venerable institution went belly up in the late 1990s, and the building stood empty for many years after that. In 2002, the upscale department store Les

Ailes de la Mode opened in the newly renovated building.

Catch a glimpse of one of Montreal's best-loved churches, Cathédrale Christ Church, less than half a block away from the former Eaton's building. The cathedral, on Avenue Union and fronting onto Ste-Catherine, is a neo-Gothic masterpiece. It was designed in the 1850s by Frank Wills, a native of a town that has an impressive cathedral of its own: Salisbury, England. Christ Church is topped by a graceful spire made of aluminium, which replaced the original stone after it was discovered that its weight threatened the structure. In 1986 the church leaders leased the rights to their lot to developers, who then propped up the entire cathedral on huge steel posts and dug out enough space underneath to squeeze in a 100-store mall, Les Promenades de la Cathédrale. Some may have decried the move as selling out, but parishioners in the late 21st century may have the last laugh. That's when the lease expires and the promenade and the soaring glass tower called Tour KPMG formerly La Maison des Coopérants directly behind the cathedral become church property. Christ Church faces Carré Phillips, a small patch of green on Ste-Catherine. Also facing the square are Birks, one of Canada's oldest jewellers and a favourite for bridal registries in the city, and The Bay department store, a red sandstone beauty dating back to 1886 with a regrettably ugly steel-covered walkway that encircles the building. Birks was given a major facelift in 2001, which has brightened up the once-subdued lighting of the store.

Beyond Carré Phillips, Ste-Catherine dips down slightly to Rue Jeanne-Mance, where Place des Arts, home to the Orchestre Symphonique de Montréal, the Musée d'Art Contemporain and the Complexe Desjardins, can fulfill many urges—for great music, contemporary arts, shopping and hotel accommodations. During the Festival International de Jazz de Montréal every July, this area is ground zero for a couple of weeks for some of the best music on the planet. The surrounding streets are wall-to-wall people as far as the eye can see, with everyone

Statue in Carré Phillips

Birks

swaying to the beat of an astonishing array of free outdoor concerts.

There are still more than five kilometres to go until Ste-Catherine runs into Rue Notre-Dame at the eastern end of Montreal's docks and calls it quits. There are a few noteworthy attractions along the way. One is the Gay Village, a small but vibrant district of dance clubs, bars, clothing stores and eateries between the cross streets of St-Hubert and Papineau. A few blocks before you reach the Village, at the corner of Avenue de l'Hôtel-de-Ville, you'll pass Henri-Henri, a hat store that has been in business since 1932 and is still one of the best places in town—if not in all of Canada—to pick up a $400 Borsalino or a beret straight from France. Henri-Henri is exceptional—and yet it's also typical in a way: it's another little jewel that pops out on Ste-Catherine when you least expect it.

Below: Place des Arts
Bottom: Shopping on Ste-Catherine

Sherbrooke St.

James Bassil

Updates by Linda Gyulai

Studded with pockets of glamour and stretches of history, the sights along Rue Sherbrooke make it a prime destination for any visitor. Attractions aside, bypassing this street would be a geographic near-impossibility: Sherbrooke spans 35 kilometres from east to west, stretching through half the island and touching upon most of downtown's diverse neighbourhoods along the way.

A 35-kilometre hike doesn't fit into most travel itineraries, so where does one find the best of Sherbrooke? A good starting point might be the corner at Avenue Atwater, a surprisingly green and lush intersection in itself. To the west are 12 acres of unspoiled land encircling Dawson College, Montreal's first English-language college. To the east, equally enticing property surrounds one of the city's many convents. One of its former convents, to be precise— Le Manoir de Belmont, once a nunnery, has since been converted into a luxurious apartment complex. While this metamorphosis may strike first-time visitors as rather surprising (if not blasphemous), many religious buildings in Quebec have undergone similar conversions. Throughout the 1950s, the province's powerful Roman Catholic clergy, anticipating rapid

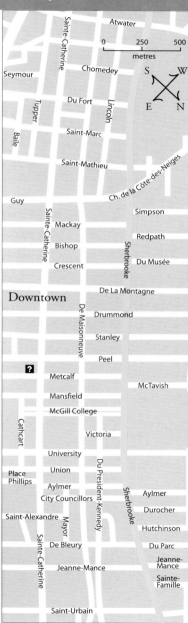

Le Manoir de Belmont

Le Grand
Séminaire

Haddon Hall

Pottery at Musée
des Beaux Arts

population growth, commissioned the construction of hundreds of churches, convents and monasteries. Two decades later, after the province had become increasingly secularized, many of these buildings remained empty. The decision to allow for their renovations towards other social purposes offended some, but most agree it is a preferable alternative to outright demolition.

The profuse vegetation and recycled religious buildings continue as one proceeds east along Sherbrooke. Behind a fence on the north side of the street is Le Grand Séminaire de Montréal. First used as a seminary in 1857, Le Grand Séminaire continues to operate as such and is still owned by the Roman Catholic Sulpician Order. Nonetheless, progress has spread into its grounds. The overgrown foliage of Le Grand Séminaire contrast with the perfectly manicured greenery on the other side of the street. These gardens act as the entryway to Haddon Hall, a regal apartment building whose architecture recalls the early years of the 20th-century. At this time, Sherbrooke served as one of the four borders for the section of the city known as the Golden Square Mile extending from Guy St. to Bleury. This district was as opulent as its name suggests: the Square Mile was home to Canada's leading industrialists and businessmen, and their wealth was reflected in the mansions lining the streets.

As Haddon Hall recalls the affluence of days past, the blocks that lie to its east showcase more current luxuries. The first glimpse of such, the Château Versailles hotel, is actually a bridge between eras. Originally built as a townhouse at the end of the 19th-century, the building's Edwardian façade, along with many of its interior mouldings and fixtures, has remained intact. The amenities that it offers, however, are geared towards the modern guest.

The real-estate values continue to rise as one crosses the busy intersection at Rue Guy. On the south side of Sherbrooke is Bice restaurant, boasting one of the most magnificent dining spaces in Montreal with its glassed-in summer terrace. If the name rings familiar, it is because the restaurant is part of an international chain with branches in Tokyo, Paris, London and New

York—each location offering an elegant blend of authentic and nouvelle Italian cuisine, and extravagant prices to match.

If dining at Bice doesn't break the bank, shopping the stretch of boutiques that follow will provide ample opportunity to do so.

Boulangerie Première Moisson

Packed in the two blocks between Guy and Rue Bishop are dozens of storefronts, each one displaying goods for the high-end consumer. For the most part, the wares consist of artwork: Impressionist paintings, glass sculptures and haute couture. If you plan on doing more than window shopping, keep in mind that many of these galleries provide viewings by appointment only.

Other boutiques provide less pricey indulgences, but indulgences nonetheless. Chocolat Belge Elegant O & M specializes in Belgian pralines and other chocolate delicacies; and La Casa del Habano caters to cigar aficionados, and Boulangerie Première Moisson offers delicious breads, pastries and quiches.

The Musée des Beaux-Arts de Montréal comprises two buildings, one on either side of Sherbrooke. The building on the north side of the street does not host exhibitions, focusing instead on the museum's permanent collection. This collection is nothing to sneeze at: works by Picasso, Rembrandt, Monet and Cézanne are to be found alongside ancient Egyptian sculptures and Canadian landscapes. The architecture of the building on the south side of Sherbrooke (designed by Moshe Safdie) has garnered mixed reviews, but the quality of the exhibitions it houses has rarely been called into question.

Continuing east, Sherbrooke briefly takes on the appearance of Fifth Avenue as one encounters a string of posh fashion boutiques—Holt

Musée des Beaux-Arts de Montréal

Renfrew, Hermès, Dior and Gucci among them. Standing just past these storefronts is Montreal's most famous hotel, the Ritz-Carlton. Recently ranked among the top 100 hotels in the world, this branch of the Ritz meets the chain's reputation with its Edwardian-style décor, marble baths in each suite and fresh fruits to greet every guest.

The Ritz stands on the corner of Rue Drummond. Two blocks east, at its intersection with Rue Peel, Sherbrooke begins to assume a different personality. Townhouses are replaced by highrises, and boutiques by banks. Many find the tone along this particular stretch of downtown to be a bit cold, but it does harbour some nice surprises. Sofitel Hotel, at Stanley and Sherbrooke, offers

Ritz Carlton Hotel

great views of downtown. Restaurant Renoir serves outdoors on a terrace during the summer. Zen restaurant is tucked in the basement of the Hôtel Omni, but it is accessible from the street—stop in any night of the week for the all-you-can-eat buffet. If you duck into the Sherbrooke branch of the Banque Scotia inside the Scotia Tower and walk past the tellers, you'll find an escalator leading down to the shopping maze of Montreal's Underground City.

All this concrete and glass is nicely balanced by the lower campus of McGill University. Often referred to as the Harvard of the North, McGill is certainly Ivy League in appearance. The university was founded in 1821 and retains many of its original buildings, scattered across 80 acres of property. Walking tours are available and the Musée Redpath, an on-campus natural history museum, is open to the public with free admission.

Musée Redpath

McGill University

Beyond the buildings of the university to the north are the Gothic towers of the Hôpital Royal Victoria and the castle-like turrets of the city reservoir. South of the main gates, the university's principal road turns into Avenue McGill-College, a wide mall that leads down to busy Ste-Catherine. In summer the promenade is bright with blossoms, and the city often arranges for photo displays along its west side. In winter its trees are festooned with tiny lights and a huge Christmas tree graces the plaza of Place Ville-Marie at the Avenue's base.

Beyond Sherbrooke between Atwater and McGill college, there are plenty of other treasures to be found on this street. Farther east one finds the sparkling new

buildings of McGill and the Université du Québec à Montréal, chic Boulevard St-Laurent, yet another museum and the restored monastery Le Monastère du Bon-Pasteur, occupants include the Quebec Culture and Heritage department. Retreating west, past our starting point, one finds the ultra-plush neighbourhood of Westmount, home to the city's elite, plenty of shops and some of Montreal's finest public parks.

St-Laurent

Sarah Louise Musgrave
Updates by Karnjit Lehal

Boulevard St-Laurent is often referred to as the dividing line between Montreal's two solitudes: the French community to one side, and the English community to the other. These days, however, quite the opposite is true. While this distinctive thoroughfare still cleaves the city's addresses into east and west, it's more of a great unifier than a great divider. More than any other street, the Main, as St-Laurent is affectionately known, brings together the different languages and cultures that make up Montreal's rich heritage. A promenade along its length offers a cross-section of local life—a journey through the past, present and even the future.

A particular blend of old world and new gives St-Laurent its colourful character. This multi-ethnic strip has welcomed just about every wave of immigration to the province since the 1800s: speakers of Yiddish, Greek, Portuguese, Cantonese and, more recently, Spanish and Thai. Haute couture boutiques, Latin salsa bars and tattoo parlours share sidewalk space with Polish sausage counters and Jewish schmatta shops whose window displays haven't changed since the 1950s.

Appropriately enough, St-Laurent begins where Montreal first took root, at the Old Port in the heart of the old city. The real fun begins at Avenue Viger, where majestic red-and-gold gates announce the entrance to a small but vibrant Chinatown. Time your trek to coincide with the frenzied lunch hour, when a range of Asian aromas compete for attention: Vietnamese noodle soups, Taiwanese bubble teas and Chinese delicacies like

Chinatown, St-Laurent

The Dragon Fountain in Dr. Sun Yat Sen Park

fried dumplings and fresh lobster. The jumble of exotic eateries, grocery stores and gift shops extends onto Rue de la Gauchetière, a brick-lined walkway that intersects St-Laurent, where vendors hawk everything from dragon beard candy to palm readings and herbal medicines. Escape the hustle and bustle in the minimalist Dr. Sun Yat Sen Park at the corner of Rue Clark.

Continuing north, you'll tread the storied sidewalks of what was once Montreal's vaunted red-light district. The stretch between Boulevard René-Lévesque and Rue Ste-Catherine, where in yesteryear peeler palaces abounded, has recently been reinvented as a different kind of entertainment district: you can catch a band at Club Soda or a play at the École Nationale de Théâtre (National Theatre School). Among the few billiard halls, strip clubs and peep shows that remain from grittier days, the Montreal Pool Room is an enduring fixture. This classic dive no longer has pool tables but continues to dish out trademark hot dogs and frites (french fries) much as it did in 1912.

A cultural institution of a different sort, the Musée Juste Pour Rire above Boulevard de Maisonneuve grew out of Montreal's internationally renowned Just for Laughs comedy festival. The permanent exhibit focuses on the history of humour, while the on-site cabaret regularly bills top pop-music acts. Across the street, the Godin, a boutique hotel, stands as a testament to an increasingly upscale attitude—as the hill gets steeper here, so do the prices.

The jet-set strip awaits just across Rue Sherbrooke. Frequented by fashionistas and visiting celebs, this section of the Main is jam-packed with some of the trendiest shopping, food and nightlife in Montreal. Boutiques showcase local designers, from the sleek styles of Nevik and street sense of Space FB to the leatherware of m0851 (formerly known as Rugby North America) and the whimsical creations of Scandale. Statuesque serving staff tend to the culinary cravings of the well-heeled at Buonanotte and Med, while floors above, chi-chi clubs with rooftop terraces start hopping as soon as the sun goes down.

Amidst the click of high heels, the bleep of cell phones and the rev of valet parking, the Ex-Centris complex is an oasis of high-tech serenity. This imposing structure screens avant-garde films from around the world in ultra-cushy, ultra-modern facilities. It's also the primary venue for the cutting-edge Montréal International Festival of New Cinema and New Media, which runs for two weeks every fall.

Before venturing north, take a short detour onto Rue Prince-Arthur, a mecca of counterculture since the 1970s. This cobblestone mall is closed to traffic—at least the motorized kind—but streams with buskers, caricaturists and acrobats, as well as budget-minded diners who flock to its patios. In keeping with the free-spirited atmosphere, most restaurants have an apportez votre vin, or bring your own wine, policy (meaning they don't have a liquor licence, but you can partake in your own purchases on the premises). Prince-Arthur spills into leafy Carré St-Louis, a gracious square with a central fountain surrounded by Second Empire homes built in the 19th-century to house Montreal's Francophone bourgeoisie.

The Ex-Centris Complex

Back on St-Laurent, the intersection of Avenue des Pins marks a crossroads of cultural chaos—in a good way. Inexpensive ethnic eats lure from every direction: lengths of links hang in the window at Slovenia, calzone emerge hot from the ovens at after-hours cafeteria Eurodeli and greasily good Portuguese chicken sandwiches are doled out at Coco Rico. La Vieille Europe, an authentic Central European grocery store, is stocked with enough cheese, salami and chocolate for a lifetime of picnics. There's food for the mind here, too. A youthful, artsy crowd populates record emporiums, handcrafted-jewellery outlets, body-piercing facilities and hip hair salons by day, then bursts on to dance floors, chills to ambient beats in lounges or swills micro-brewery products at watering holes by night.

Schwartz's Delicatessen

This stretch was once the centre of Jewish life in the metropolis. In the late 19th-century, thousands of emigrants from Romania, Poland and other Eastern European countries established shops, schools and synagogues in the area, creating a lively neighbourhood that later inspired the work of literary lions such as Mordecai Richler, Leonard Cohen and Irving Layton. Harking back to the good ol' days—or at least a time before the discovery of cholesterol—is the perpetually packed Schwartz's Montréal Hebrew Delicatessen, purveyor of the city's world-famous smoked meat. Order a medium-cut sandwich on rye with a cherry coke and half a sour pickle.

The corner of Rue Marie-Anne and St-Laurent is the nexus of the Main's Portuguese enclave,

Bookseller S.W. Welch

encapsulated by a charming blue-and-yellow-tiled park where the community's venerable members gather to chat. Steps from an African dance club, a Jewish discount clothing store and a South American market, it's a perfect place to appreciate the remarkable diversity of the area. Another such opportunity is a St-Laurent street sale, an event that takes place periodically during summer months, when the road is cordoned off to hold an absolutely bizarre assortment of merchandise: raw oysters on the half-shell, vintage clothing from fripperies, underwear by the dozen and second-hand titles from bookseller S.W. Welch.

Fans of design will revel in the span of St-Laurent north of Marie-Anne, now a high-end-décor district. Browse beautiful housewares at Côté Sud, shop for funky furniture at Biltmore or reflect on the retro stylings of Sauriol, provider of home accessories. Signs of gentrification are also in evidence on the portion of the Main that runs through the former immigrant enclave of Mile-End, between Boulevard St-Joseph and Rue Bernard. Amid new wine bars and upmarket stores, you'll find reasonably priced Indian, Italian, Thai and Peruvian meals. Grassroots eatery Sala Rossa offers Spanish tapas in an old-style dining room, while its sister establishment, Casa Del Popolo, serves up vegetarian snacks and alternative music.

Push on a few blocks farther north for a taste of Montreal's thriving Little Italy, a primo destination for foodies. The selection of restaurants and markets near Rue St-Zotique would make any nonna proud. Stop at Fruiterie Milano to browse the pasta, prosciutto, parmesan and pannetone that make this the best Italian grocery in town. For an authentic coffee-bar experience, old-school Caffe Italia comes complete with soccer paraphernalia, shaving products and some of the best espresso in the city. Sounds of merriment emerge from Piccolo Italia's numerous dining establishments any time of year, but especially during international soccer tournaments and the Montréal Grand Prix Formula One auto race (in June).

All the pleasures of the palate are brought together at Marché Jean-Talon, Montreal's largest outdoor

Student life along St-Denis

farmers' market, just east of St-Laurent off Avenue Shamrock. The market caters to gourmet shoppers as well as recent arrivals from North Africa, the Middle East, Central America and almost everywhere in between. It's the perfect place to sum up the international legacy of Boulevard St-Laurent: a unifying force from one end to the other.

Excursions

Sarah Waters

Updates by Linda Gyulai

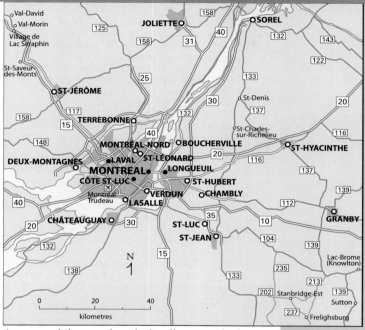

As easy as it is to get into the bustling scene in the streets of Montreal, getting out of town can be just as appealing—and surprisingly easy, too. Drive for just 20 minutes and you're out of Montreal and in rolling countryside; two hours and you're in the wilderness of the northern Laurentians—if the traffic's flowing on the bridges, that is. Whether you're looking for adventure or relaxation, there are plenty of choices for day trips out of Montreal.

One way to escape Montreal without really leaving is to take a cruise around the island. It takes about two hours to make a complete circle, and you're guaranteed to get a different perspective on the city as you take it in from the water. Croisières AML is a reliable cruise line operating out of the Old Port, with several tours departing daily from the Quai King-Edward.

Another watery option can be found barely 15 minutes from downtown Montreal with Les Descentes sur le St-Laurent, a company that offers raft and hydro-jet rides down the treacherous-looking Rapides de Lachine on the St. Lawrence River.

Laurentian Colour

Forts and Patriots

One of the simplest and best excursions is to drive east (downriver) to Sorel and then follow the Rivière Richelieu south through some of the province's richest farmlands and orchards until you reach the American border crossing at Lacolle. The Richelieu flows north from the trading areas around Lake Champlain and the Fleuve Hudson (Hudson River) and was key in the struggle between European powers (France, Britain and Holland) vying for hegemony in the region.

You could start your journey with a cruise around the Îles de Sorel, an enchanting little archipelago in the St. Lawrence that's alive with waterfowl and fish. But that would take at least a couple of hours and if time is limited it might be best to start south through the valley. Follow Highway 133 towards Chambly. This route is sometimes called the Chemin des Patriotes (Patriots' Road) in honour of the men and women who joined Louis-Joseph Papineau in the 1837 rebellion against British imperial rule. The rebels faced down the British at St-Denis-sur-Richelieu and were driven off in a skirmish at St-Charles-sur-Richelieu.

There are many reminders of the revolt along the road. The route is marked with signs bearing the image of an armed rebel in a tuque and a ceinture fléchée (a colourful woven sash), and just outside St-Denis-sur-Richelieu on Chemin des Patriotes is an early-19th-century home that is now La Maison Nationale des Patriotes. Exhibits and audio visual shows—in French only—recount the rebellion and the

Fort Chambly

battles. In St-Denis itself the insurgents' green, white and red tricolour flies over a monument erected in their honour in 1987. The nearby church has twin towers, one of which houses the liberty bell that called the rebels to battle.

The next landmark is a natural one—Mont St-Hilaire, a steep, 414-metre peak that soars abruptly out of the rolling countryside. Its lower slopes are covered with apple orchards and its upper reaches are heavily forested. An area of about six square kilometres is open to the public. You can park your car halfway up

Fort Lennox, barrack interior

the mountain and follow a series of paths to the summit for sweeping views of the valley and Montreal. The mountain was once the estate of Andrew Hamilton Gault (1882–1958), who founded Princess Patricia's Canadian Light Infantry. At the foot of the mountain is a museum dedicated to the sweetest legacy of Canada's First Nations—maple syrup. The Maison des Cultures Amérindiennes on Montée des Trente displays how sap was traditionally harvested and processed, and reveals the importance of maple products in native culture.

Farther upriver lies Chambly, an important trading and defence centre during the French Regime. Captain Jacques de Chambly built the first French fort here in 1665 to defend Montreal against Indian, and later British, attacks. The stone successor of that humble wooden stockade still guards the Rapides de Chambly, the northernmost of a series of military strongholds along the river. Fort Chambly has been restored to its 18th-century appearance and stands in a pleasant park by the river. It has an interpretation centre with displays and programs illustrating military and farming life in the 18th- and 19th-centuries.

Chambly is also the northern end of the Canal de Chambly, a 19-kilometre waterway that skirts a series of rapids and leads to the industrial city of St-Jean-sur-Richelieu. Today it's used only by pleasure craft, and the towpath has been converted into a bicycle path. From Chambly, the road heads south through St-Jean-sur-Richelieu to the next fort on the route—Fort Lennox, built by the British in 1802. It sits on an island—Île aux Noix—in the middle of the river, and a wide moat surrounds its star-shaped fortifications. Displays and costumed actors capture the tough life of a 19th-century British citizen on colonial duty. The last fort on the river is the two-storey blockhouse at Lacolle, still pocked with bullet holes from the War of 1812.

If you're travelling with kids—and even if you're not—don't miss Lacolle's Arche des Papillons, where you can walk through a magic greenhouse surrounded by clouds of fluttering butterflies. The surrounding countryside is full of orchards and growers often make their own ciders, which you can stop and sample.

Another kid-friendly favourite is the Parc Safari, about a half-hour south of the city, just north of the U.S. border. The park is full of giraffes, elephants, leopards and other transplants from around the globe, and you can either drive your own car through it or catch a ride on one of the park's buses. A little closer to Montreal, in the town of St-Constant, is the

Association Canadienne d'Histoire Ferroviaire (Canadian Railway Museum), home of the largest collection of railway equipment in Canada. This interactive museum gives visitors of all ages a chance to experience the railway adventure firsthand.

Northern Playground

Attempts in the late 19th- and early 20th-centuries to settle the low-lying rocky Laurentian Mountains didn't work out very well. The soil was often too thin for farming, but "Montreal's backyard" has since found its real wealth in recreation and tourism.

The hills, lakes and rivers of the region attract hikers, hunters, anglers, canoeists, kayakers, cross-country skiers and mountain bikers, not to mention artists and photographers. And just in case all these natural pastimes aren't enough, entrepreneurs have filled the valleys with golf courses, go-cart tracks, bungee towers and a dizzying array of bars, boutiques and fine restaurants.

One of the best ways to explore the region is on two wheels. Parc du P'tit Train du Nord—Quebec's

Laurentian Resort

longest bicycle trail at 200 kilometres follows an abandoned railway line that runs North to South between Mont-Laurier and St-Jérôme. The trail can be easily accessed at the old railway station in Ste-Agathe or via the dozens of towns along its route. In winter, cross-country skiiers and snowmobilers glide along its length. The 20-kilometre stretch between St-Sauveur and Ste-Agathe is thick with restaurants, cafés and bed-&-breakfasts—as well as Laurentian scenery. Farther north, the landscape gets wilder and the bicycle traffic thinner. North of Labelle, you can cycle for hours with just the birds for company.

But the car-bound can explore the Laurentians as well. A good place to start is St-Sauveur-des-Monts which has developed into a major resort choked with condos, name-brand outlet stores and trendy bars. Traffic on the main street in July, when the sidewalks are full of stylish diners and shoppers, can be as thick as it is on Rue Ste-Catherine in Montreal.

If a slower pace appeals, you might want to consider a visit to the Polar Bear's Club, not far out of Montreal. Here you can relax in any one of a number of hot tubs along a boardwalk that overlooks a rushing stream, and if the heat is too much, just take a quick dip in the frigid stream water. If you're prepared to travel a little farther, there's nothing quite like a visit to Ofuro Spa in Morin Heights. The beautiful site, with its charming Japanese wooden architecture, luscious garden and babbling waterfall, was clearly designed with ultimate relaxation in mind.

St-Sauveur-Des-Monts

Ste-Agathe is a favourite for tourists and weekenders, with a number of fine hotels and restaurants. From Ste-Agathe the road snakes through Val Morin and Val David, attractive villages surrounded by hills and lakes. They too have their pleasant little restaurants and bars, plus a couple of first-class inns, but Val Morin and Val David have retained their quaintness and escaped the feverish development that has marked the recent history of their more southerly neighbour.

Take Highway 15 north to St. Agathe, which merges with highway 117 and from there onto Chemin Duplessis to the Mont Tremblant ski resort. Mont Tremblant, with a vertical drop of 650 metres, is the highest mountain in the Laurentians. Intrawest, the company that developed Blackcomb on the west coast has spent billions of dollars turning the mountain into a year-round resort. It has opened two new mountain faces and added a gondola and several high-speed chairlifts. It has also built two spectacular golf

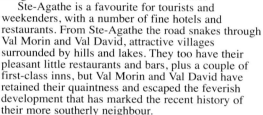

courses, opened a half-dozen resort hotels and re-created a miniature version of Quebec City at the base of the mountain. Mountain bikers use the lifts and ski trails in summer. The resort is also the setting for a summer blues festival and classical music concerts.

Beyond the resort, the road turns into Parc Provincial du Mont Tremblant, a 1,500-square-kilometre wilderness of rivers, lakes and

Mont Tremblant Resort

mountains. The road, which is closed in winter, follows the Rivière Diable (Devil's River), a well-named waterway punctuated with falls and rapids. Here you'll find some of the most wildly beautiful scenery in Quebec. Well worth a stop are Chutes du Diable (Devil's Falls) and Chutes aux Rats (Muskrat Falls), and there's a beautiful beach on Lac Monroe. The park has hiking trails and facilities for canoeists and campers. From St-Donat-de-Montcalm, take Highway 329 south to Ste-Agathe and from there follow Highway 117 or Highway 15 (the Laurentian Autoroute) back to Montreal.

Loyalist Country

After the American Revolution, colonists who wished to remain loyal to the British Crown fled north to Canada and settled in parts of Quebec, New Brunswick

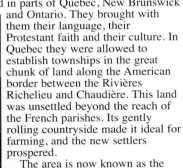

and Ontario. They brought with them their language, their Protestant faith and their culture. In Quebec they were allowed to establish townships in the great chunk of land along the American border between the Rivières Richelieu and Chaudière. This land was unsettled beyond the reach of the French parishes. Its gently rolling countryside made it ideal for farming, and the new settlers prospered.

The area is now known as the Cantons-de-l'Est, or Estrie (Eastern Townships), and its towns and villages resemble New England more than New France. They're full of fine brick and clapboard homes built on the British model, with central hallways and formal front

Parc Provincial du Mont Tremblant

rooms. The Loyalist pioneers and the British and American settlers who followed them into this region are now outnumbered by their French neighbours. The blend, however, is harmonious. Townshippers of both cultures can usually switch from one language to the other with ease and agility.

One way to get a taste of this varied and beautiful region is to drive east on Highway 10 (the Eastern

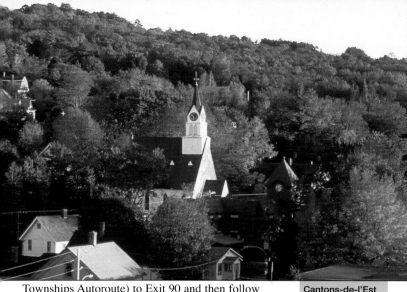

Townships Autoroute) to Exit 90 and then follow Highway 243 south along the shores of Lac Brome to Knowlton, a pleasant 19th-century town full of grand brick buildings. The streets are lined with boutiques and restaurants, and there is a summer theatre that specializes in English-language comedies and mysteries.

From Knowlton follow Highways 104 and 215 to Sutton, another pretty little Loyalist town, but the homes here are mostly white clapboard with wraparound verandahs and fanciful towers and gables. Its main street, too, has an assortment of restaurants and boutiques. Just outside town is Mont Sutton, a mountain with a major ski resort whose lifts offer summer and fall visitors a great way to view the surrounding countryside.

From Sutton drive west on Highway 237 through Frelighsburg, a beautiful village of brick homes cupped in the Pike River valley, to Stanbridge East, a good place to stop for a picnic. The village doesn't offer much in the way of restaurants, but it does have a delightful little Anglican church, an old grist mill and a general store and barn that are now the Musée Missisquoi of pioneer life. The land across the river from the mill has been turned into a wonderful little park.

From Stanbridge turn east again on Highway 202 and drive through Quebec's wine country to Dunham. Mountains protect this gentle piece of land from the northern winds and hold the southern sun, creating a microclimate just warm enough to make the cultivation of grapes possible. Most of the vineyards along the road sell their produce in on-site boutiques and some have little wine bars and even restaurants.

From Dunham you can follow Highway 202 and secondary routes 104 and 233 to Highway 10 and home to Montreal.

Antiques in
Knowlton

Other Suggested Day Trips

Terrebonne, a pretty little town on the Rivière des
Mille Îles north of Montreal, is in the heart of a fertile
farming area. Its wealth, however, comes from the
river, which 19th-century merchants harnessed to
power grist and flour mills to process grain and
sawmills to cut lumber. Much of this heritage is
preserved on Île des Moulins, a kind of industrial
theme park—carefully preserved flour mills and
sawmills as well as Canada's first industrial bakery,
built in 1802 to supply hard biscuits for voyageurs and
trappers. The old seigneurial office serves as an
interpretation centre and the "new mill," built in 1850,
houses a theatre, a cultural centre and an art gallery.

Missisquoi Musée
in Stanbridge
East

These attractions
are all open from
mid-May until
Labour Day.

The industrial
town of Trois-
Rivières sits at the
confluence of the
St-Lawrence and
Maurice Rivers.
The Maurice splits
into three channels
just before it
empties into the
St-Lawrence,
hence the town's misleading name. Its chief industry
is pulp and paper, and the odour of sulphur often
hangs heavy in the air, but the visitor who overcomes
the olfactory assault will discover the greater charms
of this place. Trois-Rivières is older than Montreal,
and its historic section is full of 18th- and 19th-
century treasures.

Quebec City's Best

Quebec City's Top Attractions

Patrick Donovan

Quebec City atop Cap Diamant

I would rather be a poor priest in Quebec [City] than a rich hog merchant in Chicago.
—English poet Matthew Arnold (1822–88)

Many might challenge Matthew Arnold's implied criticism of Chicago, but few would disagree with his praise for Quebec City. It is unquestionably one of the most historic and beautiful cities in North America. In addition to a wealth of 18th- and 19th-century architecture, Quebec City is blessed with a dramatic location atop the rugged heights of Cap Diamant (Cape Diamond). Views stretch over the widening estuary of the St. Lawrence River, with the Laurentian Mountains lending their curves to the horizon in the distance.

Château Frontenac in the snow

A nice way to get some perspective on this incredible panorama is to head for the docks and take the ferry to Lévis. When architect Bruce Price designed the Château Frontenac, the huge copper-roofed hotel that is Quebec City's principal landmark, he sketched it from across the river with the intention of giving the city a dramatic skyline. In addition to offering a glimpse of the city and its castle from this intended perspective, the view from the ferry also provides a two-level history lesson. Atop Cap

Calèche in old Quebec City

Diamant are the walls and turrets of Haute-Ville, or Upper Town. Along the river's edge are the narrow streets and tall stone houses of Basse-Ville, or Lower Town. The latter is where foundations for the city were laid by Samuel de Champlain in 1608. With time, governors, priests and army commanders moved to the Upper Town. The merchants, tradesmen and labourers (as well as thieves and hookers) scrabbled for a living down on the riverfront. After the 1759 British conquest little changed, except that the Upper Town aged gracefully and the Lower Town degenerated into an industrial slum, a state from which it was rescued only a couple of decades ago.

One of the best things to do in Quebec is to walk around with no specific destination in mind. The steep streets of the fortified Upper Town are full of nooks, crannies and tiny laneways that shoot off at unexpected angles, with discoveries at every turn. You're bound to end up at Terrasse Dufferin, a long wooden boardwalk hugging the cliffside by the Château Frontenac. The long walk to the end of the terrace, up the steps and along the boardwalk over to the Plaines d'Abraham has many breathtaking views.

The Lower Town, with some of the city's oldest areas, is also worth a stroll. The architecture of New France is at its most polished and obvious in Place Royale and Petit Champlain, though these areas often

Historic Petit Champlain

feel more like historical theme parks than genuine urban neighbourhoods. If the fake moccasins, Canadian-flag tote bags and cutesy mountie dolls start giving you a headache, walk west of the city walls for a taste of authentic local life. There you will find upscale Quartier Montcalm, bohemian Saint-Jean-Baptiste district or up-and-

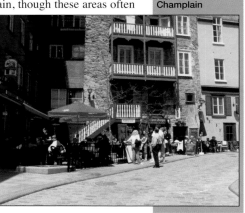

Escalier Casse-cou

coming Saint-Roch neighbourhood. These lively areas are full of interesting architecture and great non-touristy cafés.

If your feet are sore, the horse-drawn buggies—calèches—all over the city are generally a better option than tour buses. The latter have a hard time navigating the narrow streets and calèches are a quieter, more eco-friendly option. If you'd rather walk, try the excellent theatrical walking tours offered by the Compagnie des Six Associés. The tours deal with many broad themes, from medical practices in the 19th-century to the evolution of crime and punishment. A different take on history is offered by Ghost Tours of Quebec, who offer the occasional witch trial.

Quebec City has many fine museums that cover everything from history to art to … chocolate. In the Lower Town, the huge Musée de la Civilisation focuses on Quebec's relationship to the world. Two excellent permanent exhibits with interactive displays cover the history of the province and its First Nations people. If you want to learn more about the history of the city itself, head to either the Centre d'Interprétation de Place-Royale or the Musée de l'Amérique Française. The latter is housed in the large Séminaire de Québec complex, Canada's first institution of higher learning, which later evolved into Université Laval in the 1850s.

Musée de la Civilisation

Many heritage buildings are scattered throughout the city, providing various angles on local history. Among these is the Morrin Centre, which presents local history from the perspective of its English-speaking minority. This group once represented 40 percent of the total population, and a few descendants are still around today to tell their tales. It's worth stepping into the old Anglo-Victorian library full of English books located in the Centre. The François-Xavier Garneau and Henry Stuart homes also offer interesting, if infrequent, tours.

Quebec City's most important art museum is the Musée National des Beaux-Arts du Québec, located on the Plaines d'Abraham. For contemporary art, head to Complexe Méduse in St-Roch. Finally, don't miss the tiny Choco-Musée Érico, a free museum about the origins of cocoa that should be visited if only to sample the best homemade ice cream and sorbet in town.

The immense opulent churches that dot the landscape all over the city testify to the fact that religion played a crucial role in Quebec society. Notre-Dame-de-Québec, the large cathedral in the heart of the Upper Town, once ruled a diocese that stretched as

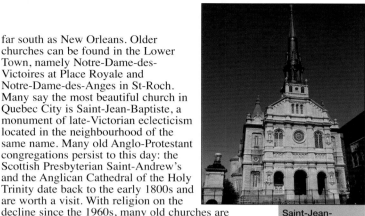

far south as New Orleans. Older churches can be found in the Lower Town, namely Notre-Dame-des-Victoires at Place Royale and Notre-Dame-des-Anges in St-Roch. Many say the most beautiful church in Quebec City is Saint-Jean-Baptiste, a monument of late-Victorian eclecticism located in the neighbourhood of the same name. Many old Anglo-Protestant congregations persist to this day: the Scottish Presbyterian Saint-Andrew's and the Anglican Cathedral of the Holy Trinity date back to the early 1800s and are worth a visit. With religion on the decline since the 1960s, many old churches are unfortunately being sold, converted or simply demolished. Among the rare examples of tasteful conversion is the former Anglican Saint-Matthew's church, now a public library surrounded by a charming 18th-century graveyard.

Saint-Jean-Baptiste

Although Quebec City is a tranquil place today, its history as a bustling military town is plainly obvious. A walk along the fortifications takes you from Parc de l'Artillerie, with its French redoubt, to the large British citadel that is still home to the Royal 22nd Régiment, with its red uniforms and large bearskin hats. Outside the walls lies Parc des Champs-de-Bataille (National Battlefields Park), site of the decisive battle between the troops of Wolfe and Montcalm that led to British control over North America in 1759. Better known as the Plaines d'Abraham (Plains of Abraham), this park is full of winding pathways and grassy knolls, which stretch for kilometres along the cliff's edge, offering great views of the St. Lawrence. On a sunny day, do as the locals do: buy some fine Quebec cheese, fresh bread and a bottle of wine from one of the many delis and boulangeries in town before strolling up to the plains for a picnic. While there, take a peek at one of the intriguing Tours Martello (Martello Towers) from the British era or the lovely Jeanne d'Arc gardens. Walk back to the old city via the tree-lined Grande Allée, Quebec's humble answer to the Champs-Elysées, with its sidewalk cafés and large nightclubs. The most interesting building along Grande Allée is the Hôtel du Parlement, or provincial parliament, with its eclectic blend of French and English architecture. To get a feel for the type of battles being fought in Quebec nowadays, it's worth dropping into the Assemblée Nationale to hear all the hooting and hollering going on during question period when parliament is in session.

Monastère des Ursulines

Picnicking on the Plaines d'Abraham

Heritage & Architecture

Sovita Chander

Updates by Patrick Donovan

The walls of Quebec

You can't turn around in Quebec City without bumping into a story about the past. The city possesses a unique architectural heritage spanning four centuries of history. Much of this heritage is intact, and has earned Quebec recognition on the UNESCO World Heritage List. It is the only city in North America to have preserved its military fortifications, which comprise a wall surrounding the old city with its gates and bastions. Within these walls are monuments, buildings, parks or residences with something to say. Some shout their visual wares, beckoning travellers with grandiose façades and far-flung reputations. Others sit squarely, solidly, stating their place in the history of everyday life. The rest whisper, yielding their rewards only through patient inquiry and observation.

From the Beginnings to 1759

Quebec City's history, and even prehistory, begins in what is now known as Basse-Ville, or Lower Town, along the banks of the St. Lawrence River. And the heart of the Lower Town, historically speaking, is

Notre-Dame-des-Victoires

Place Royale. This square has been an important

commercial site for at least 2,000 years. First Nations bands used it as a trading post, part of a vast network that covered all North America. When Jacques Cartier sailed up the St. Lawrence in 1534, he landed near the site and found the thriving Iroquois village of Stadacona. The Iroquois were gone when Samuel de Champlain arrived in 1608 to establish a settlement and open trade with the First Nations. Europeans were eager to establish a fur trade for a simple yet lucrative reason: fashion. Beaver fur made a luxuriously fine felt for the men's hats that were de rigueur for much of the period.

There's nothing left of Champlain's original settlement, though the spirit of New France lives on in this part of town. Fire destroyed Champlain's settlement in 1682 and colonial and religious officials built a church dedicated to the Virgin Mary—now called

Notre-Dame-des-Victoires—on the ruins. The parishioners of the settlement had long petitioned the Church for a place of worship in the Lower Town, as the trip to the cathedral in the Upper Town was arduous in wintertime. Looking beyond Notre-Dame-des-Victoires, we find the rest of Place Royale, which became the trading hub of New France and was where merchants lived and worked. The square was reconstructed and illustrates the vernacular architecture that developed during the French Regime. Rooted in the styles of Brittany and Normandy, Quebec's architecture evolved in response to the climate. Harsh winters resulted in raging indoor fires that burned the city down. Strict building laws were soon set up: houses had to be built out of thick stone, with dividing walls between each dwelling and non-flammable roofs. Many of these old homes still have their old barrel-vaulted basements—the gift shop in the Estebe house within the Musée de la Civilisation is a fine example that is open to the public.

Notre-Dame-des-Victoires, interior

Architecture from the New France period is scattered all over the city. The Séminaire de Québec is a vast assembly of buildings that used to house Université Laval before it moved to the suburb of Ste-Foy. The seminary was founded in 1663 by Quebec's first bishop, François de Laval, to train priests locally. It is the oldest post-secondary teaching institution in North America. Nearby, parts of the Hôtel Dieu Hospital and the Ursuline convent also date from the New France period and are open to visitors. The Ursulines run the oldest private girls' school in North America, founded in 1639.

British Rule

Though Old Quebec seems quintessentially French today, most of its architecture dates from the years of British rule. The city's commercial activities grew under British rule, particularly during the Napoleonic Wars. With Baltic supplies of timber cut off by Napoleon, the British Navy turned to its North American colonies for ships and wood. In time, Quebec City came to have the largest port in British North America. This port declined when steam replaced sails, and steel replaced wood. Ships could go farther inland, leading to the growth of urban centres like Montreal and Toronto.

Maison Thibaudeau

Many of Quebec's military structures date from the years

of British rule. These include the 4.6-kilometre wall of fortifications around Haute-Ville, extending from the Citadel on the Plaines d'Abraham, to the Prescott gate in the east, to the St-Jean, Kent and St-Louis gates to the west. The Citadel itself is an impressive structure built to protect the city from an American invasion that never came. Farther west, on the Plaines d'Abraham, are Martello towers of the type built throughout the British Empire in the 19th-century. Around 140 such towers were built at this time, including four in Quebec—three of them are still standing.

Top: Maison Chevalier
Inset: Maison Chevalier, interior

When religion played a greater role in public life, churches were important symbols of status, power and prestige. Many of Old Quebec's religious buildings date from the years of British Rule. The cathedral of the Roman Catholic archbishop of Quebec is the Basilique Notre-Dame-de-Québec on Rue de Buade. The original church was built in 1647, but one look will tell you that this is not a 17th-century structure. The Anglican Cathedral of the Holy Trinity on Rue des Jardins was built in 1804 to serve the spiritual needs of the English elite. Captain William Hall and Major

Rue Petit-Champlain

William Robe, both of the Royal Artillery, designed the cathedral in the classical tradition embodied by two London churches: St. Martin-in-the-Fields and Marylebone Chapel, both by architect James Gibb. Nearby is Saint-Andrew's, begun in 1807, the oldest Scottish Presbyterian congregation in the country.

There was a time in the 1860s when English-speakers represented nearly half the population within the fortified city, and their architectural contribution goes beyond churches. Many of the residential buildings in Old Quebec are a local adaptation on the Georgian townhouses of London and Edinburgh. Perhaps the most quintessentially British place in old Quebec is the library of the Literary and Historical Society of Québec, founded by Lord Dalhousie in 1824. The reading room is a charmingly whimsical Victorian period piece, and still functions as an English-language lending library to this day. The Society is housed in an old converted prison completed in 1813. The architect constructed the prison in accordance with the enlightened principles of the day, following the ideas of British prison reformer John Howard.

Post-Confederation Years

As in much of the Western world, symmetry and classical proportions soon gave way to ornamentation and eclecticism in the late 19th-century.

Canada came together as a country around the project of a national railroad linking the Atlantic to the Pacific coasts. Large castle-like hotels that responded to the romantic sensibilities of the day sprouted up along the railway line. Among these was the Château Frontenac, built as a luxury hotel in 1893. The château takes its name from former governor Louis de Buade de Frontenac (1622-1698). There are a few other château style buildings in the city, namely the main railway station, and the Drill Hall on Grande Allée.

The Funicular

Right outside the St-Louis Gate are Quebec's parliament buildings. The imposing main parliament building, housing the National Assembly, was completed in 1886. It was designed by architect Eugène-Étienne Taché in the French Second-Empire style. Taché coined the motto "Je me souviens," which appeared for the first time on the walls of this building. The interior is open to the public through guided tours.

Built in the same style and period is Église Saint-Jean-Baptiste, in the neighbourhood of the same name, possibly the most impressive church in the city. The current building was completed in 1884 after a fire destroyed its predecessor. Most of the buildings in the charming neighbourhood surrounding the church date from the same period.

Below: Terrasse-Dufferin
Bottom: Manège Militaire

The 20th-Century

There are few significant buildings built in the new styles of the 20th-century near Old Quebec. A notable exception is the Price Building. This 18-storey grey limestone art deco skyscraper, crowned with a copper châteauesque roof is the tallest building in the old city. It was built as the headquarters for the Price Brothers lumber firm. The cornerstone bears an inscription stating it was laid on October, 29, 1929, date of the Wall Street crash that triggered the Great Depression. The company was soon driven to the brink of bankruptcy and the building was later acquired by the government. Its uppermost floors now house an official residence for the Premier of Quebec.

Modernism

Massive infrastructure projects in the 1960s and 1970s tore down hundreds of homes to make way for highways and skyscapers. The Grand Théâtre is a probably the most successful building from this period, conceived to commemorate the Canadian Centennial of 1967. It's worth stepping in for a look at the immense cement bas-relief by artist Jordi Bonet. The inscription on the wall translates as "Aren't you sick of dying, you bunch of idiots? Enough!" Such raw language in a place of high culture stirred up controversy at the time, and is a striking testimonial of the social and cultural emancipation that took place in 1960s Quebec.

Top: Basilique Notre-Dame-de-Québec
Middle: Library of the Literary and Historical Society
Below: Séminaire de Québec
Bottom: Martello Tower

Recent Years

The most striking building of the postmodern period in Quebec is the Musée de la Civilisation, the province's main ethnographic museum. It was designed by architect Moshe Safdie to echo the heritage of Quebec City. Three historic buildings were integrated into the museum: Maison Estèbe, Maison Pagé-Quercy and the site of the Ancienne Banque de Québec.

Beyond the old city at the bottom of Côte d'Abraham, you'll find the new Jardin Saint Roch, a peaceful square surrounded by some of the city's more modern developments. Among these is the Complexe Méduse, a string of row houses that was converted into numerous art galleries, the city's foremost venue for contemporary art. A few blocks down is Saint-Joseph Street, which is slowly emerging as a new downtown for the city that comes out of a new approach to revitalization. The Place Royale project of the 1960s made local officials realize that heritage is not only about buildings—it's about the people and activities that inhabit these places and give meaning to the forms. Though Place Royale is nice to look at, many would argue that its beauty is only skin deep. The thoughtful revitalization of neighbourhoods near the city walls, most notably Saint Roch, is probably the most significant heritage accomplishment in recent years. This revitalization has gone beyond bricks and mortar by bringing a measure of real life back into old abandoned buildings. It's worth getting off the tourist trail to gauge the pulse of the living breathing changing city where locals live and play.

Festivals & Events

Sarah Waters

Updates by Patrick Donovan

Fêtes de la Nouvelle France

Winter

Many people in traditionally Catholic countries or regions tend to enter the penitential season of Lent with a hangover and something worth repenting. That's because they've partaken of that grand tradition— Mardi Gras. This one last, glorious blowout, often lasting a couple of weeks, prepared the devout to endure the 40 days of fasting and mortification that led up to the glory of Easter. Lent is less rigorous than it used to be and not as widely observed, but the carnival tradition persists. There are street parties, fireworks and parades and people eat too much, drink too much, sing too much and pursue romance with commendable vigour. All this is very well in places like New Orleans, Rio de Janeiro and Nice. But Quebec City has managed to create a similar bacchanalia in one of the harshest climates in the world.

Dozens of imitators have sprung up across Canada—Montreal's Fête des Neiges and Ottawa's Winterlude, for example. But Quebec City's party, the Carnaval de Québec, is the granddaddy of them all. The first winter carnival was held in 1894. It was a

Bonhomme Carnaval

fairly modest event with some religious overtones, but it had a parade, as well as a ball for the elite and street parties for humbler folk. It wasn't until 1955 that the Quebec Winter Carnival became an annual event, thanks to members of the city's chamber of commerce who were looking for a way to perk up the anemic midwinter economy and attract some visitors. The chamber beefed up the parade and the balls and introduced Bonhomme Carnaval, the snowman mascot with a tuque and ceinture fléchée (a colourful woven sash) for a dash of Quebec patriotism.

Both Bonhomme and the Carnival continue to brighten the dead of winter with two weeks of parties and sporting events that attract more than 100,000 fun seekers in January and February. That's not to say that the Carnival hasn't had its problems, but since 1996 the organizers have been making serious efforts to revitalize their big party and clean up its sometimes riotous image. There is a definite emphasis on good, clean family fun, so along with the traditional balls and street parties, there are more kid-friendly activities: slides and rides at the ice park built on the Plains of Abraham, for example, and junior lessons in ice sculpting. Every weekend, a large parade, complete with magnificent floats, great bands and hilarious clowns, winds through the streets of the city. Bonhomme Carnaval, the pudgy snowman with the big smile, pops up everywhere. Most of the carnival's traditional events—dogsled races, ice-sculpture-carving contests, boat races across the half-frozen St. Lawrence, ski and snowmobile races, street parties—are still going strong.

Dogsled races at Carnaval de Québec

Spring

After the riotous celebrations of winter, spring festivities in Quebec are a time for sobering up with events geared to film and literature buffs. The 3 Americas Film Festival hits the city in late March with screenings of innovative movies produced in North, Central and South America. The Salon International du Livre de Québec, held in mid-April at the Quebec City Convention Centre, is a large affair bringing together a wide range of French-language publishers, authors and comic book artists. If it's English-language literature you're after, the Morrin Centre's Writers Series hosts bi-weekly readings by well-known English-Canadian writers around the same time.

Top and bottom:
Expo-Québec

Summer

The first event of summer, and one of the most riotous, is Quebec's Fête Nationale, or Saint-Jean-Baptiste day, celebrated on June 23 and 24. Young people from around the province take over the streets and engage in copious amount of drinking and flag-waving. The first evening culminates in a large musical show on the Plains of Abraham, followed by a bonfire. It's probably best to leave your Canadian flag at home during these festivities (if you have one), though you can certainly pull it out a week later for Canada Day on July 1. This is a quieter celebration which includes free Canada Day cake on Terrasse Dufferin, compliments of the Château Frontenac.

The new Grand Rire comedy festival usually hits Quebec around mid-June, bringing together hundreds of stand-up comics and street performers in locations throughout the city. Follow the smiling blue faces. Most of the entertainment is in French, though there are a few evenings of English programming.

The city's biggest party is the summer festival, Festival d'Été de Québec, held in early July. This large festival brings together performing artists, street theatre and an impressive palette of well-known international musicians. It is necessary to purchase a festival pass to get closer to the stages, though it's also possible to "squat" near some of the shows for free. The Festival Off is held around the same time, involving original up-and-coming musicians from Quebec who show off their talent at free shows in smaller venues throughout the city—this is your chance to hear a rockabilly band from Montreal that sings in Japanese (Les Doux Cactus), or a Hawaiian Country ukulele trio from Quebec City (Le Train qui Roule).

A couple of events held just outside the city are also worth considering. The Grands Feux Loto-Québec takes place at the end of July and the beginning of August. These fireworks displays are staged in a spectacular setting at the foot of Chutes Montmorency. Farther downstream from Quebec lies the shrine of Sainte-Anne-de-Beaupré, built in honour of the mother of the Virgin Mary. St. Anne's Feast Day is celebrated on July 26 with due religious ceremony but it is also something of a festival. Gypsies and some First Nations bands hold St. Anne in particular esteem, and they flock to the site in late July. Many of the First Nations celebrate in traditional costumes and the Gypsies often arrive in caravans of mobile homes.

August begins with the Fêtes de la Nouvelle France, which recalls the era of the 17th- and 18th-century French Regime

Fêtes de la Nouvelle France

with military displays, parades and re-enactments, as well as storytellers, musicians, singers, dancers and street performers. Other festivals in August include Plein Art, a 10-day crafts exhibition held in a tent on the esplanade near the parliament buildings; and the Festival International de Musiques Militaires, bringing together military bands from across Canada and Europe.

Expo-Québec has marked the end of summer in Quebec for more than 90 years. With more than 300,000 visitors each year, the event features some of the region's prime livestock, especially beef cattle, and agricultural exhibits. It comes with all the usual bells and whistles of a major country fair. Expo runs in conjunction with the Carrefour Agro-Alimentaire, a food fair that showcases all the culinary specialties of the region.

Autumn

Two emerging festivals are held on Labour Day weekend: the Québec City Celtic Festival, and the Fête arc-en-ciel. The former, held around the Morrin Centre, celebrates the city's Breton, Irish, Scottish, and Welsh heritage. Free workshops and performances take place throughout the day, with concerts and whisky tastings in the evenings. The Fête arc-en-ciel, held mostly in Faubourg Saint-Jean-Baptiste, is Quebec's Gay Pride Festival involving music shows, a street fair and film screenings.

If you're in town around the second week of September, you might want to explore the Festival des Journées d'Afrique. There are a variety of free concerts for the whole family and a number of indoor concerts by acclaimed international artists.

Autumn comes relatively early to the Quebec City region, and the leaves start to turn as early as mid-September. The city celebrates this change with a Festival des Couleurs on nearby Mont Ste-Anne, an 800-metre-high ski hill that affords a dramatic view of the surrounding countryside. Another autumn event that has been turned into a festival is the return of the snow geese. Great clouds of these magnificent white birds, which spend their summers at the northern tip of Baffin Island, descend on the marshes and farmlands before continuing their flight to their winter nesting grounds. One of their favourite stopovers is Cap Tourmente, and the local residents celebrate the visit with the Festival de l'Oie des Neiges de Saint-Joachim. Sandwiched between those two natural events are shows, craft displays and guided walking tours of the birds' favourite haunts.

Festival d'Été de Québec

Shopping

Lorraine O'Donnell

Updates by Tom Welham

Shopping on Rue Trésor

To know Quebec, is to go shopping. You'll discover all kinds of hidden treasures when you do; Quebec has wonderful things to buy, especially local products that make good souvenirs. There are antique and newly handcrafted household goods brimming with character. There is clothing made and worn by Quebeckers because it suits their boiling summers and freezing winters. And there are the fruits of many artists and artisans: paintings, sculpture, jewellery.

But shopping somewhere new is about more than buying things. It also gives you a glimpse of real life, the chance to encounter local people going about their business and to see what they eat, wear and use to work and play. It can take you off the beaten track and into interesting neighbourhoods. This is especially true of Quebec City, with its range of markets and malls, department and discount stores, running the gamut from humble to upscale, dusty to dazzling.

The brief guide that follows introduces you to some of the best places to shop in Quebec City. It is organized by district, starting with the old city centre, where you will most likely be spending a lot of time, and moving outwards to some of the other areas that are also worth a look.

Rue St-Louis

Old City Centre

You can find all kinds of souvenirs in the upper part of the old city centre. For kitschy knick-knacks and T-shirts, look into the shops on Rue St-Louis. Nearby in the landmark Château Frontenac is Lambert & Co., featuring regional crafts like colourful striped wool socks in the old Charlevoix style. Rue du Trésor is a fun open-air market of locally produced prints

Charlevoix socks at
Lambert & Co.

and paintings, many of the city itself. At the end is Rue de Buade, site of the well-known tobacconist J.E. Giguère, with its Quebec-made pipes and Cuban cigars. Over on Côte de la Fabrique is a small branch of the famous Simons department store, founded in Quebec and known for its house brands of women's and men's clothing. Down the street, you can buy fine handmade sweaters and moccasins at La Corriveau and high-end jewellery at Zimmermann. Now turn onto the main shopping street of the area, Rue St-Jean. Here, you'll find everything from candy to more clothes. The chic Librairie Pantoute has a large selection English-language books—best sellers, cultural, arts and tourist.

Shopping in the lower section of the old city is more varied. The Quartier du Petit-Champlain, the oldest commercial district in North America, offers high-quality, handcrafted goods. There are Quebec designer clothes at Oclan. On Rue du Petit-Champlain, all kinds of handicrafts, ranging from lace to art, including sculpture and paintings, are sold. The store Transparence showcases a dazzling array of glassware, Sculpteur Flamand features wood carvings in the traditional Québécois style, while down the street La Soierie Huo sells graceful, modern hand-painted silk and wool scarves.

In the Old Port area is Rue St-Paul, famous for its shops selling antiques and decorative items. Gérard Bourguet Antiquaire sells 18th- and 19th-century pine furniture, while Décenie features great pieces from the 1960s, such as

Rue St-Jean

modern dishes and vinyl chairs. Nearby is the Marché du Vieux-Port on Quai St-André, open year-round. At the heart of the port area revitalized for the City's 400th anniversary, the Marché is the best place to sample a wide variety of local produce, with everything from apple cider, fresh blueberries and emu steak. An autumnal weekend visit is highly recommended as it allows you to enjoy the sights, sounds, and tastes of Quebec, coupled with giving you an insight into the locals' joie de vivre!

Basse-Ville (Lower Town)

Antiques on Rue St-Paul

The differences between the old city centre and the Lower Town are many, and nowhere does this become more apparent than in the stores. If you consider the old centre too upscale, then gritty Basse-Ville is the place for you. It's an old working-class district, now also populated by artists, students and immigrants, and many of its stores are unpretentious and eclectic.

This being said, parts of Rue St-Joseph E. have been returned to their former glory. Once Quebec City's main shopping street, it suffered a giant setback in the 1960s, when new suburban shopping centres enticed its clientele away. To compete, five blocks of St-Joseph E. were enclosed and turned into a hideous mall during the next decade, but this "improvement" only hastened the area's decline. Finally, in 2000, the roof was taken off three blocks (between Rues de la Couronne and St-Dominique), and in 2007 the remaining sections were removed. This led to a frenzy of renovation that has resulted in a real revitalization of the city's true downtown. Some of the highlights include the revamped Laliberté, whose fur coats are famous (you can even visit the shop's fur workshop); Baltazar, with its hip decorative and culinary objects; Mountain Equipment Co-op, known for excellent outdoor gear; visit Benjo, a toy store that has to be experienced, and at the Maison de thé Cameille Sinensis you can sample any one of the myriad of teas available.

Suit at Oclan

Farther west on St-Joseph E., you'll find Basse-Ville bargains. X20 sells its own line of funky street wear. For a worthwhile detour: see and sample the bright rows of cupcakes and other baked goods at Royaume de la Tarte (on Avenue des Oblats at Rue Durocher). On Rue St-Vallier O. there are a number of East Asian and Latin American import stores. There's also Magasin Latulippe, with its enormous selection of camping, fishing and hunting gear and sturdy outdoor wear.

If you follow this street back to its east end, you'll come to the wonderful thrift shop Comptoir Emmaus: four giant floors of inexpensive used clothing, books, furniture and housewares. Here you can find that

Handmade paper at Copiste du Faubourg

pineapple-shaped ashtray you've always wanted. Be sure to check out the second-floor pneumatic-tube system for making change!

Haute-Ville (Upper Town)
Rue St-Jean west of Côte d'Abraham, is the colourful commercial heart of the friendly St-Jean-Baptiste neighbourhood. Cafés peacefully co-exist here with upscale sex shops (gay and straight) and stores selling cool clothing and local and imported furniture and decorative items. You'll also find purveyors of fine food, including the oldest grocery store in North America, J.A. Moisan.

Continuing west down Rue St-Jean until it changes its name to Chemin Ste-Foy, you come to Avenue Cartier, which serves the richer, older, more orderly clientele of the Montcalm neighbourhood. As well as many restaurants, cafés and specialty food shops, Cartier has a number of good women's fashion boutiques. One with consistently attractive collections is Boutique Paris Cartier. The mini-mall Halles le Petit Cartier will interest gourmets. On Boulevard René-Lévesque E. just east of Cartier are some exclusive Quebec designer shops. Pop into Autrefois Saïgon to see an intriguing line of women's clothing made here but possessing an East Asian flavour.

Suburbs
To really cover the Quebec shopping scene, follow the locals to the suburban malls. These centres sell all kinds of clothing, household items and food, and they have good parking facilities as well as services like stroller loans. Plus they offer shelter and entertainment when it's too cold to be outside. What they lack is local flavour and charm. Probably the most interesting is Galeries de la Capitale; it has an enormous indoor playground featuring a rollercoaster and an ice rink. For sheer size, visit Place Laurier in the suburb of Ste-Foy. With 350 stores, it's the largest shopping centre in eastern Canada. Close by, Place Sainte-Foy has big department stores, including another Simons and the huge Ailes de la Mode. The Sainte-Foy malls are easily accessible on the city's bus system.

But all is not hopelessly suburban in Ste-Foy. Witness the lively outdoor food and flea market on Avenue Roland-Beaudin, open every Sunday from May to late September. You can browse and haggle your way through reams of the lovely stuff cast off by people anxious to mine new treasures at (where else?) the nearby malls.

Dining

Patrick Donovan

It comes as no surprise that Quebec City has the highest density of French restaurants on the continent. Some of the finest chefs in the country ply their trade in very sumptuous locales here. The city also boasts humbler bistros serving tasty soups, baguettes and plenty of coffee.

The city's finest and most expensive restaurants are located within the old city. Farther from the walls, Grande Allée has many charming terraces, but most restaurants on this stretch offer subpar overpriced tourist fare. Your best bets for a good concentration of mid-price restaurants serving excellent food are Rue Saint-Jean and Avenue Cartier.

Haute Cuisine

Although similar to what one would find in France, Québécois haute cuisine uses local ingredients in very interesting ways. In addition to beef and pork, caribou or venison may be offered. The meat may come braised in maple syrup, marinated in Arctic tea leaves or served with Saguenay berries.

There are two major restaurants serving haute cuisine in the lower town. L'Initiale is one of four restaurants in Canada to carry the prestigious Relais & Chateaux label. The Laurie Raphaël, located nearby, has a more eclectic menu with occasional Asian touches. Both offer innovative food in a sleek contemporary décor and are frequently cited as the best restaurants in the city. The cuisine is referred to as cuisine du marché (market cuisine), since

Terrace Dining

Inside Laurie Raphaël

Le Saint-Amour

Le Continental

menus change regularly in accordance with the availability of fresh produce at the market.

In the upper city, cuisine du marché can be sampled in two romantic venues. Food at Le Saint-Amour tastes as poetic as it sounds with lavish dish names and a glass-roofed courtyard with art nouveau detailing. Others would argue that the oak-paneled dining room of Le Champlain, located in the iconic Château Frontenac, is more romantic. Chef Jean Soulard, the first Canadian to win the "Master Chef of France" award, lives up to his reputation in this venue with fine views of the Saint Lawrence.

If you're interested in sampling Québécois haute cuisine at half price, try Le Café du Clocher Penché in Saint Roch. A three-course lunch will set you back less than $15, while evening prices hover in the $17 to $24 range.

Traditional Québécois Cuisine

Traditional Québécois cooking is tasty comfort food—think meat pies, heavy soups, and hearty stews. Les Anciens Canadiens, located in a tiny old house dating back to 1675, provides excellent food despite the somewhat staged touristy atmosphere. For a more authentic Québécois greasy spoon, le Buffet de l'Antiquaire in the lower city serves up a good "Assiette Québécoise."

Italian cuisine

Quebec City boasts many excellent Italian restaurants. At the heart of the tourist action lies Au Parmesan on Rue St-Louis, a wildly atmospheric place with a wandering accordionist and loads of bottles and knick-knacks lining the walls. Cuisine from the Parma region of Italy is featured and the chef makes his own prosciutto and smoked

salmon on site. Other notable establishments offering
Italian cuisine include Le Graffiti on Avenue Cartier
and the little-known Ciccio Café on Rue Claire-
Fontaine. For more affordable Italian food, try Les
Frères de La Côte, a Mediterranean restaurant
specializing in wood-fired pizzas
that is run by two boisterous
brothers from the south of France.

Le Café Clocher
Penché

Cafés, Bistros, Crêperies, and Wine Bars

The most quintessentially French
bistro in Quebec City is certainly Le
Café du Monde, a huge sprawling
place in the ferry terminal of the old

Le Graffiti

port. Quiches, moules-frites and pâtés grace the menu,
and the atmosphere of a Parisian brasserie is
unmistakable. The service will remain friendly as long
as you refrain from snapping your fingers and yelling
"Garçon."

If you're looking for something cozier, there are
many smaller cafés worth sneaking into for a bowl of
coffee. Chez Temporel on Rue Couillard is a favourite
with local students, serving up affordable soups and
the best cheese croissant in town. Le Petit Coin Latin
on Rue Ste-Ursule has one of the loveliest terraces in
Quebec City. The specialty here is Swiss raclette:
cheese and meats grilled on a small portable oven.

Le Moine Échanson, at 484 Rue Saint-Jean in artsy
Saint-Jean-Baptiste, is a welcome new addition to the
city's gastronomic scene, and one of the more original
places in town. This wine bar's menu changes
regularly, focusing on new European regional
specialties every few weeks. These are served up in
small tapas plates alongside an appropriate wine and
excellent home-baked bread.

Although crepes are available all over Quebec City,
most of the old town creperies are disappointing. There
is hope outside the city gates at Le Billig on Rue Saint-
Jean. This Breton-run establishment is worth the walk.
"La Savoyarde", a wonderful artery-clogging
concoction of potatoes, lardoons, and melted
Québécois migneron cheese is sure to please.

Les Frères de
La Côte

Non-Western Cuisine

Quebec is not exactly multicultural but there are still

a few establishments that dish out excellent non-Western food.

For Chinese food in the old city, L'Élysée Mandarin is your best bet. They probably offer the best value for money in the old city at lunch. A three-course meal with a full dim

A beautiful presentation from Yuzu Sushi Bar

sum plate in an impressive old dining hall is available for less than $10.

There are many restaurants serving good, affordable Thai, Cambodian and Vietnamese food all over town. The best of the lot is probably the Cambodian-run Restaurant L'Apsara, located in an old bourgeois mansion next to the city walls. It's a bit more expensive than the others, but the food is worth the price.

If you're looking for sushi, the classiest place in Quebec City is the chic and very expensive Yuzu Sushi Bar at 438, in Saint Roch, nominated as having the nicest restrooms in Canada! More affordable Japanese food can be found at Le Tokyo, a bring-your-own-wine establishment on Rue Saint Jean.

The Aviatic Club

The best place for a taste of North Africa is probably Le Carthage on Rue Saint Jean. On certain nights, belly-dancing shows accompany the tajine and couscous. For more modest fare, the small Tunisian-run Salon de thé Le Sultan is located nearby and serves up delicious mint tea and sandwiches.

Indian restaurants are few and far between in Quebec City. The best is the newly-opened Restaurant Taj Mahal.

For North-American Indian cooking, Nek8arre at the Wendake reserve treats its guests to interesting Huron-Wendat food. Buffalo, caribou, deer and clay-baked fish are served up with corn and wild rice.

Last but Not Least

A section on dining in Quebec City would be incomplete without mentioning poutine, a staple of Québécois junk food. Although the dish is now available nationwide, even in big chains like McDonald's, this artery-clogging concoction of French fries, brown sauce and squeaky cheddar cheese curds is best sampled in Quebec City. Ask any resident where the best poutine in town is and most will point you to local fast-food chain Chez Ashton (many locations). For a classier poutine with three-pepper sauce, stop into Café au Bonnet d'Âne in Saint-Jean-Baptiste.

Quebec City
by Area

Lower Town

Patrick Donovan

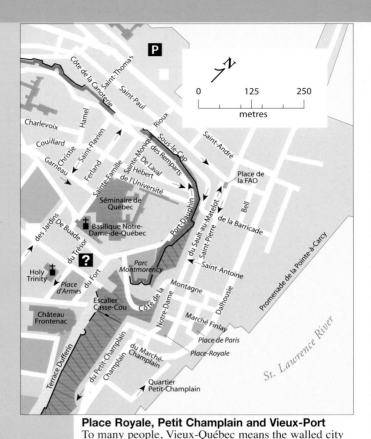

Place Royale, Petit Champlain and Vieux-Port

To many people, Vieux-Québec means the walled city
on the hill with its warren of narrow, twisted streets
spreading out from the castle-like bulk of the Château
Frontenac. In fact, Haute-Ville, or Upper Town, is the
newer part of the old city. To introduce yourself to
Quebec City's real birthplace, you can stand on
Terrasse-Dufferin at the edge of the Upper Town and
look over the wrought-iron guardrail. The steep roofs
below cover some of the oldest buildings in North
America. In 1608 Samuel de Champlain landed down
there on the narrow strip of land between the St.
Lawrence River and the cliff, cut down some trees and
built himself a trading post. That first rude settlement
comprised a moated manor house and some
storehouses and outbuildings. Fire and war have
destroyed any trace of Champlain's post, but many of
the walls and foundations of the current buildings date
to the prosperous days of the early 1700s.

The year 1608 also saw Jean Duval tried and found

guilty of treason for trying to kill Samuel de Champlain and take over the new French colony. Champlain had Duval beheaded — a darker element of the city's history. You can investigate this more mysterious side of the city's past after dark by taking a walking excursion through haunted sites with Ghost Tours of Quebec.

As recently as the 1960s, the Lower Town by the harbour was a rundown slum. Revitalization work began at Place Royale, a gathering place where various Amerindian nations met as early as 2,000 years ago. The new settlers began to use it as a marketplace in 1673. The restorers certainly succeeded in recapturing the look of the French Regime, but unfortunately, they also managed to suck much of the life out of the place which now looks rather like a film set.

Notre-Dame-des-Victoires

Still, the humble church on the square, Notre-Dame-des-Victoires, is worth battling the crowds to see. Built in 1687, it was a favourite of New France's first bishop, François de Laval. Hanging from the ceiling is a replica of the boat Brézé, one of the few remaining examples of ex-voto offerings left by devout sailors who arrived in Quebec. When caught in one of the frequent storms in the Gulf of the St. Lawrence, they would promise to build an exact replica of their boat if providence saved them.

Just down the hill from Place Royale towards the harbour is Place de Paris, a once bustling market now dominated by a chunk of modern sculpture that was a gift from the city of Paris and provides a little comic relief for tourists and locals

Place Royale

who wonder whether the real gift is inside this large white box. Behind this odd monolith are several houses and the reconstructed Batterie Royale, topped with 10 French cannons. Notice the different types of roofing on the houses, chosen to showcase the variety of roofing styles in New France. Many of the original houses in this part of the city were built out of wood and had shingle roofs. Time after time the city burned down from large indoor fires in the harsh winter, until

Batterie Royale

reconstructions used stone and tin roofs. To learn more about the early days of New France, you can visit the new Centre d'Interprétation de Place-Royale, housed in the two interesting postmodern buildings on the square.

Between 1797 and 1897, Quebec City's 40 shipyards turned out 2,500 ships. The Quartier du Petit-Champlain, hugging the cliff to the west beyond the funicular and the Breakneck Stairs, was where the shipsmiths, spar- and block-makers, riggers, chandlers and tow-boat owners lived, most of them poor Irish

Quartier du Petit-Champlain

immigrants. This area witnessed the birth of the first labour union in the country. Restored and sanitized by a citizens' co-operative a decade after Place Royale's revitalization, this area is worth a wander for the craft shops, cafés and atmosphere.

On the other side of the Lower Town, the modern port offers something of a relief from the tourist throngs at Place Royale. Watch yachts from benches along the water or view the city from a ferry ride.

The magnificent Nouvelle Douane, or "new" Customs House (actually built in 1856), on Quai St-André is still what it claims to be, and it glares across at the equally magnificent Société des Ports Nationaux building (built in 1914) on Rue de Quercy. Between them is a restful little park with fountains and rows of mountain ash trees. The contemporary grey building next door houses the free Naval Museum of Quebec, a chance to learn about Canada's recent military history.

Going back towards the cliff, the imposing buildings of the old financial district tower over the narrow rues du Sault-au-Matelot, St-Antoine and St-Pierre. Until the 1960s, this was the Wall Street of Quebec; it even had its own stock exchange for a few years. Now there's not a bank to be seen — just restaurants, hotels, art galleries and one of the most

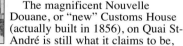

The New Customs House

interesting museums in Canada, the Musée de la Civilisation on Rue Dalhousie.

The museum, built in 1988, was designed by Moshe Safdie (who also conceived Montreal's Habitat '67 and Ottawa's National Gallery) to blend in with the old buildings that surround it.

Nouvelle Douane

With a special mission to explore Québécois culture and its relationship to the world, the museum consists of 11 exhibition spaces arranged around a vast bright entrance hall, which in turn is dominated by a cement sculpture featuring pools of water that represent the spring break-up on the St. Lawrence River. Aside from permanent, temporary and travelling exhibitions, the space hosts concerts, film screenings, poetry readings and political debates. The pièce de résistance is the fabulous dressing-up room in the basement, with extraordinarily creative costumes available for adults and children alike to try on for size.

Across the street, Robert Lepage, Quebec's internationally renowned playwright and filmmaker, was inspired to add some blocks of black granite to the back of the old fire station. The building is now the home of his production company, Ex Machina. All his shows are created, rehearsed and produced here, but this is not a performance space.

Nearby, you'll find the small Place FAO, which has won scores of architectural prizes for having transformed an ordinary street corner into a unique public space. From here, walk down Rue St-Paul, renowned for its excellent antique shops. If you duck into one of the narrow passageways between houses on this street, you'll discover Rue Sous-le-Cap, one of

Musée de la Civilisation

Quebec City's hidden gems: a dark, narrow street that hugs the cliff and is criss-crossed with picturesque stairways and galleries.

The contemporary eco-friendly glass building on Rue St-André was built as the hub of Quebec's 400th anniversary celebrations in 2008, hosting exhibits and special activities. The following year, it will reopen as the Parks Canada Discovery Centre, with exhibits focusing on immigration, the Saint-Lawrence, and heritage sites in Canada.

The Marché du Vieux-Port is the next stop. Here you can buy a snack from the farmers of Île d'Orléans, whose ancestors sold their wares at Place Royale during the French Regime, or sample some of the fine ciders and kirs produced locally. As you munch your apple, take a look

Above: Vieux-Port
Below: Marché du Vieux-Port

at the railway and bus station, built to resemble a château. If you step inside and look up at the magnificent skylight, you'll see its stained-glass map of North America.

St-Roch and St-Sauveur

Beyond the Dufferin-Montmorency viaduct is another part of the Lower Town, vibrant with life and devoid of tourists. As recently as 1990, St-Roch was a bleak urban wasteland with decaying buildings punctuated by empty parking lots. Since then, the neighbourhood has undergone one of the most thorough revitalization cures imaginable. It is now home to pricey sushi bars, hip nightclubs and some of the most expensive condos in the city. At the moment, it is an interesting place where wealthy urban bachelors in chic lofts rub shoulders with bohemian artists and much of the old working-class population.

A good place to begin is the Jardin St-Roch at the bottom of Côte d'Abraham. This is where the city's revitalization efforts began. Inaugurated in 1992, this tree-filled square, with its lovely waterfall, was initially a strange oasis surrounded by grim parking lots. Today, many tasteful new buildings frame it. Among these is Complexe Méduse, the premier venue for contemporary art in Quebec City. In the mid-1990s, several artists' collectives came together to convert a string of row houses into a vibrant complex that now houses numerous art galleries.

Railway and Bus station

From the park, walk down towards Rue St-Joseph, the main commercial artery of St-Roch. Until a few years ago, St-Joseph was listed in the Guinness Book of World Records as the "longest covered street in the world." Despite this honour, it was also one of the dreariest places in the world: a strip of shops on the verge of bankruptcy under a low, claustrophobia-inducing

Wall Mural
in St-Roch
neighbourhood

roof that concealed many interesting 19th-century buildings. The roof, built in 1972, was an urban renewal error, and all of it was demolished in the past decade. This made way for an up-and-coming urban street with new chic shops, excellent bakeries and unique art galleries.

The massive Église Saint-Roch, a church built during World War I, deserves a peek for its impressive stained glass. Further down St-Joseph is the city's main library, the very modern Bibliothèque Gabrielle-Roy, built in 1983. Nearby is the beautifully restored Édifice de la Fabrique on Boulevard Charest E., an industrial brick building with a prominent turret and clock tower. It now houses Université Laval's faculty of fine arts, though many still refer to it as Dominion Corset. Don't laugh: in its heyday, this factory employed over 1,000 single women, who produced as many as 21,000 corsets and brassieres per day.

The smaller back streets of St-Roch and the neighbouring St-Sauveur district are worth exploring. The tightly packed housing on streets such as Jérôme, Arago and du Roi in St-Roch and Aqueduc, des Oblats and Victoria in St-Sauveur are a jumble of styles. Tiny old houses with mansard roofs are jammed in among those from every successive era.

In the heart of this working-class neighbourhood is a large complex that dates back to the French Regime and contains the oldest surviving church in the city. The Hôpital Général on Boulevard Langelier was founded in 1693 by Quebec's second bishop and still looks after the poor and dying. With a little advance notice, sisters from the Augustinian order will give you a guided tour of the museum and the beautiful Notre-Dame-des-Anges chapel (built in 1673), Quebec City's best-kept secret. At the cemetery outside, the remains of the Marquis de Montcalm were recently re-interred next to the soldiers who fell with him on the Plaines d'Abraham.

Upper Town

Mary Ann Simpkins
Updates by Tom Welham

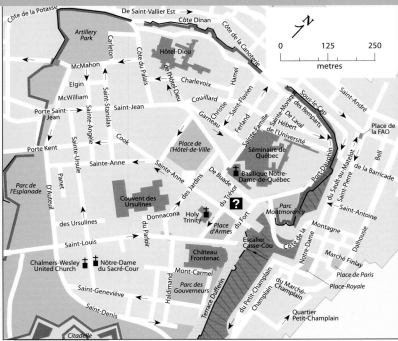

Château Frontenac

The doughty French settlers who founded Quebec City in 1608 built their homes and warehouses with convenience in mind, not security. Theirs was a trading venture, after all, and what better place to build it than on the banks of the St. Lawrence River, where boats and canoes could easily land? A few skirmishes with English fleets, however, revealed their vulnerability, and soon the colonists hacked a trail up the sheer rock face of the heights and founded Haute-Ville, or Upper Town, in 1620. At the top, Samuel de Champlain built a small fortress, where his statue now stands between the Château Frontenac hotel and a wildly modernistic globe that commemorates UNESCO's decision to designate the entire old city a world heritage site. Champlain's statue faces Place d'Armes, a space that served as a military parade ground during both the French and British regimes. The best way to tour Upper Town is by foot. You can easily walk the route in an hour, but leave more time for stops along the way.

Start at the turreted Musée du Fort on the corner of Place d'Armes, where taped commentary and lights flashing on a panoramic model of the city chronicle Quebec's military conflicts. Much livelier is Quebec Expérience on Rue du Trésor. Blazing guns, gushing water, three-dimensional figures and other special effects give you dramatic snapshots of the city's history. The English-speaking population of Quebec City has dwindled since the mid-1800s, dropping from half the population to less than two percent today, yet three of the churches in Upper Town are Anglophone. The one you see backing onto the northeast corner of Place d'Armes is Cathedral of the Holy Trinity, the mother church of the Anglican diocese of Quebec and the first Anglican cathedral built outside the British Isles. King George III, no doubt unclear on Canada's timber resources, shipped over oak from Windsor Castle's royal forest for construction of the pews. A balcony pew has been reserved since 1810 for royalty or royalty's representative. Guided tours of the cathedral, offered daily from May to Thanksgiving in October, recount the fascinating history behind some of the memorial plaques and the burial of the Duke of Richmond under the main altar. Craftspeople set up shop on the church grounds in the summertime, but artists hang their paintings and engravings of Quebec City year-round on the walls lining Rue du Trésor, which leads eastward from Place d'Armes and was where the early colonists came to pay their taxes to the governor of New France.

Cathedral of the Holy Trinity

Basilique Notre-Dame-de-Québec

At the end of this short street, turn left on Rue de Buade to reach the entrance to the Basilique Notre-Dame-de-Québec, the cathedral of the Roman Catholic archdiocese. The glorious interior is lavishly decorated with statues, stained glass and a sumptuous gilded canopy over the main altar. In summer the

151

church stages Feux Sacrés, an impressive sound-and-light show that focuses on the building's architectural and religious history. The ornate iron gate next to the cathedral guards the Séminaire de Québec, founded by Bishop Laval in 1663 to train priests for the parishes of New France. The first institution of post-secondary education in North America, it eventually evolved into Université Laval. In 1954, the university moved to modern quarters in suburban Ste-Foy, but the old Séminaire still houses the architecture school. It also houses the Musée de l'Amérique Française, which traces more than three centuries of French history and culture in North America through temporary and permanent exhibitions. Don't miss the seminary's stunning external chapel, with its Second Empire trompe-l'oeil interior and Canada's largest collection of relics.

Top: Basilique Notre-Dame-de-Québec, interior Inset: An ornate iron gate guards the Séminaire de Québec

Right: Musée de l'Amérique Française

Follow the seminary's high stone wall down Rue Ste-Famille to the street's end. At this point, if you turn right on Avenue des Remparts you'll come to Parc Montmorency, which has been lined with a row of British cannons since 1832.

If you turn left at the end of Ste-Famille, you'll reach one house that survived the British

Hôtel de Ville (city hall)

bombardment, the home of the Marquis de Montcalm, the general in charge of the French forces. A plaque identifies the burgundy-coloured house. The wood facing was installed over the stone around 1850 as protection against the fierce north-easterly winds. Go back up Rue Ferland and just before turning the corner onto Rue Couillard, you'll see a small doorway on your right. It leads into the convent of the Bon-Pasteur and was used by unwed mothers-to-be who needed the nuns' help but wanted to avoid the prying eyes on the more public Rue Couillard. The 19th-century convent is now a museum, and you can enter through the front door no matter what your condition. Rotating and permanent exhibits fill three floors, and friendly nuns will play an English video about their order for you and answer questions about the displays ranging from the cloth-enclosed nuns' rooms to religious art.

A block away, at the corner of Rue St-Flavien and Couillard, is one of the few historic homes open to the public. Stuffed with Victorian furniture and decorations, the Maison François-Xavier Garneau retains the typical decor of a 19th-century bourgeois home. Built in 1864, the two-storey neoclassical home topped with a widow's walk is named after French Canada's first historian, its most famous occupant — his statue sits near the St-Louis gate. On weekends, you might run into the man responsible for preserving the home, former Canadian national cycling champion (now owner of an international cycling products company) Louis Garneau.

The home of the Marquis de Montcalm

It's hard to avoid the influence of nuns in Quebec City. After the church established a presence in the colony, dozens of religious orders poured into the city. One of the first to arrive was a group of Augustinian nuns, who opened a hospital in 1644, the first in North America north of Mexico. Hôtel-Dieu still operates, as does the adjoining convent and its museum on Rue Charlevoix next to the small church at the side of the massive greystone hospital.

Convent of the Bon-Pasteur

Rue St-Jean was the city's fashionable shopping street from the late 1800s to the 1950s, but now it's a mishmash of souvenir shops, clothing stores and restaurants. Walking past these towards the St-Jean gate, turn right down Rue St. Stanislas and you will come to a blue limestone Celtic cross. This impressive monument was donated to the city by the Stokestown Park Famine Museum in Ireland in recognition of the compassion shown by the people of Quebec towards the Irish refugees during the Potato Famine. Off to the left is the Parc de l'Artillerie. This national historic site run by Parks Canada transports you back into Quebec's military history, a passage reinforced by guides acting as characters from the different periods. The reception centre for the complex is the Federal Arsenal, a turn-of-the-century munitions factory that closed in 1964. A short walk

Hôtel-Dieu

away looms the imposing Dauphine redoubt. The French began building the whitewashed fort in 1712, later turning it into barracks. Inside you'll find French soldiers, but also a cook from the Royal Artillery Regiment. After the Conquest, the redoubt housed British troops.

Head up towards Rue St-Jean, on Rue d'Auteuil which runs parallel to the city's walls. Turn left down Rue Dauphine, and continue along until you reach an imposing stone building on your right. Enter under the arch into chaussée des Écossais. On your right, you have the newly renovated Morrin Centre. Dating from 1808, this imposing building has had many incarnations, and each has left its mark. Originally built as a prison and the scene of a number of public executions, it was converted in the 1860s to house a Presbyterian college of higher education. If you look at the windows, you will notice where the prison bars were removed. In 1868, the library of the Literary and Historical Society of Quebec moved in and has remained there ever since even after the closure of Morrin College in 1902. Today, the Morrin Centre operates as an English-speaking cultural centre. On your left you have the Manse, or minister's residence, of St. Andrew's Presbyterian Church erected in 1837. Continue through chaussée des Écossais, and turn right onto Rue Ste-Anne and rejoin Rue d'Auteuil.

The Upper Town was the preserve of religious organizations, the city's administration and the wealthy, as you can see at 69 d'Auteuil, considered the Upper Town's most beautiful house. Any similarity between it and Ottawa's parliament buildings is understandable: this was the residence of their builder, Thomas McGreevy. In contrast to the flamboyance of McGreevy's home, Chief Justice Sewell chose the stolid English Palladian style for his residence, erected in 1803 at the corner of d'Auteuil and Rue St-Louis.

The St-Louis gate on Rue St-Louis is the principal entrance to Vieux-Québec. When the British garrison departed, the city tore down many gates. Some people clamoured for the walls to be demolished as well, but the governor general at the time, Lord Dufferin, persuaded them to save the walls and had this gate and others rebuilt. The road to the left of the gate leads to the Citadelle. On the right, dug into the wall, is the magazine the British used to store gunpowder. It serves as an interpretation centre

Parc de l'Artillerie

and has a scale model of the city depicting the evolution of the walls, from those constructed by the French in 1690 to those put up by the British in 1790. Back on St-Louis, head for the city centre. At Rue Ste-Ursule, make a short detour to your right and take a peek into the church of Notre-Dame-du-Sacré-Coeur. Its richly coloured stained-glass windows diffuse a gentle light onto walls crammed with marble plaques giving thanks for favours granted. Across the street, Chalmers-Wesley United Church offers free Sunday-night concerts in summer on its century-old organ.

No. 69 Rue d'Auteuil

Returning to St-Louis, keep your eyes peeled for a souvenir of the British bombardment: a cannonball lodged in the base of a tree. If you turn left on Rue Donnacona, you'll come to the great sprawl that is the Monastère des Ursulines, home to an order of nuns who arrived in Quebec City in 1639. Its stone walls still house the oldest continuously operating girls' school in North America, a beautiful chapel and a delightfully eclectic museum. The four rooms of the Musée des Ursulines display the parchment signed by Louis XIII approving the opening of a monastery and school in New France; altar cloths finely embroidered with silk and gold thread; and porcupine-needle baskets. Farther down St-Louis are some of Haute-Ville's oldest houses. The white house with the steep red roof, for example, was constructed in 1677. It's now the restaurant Aux Anciens Canadiens. The stately white building with blue trim was built about 1650 and is where the French formally surrendered the city to the British in 1759. Oddly enough, it now houses the French consulate.

The Château Frontenac only emerged as the city's most recognizable symbol in 1893. William Van Horne and other businessmen had the turreted, copper-roofed hotel constructed on the site of the demolished governor's palace. The wooden boardwalk in front of the château is called Terrasse-Dufferin, a fitting recognition for Lord Dufferin's saving of the fortifications. Delving back into this past, the Terrasse is the scene of extensive archaeological and reinforcement work. In the summer of 2008, the public will have the unique opportunity to tour the site, with work set to be completed in 2009.

The St-Louis gate

The Walls and Beyond

Sarah Waters

Updates by Patrick Donovan

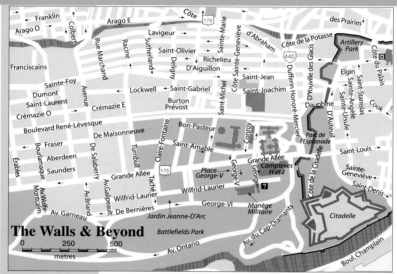

The Walls & Beyond

0   250   500
metres

Cannons along the walls of Quebec

There's something very seductive in the grey stone walls of Vieux-Québec. Tourists have been known to disappear behind the St-Louis gate, never to re-emerge until it's time to go home. And they no doubt have a wonderful time exploring the cobbled streets and 18th-century buildings of the old city. But their view of Quebec remains somewhat skewed and one-dimensional. Staying behind the walls is a delightful but limiting experience. To get the whole picture, you may want to step beyond the sheltering walls and explore the other facets of the city.

The Fortifications

A good way to start would be to skirt the edges of the historic city and examine its fortifications before you venture outside of the walls. There are two parts to this exploration: the walls and the citadel. Let's start with the walls. The city has always been fortified, but the French authorities didn't begin the present walls in earnest until after British troops took Louisbourg on Cape Breton Island in 1745. The construction turned out to be a bit late. The walls were still unfinished when General James Wolfe conquered the city in 1759. It was then that the British completed the walls fearful of an invasion from the newly-created United States of America. By the late 19th-century, North America was a fairly peaceful place and the walls no longer served a military purpose. However, Canada's governor general from 1872 to 1878, Lord Dufferin, insisted they not only be preserved but also adorned with medieval-looking turrets and towers. The only parts demolished at this time were the narrow gates, widened to let traffic through. Quebec City owes much of its French-regime charm to the whimsical tastes of an English aristocrat.

Fortifications of Quebec

At the interpretation centre at the wall on Rue St-Louis, Parks Canada gives an excellent overview of the history of the fortifications and their construction. You can take a 90-minute walking tour from here, or explore on your own. It's just a short stroll over to the St-Louis gate, and there you can begin to get a real feel for the ramparts. The wall is an impressive 1.5 metres thick and close to 5 metres high. Three ornate main gates, the St-Louis, Kent, and the St-Jean, puncture its stone solidity. At the northern end of the section is Parc de l'Artillerie, a pleasant green space that holds relics of some of the oldest sections of the fortifications. The park's old foundry has a beautiful scale model of what Quebec City looked like at the beginning of the 19th-century. Nearby is the Redoute Dauphine, parts of which date to 1713, and the decrepit Nouvelles Casernes. Beyond the park the fortifications swing east

The St-Jean gate

Redoute Dauphine

157

along the clifftops overlooking the Lower Town. The walls along Avenue des Remparts eventually lead to the Château Frontenac. Just in front of the château is Terrasse-Dufferin, a wide boardwalk along the cliffs that leads to the narrower and more precipitous Promenade des Gouverneurs, which in turn leads you to the next stop on the tour: the Citadelle de Québec.

La Citadelle is a post-Conquest addition. The British built the citadel between 1820 and 1831 to defend the city against an American attack that never came. Still an active military post, it is home to the Royal 22e Régiment and visitors may join a guided group tour of the interior. It is also possible to take a separate tour of the official Governor General's

The Van Doos Band on parade

summer residence. The Governor General is the British monarch's representative in Canada and has had a residence in Quebec City since 1872.

The National Battlefields Park

The western walls of the fort overlook the Plains of Abraham, now with the Des Brave Park. Gently rolling greenery stretches out along the cliffs overlooking the St. Lawrence River. It could be said that Canada's fate was sealed on this pleasant tract of land on September 13, 1759, when General James Wolfe and his battle-hardened British soldiers defeated a French garrison force commanded by the Marquis de

Former Governor General's residence

Montcalm. The battle claimed the lives of both commanders and essentially ended French dreams of a North American empire.

Monument on the Plaines d'Abraham

Start your visit at the Discovery Pavilion, the turreted stone building backing onto the park close to the pedestrian bridge leading to the citadel. A multimedia exhibition entitled Odyssey offers a historical film. The Pavilion is also the starting point for Abraham's Bus, a 35-minute tour which provides a quick overview of the park's highlights if you're in a hurry or don't feel like walking.

Reminders of the park's martial past litter the landscape in the form of old cannons, plaques and monuments to both leaders, and several panels describing the battle. Two Martello Towers are located in the park. Tower #1 is open to the public and presents exhibits on military engineering and meteorology. Tower #2 allows you to immerse yourself in 1814 military life, in a dinner theatre atmosphere. Enjoy a meal typical of the period while helping British soldiers solve a mystery (drop by the Discovery Pavilion to find out when this activity is held). These round stone towers were cutting-edge military technology when built in the early 1800s as outer defences for the citadel. The walls that face away from the citadel are solid and thick to fend off attack. The walls facing the citadel, however, are much thinner and could be easily destroyed by the citadel's cannon, ensuring that attackers could not use them for defence.

For something a little less militaristic, pause at the Jardin Jeanne d'Arc. This flower-filled oasis, with its statue of the Maid of Orléans, is located at the entrance to the park between Avenue Taché and Place Montcalm.

Farther along is the Musée National des Beaux-Arts du Québec, well worth a visit. It has one of the finest art collections in Canada, with more than 22,000 pieces that illustrate the development of painting, sculpture and decoration in Quebec from the 18th-century to the present. Besides a permanent retrospective of two Quebec artists, Jean Paul Lemieux and Jean-Paul Riopelle, the museum displays landscapes, portraits and a fascinating exhibit of religious art and artifacts drawn from churches all over the province. But the Musée is not all art. One of its two buildings, the Édifice Baillairgé, a beautiful Renaissance-revival structure, was designed in 1871 by renowned architect

Martello tower on the Plaines d'Abraham

Musée du Québec

Charles Baillairgé to serve as a prison. The museum has preserved an entire cell block and uses it to portray prison life in the 19th-century.

Along Grande Allée

When you emerge from the museum, walk down Avenue Wolfe-Montcalm and turn right onto Grande Allée to head back towards the old city. This stretch of Grande Allée is about as stately and elegant a street as any in North America. It's lined with some fine old homes, churches and public buildings in styles that range from neo-Gothic to Beaux-Arts, with a heavy dose of Second Empire, which was very popular with the 19th-century bourgeoisie who made their homes here.

At No. 115, for example, is something that resembles a country cottage with its steep roof and dormer windows. Built in 1850 when this part of the city was out in the country, it's named Maison Krieghoff for its most famous resident, the painter Cornelius Krieghoff, who lived in it for a few years. Next door is the graciously proportioned Ladies' Protestant Home, with its massive cornice and lantern. No. 82 is a piece of pure Regency, the Maison Henry-Stuart, with its row of French windows and massive overhanging roof. Maison Henry-Stuart and its pretty gardens are open to the public, and afternoon tea is

Café on Grande-Allée

served here. The fanciful jumble of towers and battlements at 530 Grande Allée that looks a little like a fortress is actually the church of Saint-Coeur-de-Marie, built by Eudist priests in 1919. Further west and just two blocks north of Grande Allée on Rue de la Chevrotière is a far more significant religious building. It's the former Mother House of the Soeurs du Bon-Pasteur (Sisters of the Good Shepherd), a religious order dedicated to the

education of abandoned and delinquent girls. Its austere walls hide one of the most exuberantly beautiful places of worship in the city, a neo-Baroque chapel designed by Charles Baillairgé.

Just across the street from the former nuns' residence is the

Maison Krieghoff

Édifice Marie-Guyart, Quebec's tallest building. Its top floor, the 31st (at 221 metres high), is an observatory with a magnificent, 360-degree view of the city and the surrounding countryside. There's a fee to get in, but it's worth it. For a similar view at no fee, walk a few blocks up to l'Astral, the rotating restaurant at the top of Loews Le Concorde. You'll need to eat something to stay and enjoy the view, but their lunch specials are surprisingly affordable.

If you head back to Grande Allée and continue the trek east, you'll come to the Hôtel du Parlement, where the province's legislature—the Assemblée Nationale— meets in Second Empire splendour. The building faces the walls, so to get to the main entrance you have to skirt its southern side.

Maison Henry-Stuart

You'll appreciate the beauty of the Hôtel du Parlement if you walk all the way down to Avenue Dufferin, where the 150-year-old Fontaine de Tourny was donated by a local businessman, who had it restored and erected as a 400th anniversary gift to his native city. Eugène-Étienne Taché, the architect who designed the parliament building in 1875, went out of his way to showcase the men and women who built the province. Bronze statues of people such as Samuel de Champlain; Paul de Chomedey, Sieur de Maisonneuve; Marguerite Bourgeoys, Jeanne Mance and others fill 22

Soeurs du Bon-Pasteur chapel

niches along the façade and up the sides of the central tower. A First Nations family in bronze poses at the main door and just below them, a First Nations fisherman stands at the edge of a fountain, his spear poised to catch a fish. In less politically correct times (say, in the late 1970s), this door was called the Porte des Sauvages, or Door of the Savages.

There are frequent free tours of the building and it's worth going inside even if only to see the two parliamentary chambers. The ornate Red Room on the left of the main door is where the appointed Legislative Council used to meet. When it was disbanded, the room became the main meeting room of parliamentary commissions and

committees. Today, laws are hammered out in the less ornate Blue Room on the right of the main door.

When you exit the Hôtel du Parlement you'll nearly be back at the St-Louis gate, but before you return to the charms of the old city, look across Grande Allée at the Manège Militaire, or Armoury. It too was designed by Eugène-Étienne Taché. The pleasant green space in front is Place George V, and there a monument that honours the memory of two British soldiers who died fighting a fire in Faubourg St-Sauveur in 1889.

Top: Hôtel du parlement
Inset: Detail on statue

Faubourg Saint-Jean-Baptiste

It's worth going down the hill beyond the parliament to discover one of the city's most charming and non-touristy neighbourhoods: Faubourg Saint-Jean-Baptiste. The neighbourhood is frequently referred to as the "People's Republic" of Saint-Jean-Baptiste, since it is a bastion of leftist students and artists in the heart of conservative Quebec City. Most of the quirky homes in this former working class area were built between the 1840s and the early 20th century. There is a certain charming grit to Saint-Jean-Baptiste that is lacking in other parts of the upper city; power lines are tangled like clotheslines across the streets, most of which are too narrow for trees.

Westward, beyond Porte Saint-Jean, the main street Rue Saint-Jean has all the trappings you expect from a great neighbourhood once you move the walls. There's a bakery on every street corner, a butcher, a poissonier, a chocolatier, European delis, health food stores, and excellent gelato shops. The old Saint-Matthew's Anglican Church has been respectfully converted into the neighbourhood library, with Sir Walter Scott's brother and Queen Victoria's supposed half-brother buried in the city's oldest graveyard, now a public park favoured by gelato-eaters. The streets and bars

Manège Militaire

surrounding Saint-Matthew's are where Quebec's gay and lesbian population congregate. Farther along Rue Saint-Jean, the towering Catholic Saint-Jean-Baptiste Church has a beautiful late-Victorian interior with lovely Portuguese floor tiles—it is perhaps the finest church in the city.

Excursions

Mary Ann Simpkins

Updates by Tom Welham

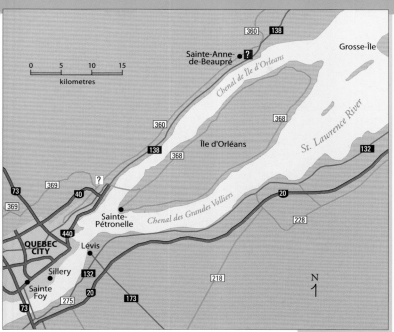

The area around Quebec City, beyond the old walls and Grand Allée, is rich in history and natural beauty. Within a short distance of the citadel are marvellous gardens, a waterfall higher than Niagara Falls, a shrine that attracts pilgrims from all over the world and a traditional First Nations village.

Take Sillery, for example, just west of the Plaines d'Abraham, where the governor general of the United Province of Canada had his home in the 1800s. In those days, nearly half the city's population was English-speaking and the wealthy ones lived in grand homes near the vice-regal residence. Fire destroyed the residence in 1966 and the grounds became a public park—the Bois-de-Coulonge on Chemin St-Louis, which is filled with flower gardens and walkways to some great viewing spots over the St. Lawrence River.

The Bois-de-Coulonge

Fire also wrecked a smaller home on the estate. A replica was erected in 1929. Villa Bagatelle is a rare example of rural Quebec Gothic architecture. The barren, modernized interior that features rotating exhibits on aspects of Quebec society is overshadowed by the English-style garden, which

Villa Bagatelle

demonstrates the diversity possible in a small space.

The Governor General's summer residence was a few kilometres away, in the centre of Sillery. Additions over the years have turned Domaine

Domaine Cataraqui

Cataraqui on Chemin St-Louis into an elegant neoclassical villa. Purchased by the provincial government after the death of the last owner, Catherine Rhodes, the house was restored to the style of the 1930s, when Rhodes lived here with her husband, the artist Henry Percyval Tudor-Hart. Some furnishings, photographs and paintings belonging to the couple remain in the house, which also serves as the provincial government's official reception centre and an art gallery, hosting three major exhibitions a year.

Just as elegant are other buildings on the estate, such as the stable and Tudor-Hart's studio. The artist treated the front lawn as a canvas, using dynamite to duplicate the contours of the waves that ripple over the St. Lawrence, visible at the end of the property. You can easily spend an hour wandering among the flower beds and along trails through a forest of catalpa, Japanese ginkgo and other species. This is an idyllic setting for the various musical groups that perform Wednesday evenings and Sunday mornings in summer.

Nearly directly below, at the base of the cliff on Chemin du Foulon, is the Maison des Jésuites. The

Jesuits set up their first permanent mission in North America beside the St. Lawrence where First Nations people fished for eel. Fire demolished the original home. The present stone house was built around 1730, with the second floor being added about 100 years later. Inside are photographs, amulets and other artifacts unearthed on digs here, and

Maison des Jésuites

a copy of a 1769 romance novel written by a resident, Frances Brooke—the first English-language book published in Canada. The Jesuits tried to persuade the Montagnais, Algonquin and Attikamek nations to settle among them, but only a few stayed here permanently. The Amerindian camp in the backyard is a reminder of their presence, as are the wooden crosses across the street in the First Nations cemetery.

Back up the cliff, nearly adjacent to the bridges connecting the north and south shores, is the Aquarium du Québec. The collection of more than 3,500 specimens ranges from pythons to piranhas. Small

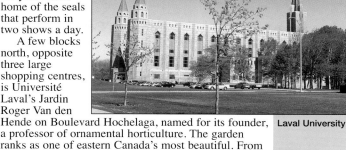

Laval University

outdoor pools are the year-round home of the seals that perform in two shows a day.

A few blocks north, opposite three large shopping centres, is Université Laval's Jardin Roger Van den Hende on Boulevard Hochelaga, named for its founder, a professor of ornamental horticulture. The garden ranks as one of eastern Canada's most beautiful. From May to September the public can tour the six hectares, filled with more than 2,000 plant species from Europe, Asia and North America.

North of the city, the Réserve Indienne de Wendake is the only Huron reserve in Canada. Converted by the Jesuits and allied with the French, the Huron left what is now Ontario more than 300 years ago to settle here. A wooden palisade circles the re-created traditional Huron village, which offers a glimpse into the lives of the ancestors of the present residents. Inside the longhouse, a full-sized doe hangs from the rafters and someone might be tanning a beaver skin by the smokehouse. The village restaurant serves typical aboriginal food, and its row of tiny shops sell everything from herbal remedies to recordings of Huron music. The Traditional Huron-Wendake Village is open year-round, with dance and song performances from May to September.

Traditional Huron-Wendake Village

Many locals will tell you that an important part of Quebec City's charm is its proximity to the great outdoors. Heading north along Highway 73, you wend your way up into the Laurentian Mountains, first passing the picturesque town of Lac Beauport on your right where you can go night skiing at Le Relais. Proceeding north you pass Stoneham village and ski station on your left. About forty minutes from downtown you continue on to Parc de la Jacques Cartier, a year-round destination for those in search of tranquility and/or adventure. In spring, summer and fall, it is possible to hike, bike and canoe in the park (rentals are available). The full range of nature interpretation activities are not to be missed, with the possibility of seeing some of the more reticent local residents including moose, beaver and even wolves. In winter, there is a network

Île d'Orléans

of backcountry ski and snowshoe trails, serviced by a series of huts and cottages—the ultimate Quebec backcountry winter experience!

Île d'Orléans, a small island that is a 15-minute drive east of Quebec City, remains rooted in the past. The entire island was named a historic district by the Quebec government in 1970. The first settlers arrived in 1649 but most buildings date from the 18th- and 19th-centuries. Driving the 67-kilometre road around the island reveals a bucolic landscape, a vista of farms, stone manors and churches interspersed with a few artisans practising time-honoured crafts. Join the city families out picking apples in the fall, sample the exquisite crème de cassis at Cassis Monna et filles in St-Pierre and be sure to visit one of the island's vineyards.

When he set out to conquer Quebec in 1759, General James Wolfe set up his headquarters at the western tip of Île d'Orléans, in Ste-Pétronille, the smallest of the island's six parishes. His takeover of the island wasn't always peaceable. The Manoir Mauvide-Genest in St-Jean, for example, rated the finest example of rural architecture under the French Regime, still bears the pockmarks of British cannon fire in its stone walls. The Norman-style manor is today a museum and restaurant.

Elsewhere on the island, the Parc Maritime de St-Laurent celebrates the shipbuilding heritage of St-Laurent parish with exhibits and on-site demonstrations of wooden boat-building. As well, a blacksmith demonstrates traditional techniques at the Forge à Pique-Assaut and weavers spin rugs at the Economusée du Tapis in St-Pierre. To see other works by local craftspeople, visit the parish church, Canada's oldest village church.

On the mainland, just east of the Île d'Orléans bridge, the Pont d'Île, Chutes Montmorency plunges 83 metres, a drop nearly one and a half times greater than that of Niagara Falls. For a superb view, cross the pedestrian bridge suspended over the falls. The cable car offers another panorama, as well as an alternative to climbing the 400 stairs connecting the upper and lower boardwalks. Perched on top of the cliff close to the falls is a Palladian-style villa, a replica of the

Chutes Montmorency

original constructed around 1783 for the governor of Quebec, later rented by the Duke of Kent. A small museum tells the history of the graceful white wooden building, which also houses an art gallery, bar and restaurant. The Chutes are perhaps at their most spectacular in winter when you can see the Pain de Sucre (the Sugarloaf) at the foot of the falls that is formed when the spray freezes.

Farther east along Highway 138 sits Basilique Sainte-Anne-de-Beaupré. Pilgrims have been coming to this site since 1658; it is considered the oldest Christian shrine in North America. More than one million visitors a year still come to pray inside the most recent church on this site: a concrete edifice warmed by glimmering mosaics, carved stones and 200 stained-glass windows. On the opposite side of the basilica, the round Cyclorama features a museum and a panoramic painting of Jerusalem. One floor covers the history of the pilgrimages, displaying photographs along with earrings, necklaces and other offerings to St. Anne. The second floor displays the church's treasures, from silver chalices to an 18th-century gilded altar.

Basilique Sainte-Anne-de-Beaupré

The shrine and its little town sit at the foot of Mont Ste-Anne, an 800-metre-high mountain that offers some of the best alpine and cross-country skiing east of the Rockies. The resort has 65 downhill trails totalling 84 kilometres, and 17 night ski runs. The cross-country network, the largest in Canada, has 223 kilometres of trails, while a large fun park and two halfpipes lure snowboarders. The resort also offers a skating rink, dog sledding and a ski museum. In summer, Mont Ste-Anne transforms into a world-class mountain bikers' paradise with rentals on site. Hikers can also take advantage of an extensive trail network, sightseers can ride the lifts and golfers play on the two courses that grace the foot of the mountain.

Skiing at Mont Ste-Anne

In summer, take the ferry from Quebec City to Lévis and catch one of the shuttle buses that meander around the city. Among the stops is Fort No. 1, built early in the 19th-century to fend off an American attack that never came. The guides who lead tours wear costumes modelled on the uniforms of the Royal Engineers, but the fort is no longer a military installation. It was used as a storage depot for

Celtic Cross

ammunition through two world wars and was finally decommissioned in 1948.

East of Lévis, close to the town of Montmagny, sits Grosse Île. For more than 150 years the small island was the main gateway to Canada for thousands of immigrants and the quarantine station for those afflicted with cholera, typhoid and black plague. A sense of sadness pervades this final destination for so many. The sightseeing trolley visits the Celtic cross, the Catholic church, the hospital, Irish Cemetery and the Disinfection Building, where pipes over narrow shower stalls sprayed each ship passenger with mercury chloride. The only way to reach this island, operated by Parks Canada, is on licensed boats.

East of Ste-Anne-de-Beaupré, on the right before climbing the hill lays the Cap Tourmente National Wildlife Area. This site is home to more than 300 species of birds, 45 species of mammals, and 700 species of plants and trees. Visit the interpretation centre, view the birds from the shore-side hides and hike along the extensive network of trails that lead to some spectacular view points over the St. Lawrence and back to Quebec City. Continuing farther east on Highway 138, about an hour from Quebec City, you come to Le Massif, a world-class ski station that offers the unparalleled experience of skiing down hill towards the frozen expanse of the St. Lawrence! Upon reaching Baie St. Paul, you are in the heart of the Charlevoix region, an area that has long been a magnet for artists—even the smallest village boasts a gallery. The scenic landscape leads to Pointe-au-Pic, where a turreted stone castle, Manoir Richelieu, was recently renovated to celebrate its 100th anniversary. Opposite the hotel, try your luck at the casino. Or hop aboard a boat for a whale-watching tour or a ride down the majestic Saguenay fjord.

Golf at Mont Ste-Anne

Listings: Contents

Getting There

Montreal

Located along the shores of the St. Lawrence River, Montreal is easy to get to by air, highway, rail and water.

By Air

Pierre Elliott Trudeau International Airport: Located 18 kilometres west of downtown Montreal, the airport is accessible from Highways 20 and 40 and by commuter train or shuttle bus. It is a 20-minute drive from the city centre. The airport handles regular scheduled flights from local and international destinations. Some 20 major airlines offer regularly scheduled flights.

By Road

By car or by bus, travellers can reach Montreal by several major routes. Highways 20 and 40 enter Montreal from the west. Hwy. 20 also enters Montreal from the northeast, hugging the north shore of the St. Lawrence River. Hwy. 10 enters Montreal from the east over the Pont Champlain (Champlain Bridge). Hwy. 15 runs towards Montreal from Quebec's southern border, shared with New York State, and from the north. Out-of-town buses arrive and depart from the Montreal Bus Terminal (formerly the Terminus Voyageur), at 505 Boul. de Maisonneuve E. (corner of Berri). Adirondack Trailways and Greyhound Lines offer rides to New York City, and Orléans Express covers Quebec City and other destinations in the province. From May to October, the Rout-Pass entitles holders to unlimited bus travel for 15 consecutive days in Quebec and Ontario. Call the station at 514-842-2281 for bus company fares and schedules.

By Rail

Train travellers arrive at Gare Centrale (Central Station), 895 Rue de la Gauchetière O. Montreal is served by the VIA Rail Canada system, the network that provides all rail service throughout Canada. Amtrak provides daily service to New York and Washington. VIA Rail offers a Canrailpass, valid for one month, which allows the holder 12 days of train travel across Canada. Central Station is located directly beneath the posh Hôtel La Reine-Élisabeth (Queen Elizabeth Hotel) and across from the Hilton Montréal Bonaventure. The station also serves commuter rail lines and is connected by indoor tunnels to Montreal's subway system and several underground shopping centres. Call 1-800-561-3949 or 514-989-2626 for train schedules and fares.

Quebec City

Located 253 kilometres northeast of Montreal along the St. Lawrence River, Quebec City is easily accessible by air, road and rail.

By Air

Jean Lesage International Airport: The airport is located 16 kilometres west of downtown Quebec City along Route 138 and Autoroute 540. The airport offers scheduled flights with Air Alliance, Air Canada, Air Nova, Air Atlantic, Northwest Airlink and charter flights with Aeropro, Aviation Portneuf and Aviation Roger Forgues. For information on flights, call 418-640-2700. There is no longer any bus shuttle service available from the airport into the city. A taxi costs about $27 from the airport to downtown.

By Road

Quebec City is served by Highway 20 along the south shore of the St. Lawrence River and Hwy. 40 from the north. Buses arrive at the Bus Terminal, 320 Rue Abraham-Martin. Intercar Côte-Nord links Quebec City with a number of northern towns, and Orléans Express Coach Lines links the city with the rest of Quebec. From May to October, the Rout-Pass entitles holders to unlimited bus travel for 7, 14 or 18 consecutive days in Quebec and Ontario. Call 418-525-3000 for information.

By Rail

Via Rail Canada offers daily service

between Quebec City and Montreal with regular and first-class cars. Call 1-888-842-7245 for information and reservations. Trains arrive and depart from Gare du Palais, 450 Rue de la Gare-du-Palais in downtown Quebec City. Call 418-524-4161 for information.

Travel Essentials

Money

Currency can be exchanged at any bank at the prevailing rate. If you use a small local branch, it's best to call ahead to confirm its capacity to exchange, on the spot, any currency other than American funds. There are currency exchange booths at the airport. Banks are generally open from 10 a.m. to 4 p.m. Units of currency are similar to those of the United States, except for the Canadian one-dollar (loonie) and two-dollar (toonie) coins.

Most major North American credit cards and bank cards, including American Express, Carte Blanche, Diners Club, EnRoute, MasterCard and Visa, are accepted almost everywhere. Travellers' cheques can be cashed in major hotels, some restaurants and large stores. Many stores and services will accept U.S. currency, but the exchange rate they offer may vary greatly. Since there are no laws enforcing foreign currency rates of exchange, it is strongly recommended that you convert to Canadian funds before you make your purchases.

American visitors may also use bank or credit cards to make cash withdrawals from automated teller machines that are tied into international networks such as Cirrus and Plus. Before you leave home, check with your bank to find out what range of banking services its cards will allow you to use.

Passports

American citizens are required to carry proof of citizenship, such as a U.S. passport or a birth certificate, plus photo identification. Naturalized U.S. citizens should carry a naturalization certificate, plus photo identification. Permanent U.S. residents who are not citizens are advised to bring their Alien Registration Card (Green Card) or a valid 1551 stamp in their passport. Note that other documents such as a driver's licence or voter registration card will not be accepted as proof of U.S. citizenship. Visas are not required for U.S. tourists entering Canada from the U.S. for stays up to 180 days.

Citizens of most other countries must bring a valid passport. Some may be required to obtain a visitor's visa. For details, please consult the Canadian Embassy or consulate serving your home country.

Customs

Arriving

As a non-resident of Canada, you may bring in any reasonable amount of personal effects and food, and a full tank of gas. Special restrictions or quotas apply to certain specialty goods, and especially to plant, agricultural and animal-related materials. All items must be declared to Customs upon arrival and may include up to 200 cigarettes, 50 cigars, 200 grams (6.5 oz.) of manufactured tobacco and 200 tobacco sticks. Visitors are also permitted 1.14 litres (40 oz.) of liquor or 1.5 litres of wine or 8.5 litres (24 x 12-oz. cans or bottles) of beer.

You may bring in gifts for Canadian residents duty-free, up to a value of $60.00 (Canadian) each, provided they do not consist of alcohol, tobacco or advertising material. For more detailed information, call the Canada Border Services Agency's Automated Customs Information Service (ACIS) at 1-800-461-9999, or visit the Canada Border Services Agency on-line at www.cbsa-asfc.gc.ca.

Departing

For detailed customs rules for entering or re-entering the United States, please contact a U.S. Customs office before you visit the province of Quebec.

Information is also available on the U.S. Customs and Border Protection (CBP) Web site at www.customs.ustreas.gov. Copies of the U.S. Customs information brochure *Know Before You Go* are available from U.S. Customs offices or on the CBP Web site (under "Publications"). It is generally recommended that you try to pack the things you'll need to declare separately.

Travellers from other countries should also check on customs regulations before leaving home.

Taxes

Most goods and services are subject to a federal tax (GST) and a provincial tax (PST) in Quebec. Foreign residents may be entitled to certain tax rebates on tourism-related goods and services. If you keep all sales slips from your visit you will be able to claim tax rebates upon your departure. For more information, visit the "Tax Refund for Visitors" page at www.cra-arc.gc.ca/visitors/tax-e.html, or phone 902-432-5608 or 1-800-668-4748 (Canada).

Goods and Services Tax

(GST, or TPS in French)

The federal Goods and Services Tax is 7%. This is a value-added tax that applies to most goods, purchased gifts, food/beverages and services, including most hotel and motel accommodation.

Provincial Sales Tax (PST, or TVQ in French)

The Quebec provincial sales tax is 7.5% of the original price plus GST. A PST refund form can also be obtained by contacting Revenue Quebec at 514-873-4692, or ask a retailer for a form.

Getting Acquainted

Time Zone

Montreal and Quebec City fall within the Eastern Standard Time Zone.

Climate

Here are average Montreal temperatures, highs and lows; fluctuations from the norm are common:

January	21°F to 5°F	
	–6°C to –15°C	
February	25°F to 7°F	
	–4°C to –14°C	
March	28°F to 19°F	
	–2°C to –7°C	
April	52°F to 34°F	
	11°C to 1°C	
May	66°F to 45°F	
	19°C to 7°C	
June	73°F to 55°F	
	23°C to 13°C	
July	79°F to 59°F	
	26°C to 15°C	
August	77°F to 57°F	
	25°C to 14°C	
September	68°F to 48°F	
	20°C to 9°C	
October	55°F to 39°F	
	13°C to 4°C	
November	41°F to 28°F	
	5°C to –2°C	
December	27°F to 12°F	
	–3°C to –11°C	

Average annual rainfall:
28.98in./73.63 cm.

Average annual snowfall:
89.6in./226.2 cm.

Average temperatures are
5.4°C (41°F) in spring,
19.4°C (66.2°F) in summer,
11.4°C (51.8°F) in autumn,
–6.1°C (21.2°F) in winter.

Here are the average Quebec City temperatures, highs and lows:

January	18°F to 1°F
	–8°C to –17°C
February	21°F to 3°F
	–6°C to –16°C
March	32°F to 16°F
	0°C to –9°C
April	46°F to 28°F
	8°C to –2°C
May	63°F to 41°F
	17°C to 5°C

June	72°F to 50°F
	22°C to 10°C
July	77°F to 55°F
	25°C to 13°C
August	73°F to 54°F
	23°C to 12°C
September	64°F to 45°F
	18°C to 7°C
October	52°F to 36°F
	11°C to 2°C
November	37°F to 25°F
	3°C to –4°C
December	23°F to 9°F
	–5°C to –13°C

Average annual rainfall:
34.69in./88.13 cm.

Average annual snowfall:
132.6in./337 cm.

Average temperatures are
3.2°C (37.4°F) in spring,
17.7°C (64.4°F) in summer,
9.5°C (50°F) in autumn, and
–8.3°C (17.6°F) in winter.

Guides and Information Services

Tourisme Quebec operates more than 200 tourist information offices province-wide to provide regional information and seven Maisons du Tourisme, with more extensive services. For information call 1-877-266-5687 (Canada and the United States); fax 514-864-3838; email: info@bonjourquebec.com; or write to Tourisme Quebec at P.O. Box 979, Montreal, QC H3C 2W3. Also, visit Tourisme Quebec's Web site at www.bonjourquebec.com for comprehensive information about accommodations, camping and attractions throughout the province of Quebec.

Montreal

- L'Hôtel de Ville de Montréal (Montreal City Hall). 275 Rue Notre Dame E., Montreal, QC H2Y 1C6; 514-872-1111; www.ville.montreal.qc.ca. For a guided visit: email: bam@ville.montreal.qc.ca;

www.ville.montreal.qc.ca.
- Infotouriste Centre. 1001 Square Dorchester, Montreal, QC H3B 1G2; 514-873-2015 or 1-877-266-5687 (North America). Near the Peel Métro station, the Infotouriste Centre handles travel planning, hotel reservations, car rentals, attractions and guided bus tours. Visit www.tourisme-montreal.org for regional information.
- Tourisme Montréal's Greater Montréal Convention and Tourism Administration Bureau. 1555 Rue Peel, Suite 600, Montreal, QC H3A 1X6; 514-844-5400; fax 514-864-3838. Regional information is available at www.tourisme-montreal.org/meet, or visit www.montrealcam.com to see Montreal in real time via the Greater Montreal LiveCam Network.
- Tourist Information Centre of Old Montreal. 174 Rue Notre-Dame E. Located near the Champs-de-Mars Métro station, the centre supplies bus maps, road maps, telephone cards, museums passes and bicycle-path passes as well as brochures about attractions. www.oldportofmontreal.com

Quebec City

- Ville de Québec (Quebec City Hall). 43 Côte de la Fabrique, Quebec City, QC G1R 5M1; 418-641-7010. Ground floor houses the Urban Life Interpretation Centre of the Ville de Quebec, 418-641-6172.
- Maison du Tourisme. 12 Rue Ste-Anne. Located across from the Château Frontenac, the Infotouriste Centre provides extensive local information plus hotel and car rental reservations. Visit www.bonjourquebec.com.
- Office du Tourisme et des Congrès de la Communauté Urbaine de Québec. 399 Rue St-Joseph E., Second Floor, Quebec City, QC G1K 8E2; 418-641-6654; fax 418-641-6578; www.gouv.qc.ca.

- Vieux-Québec Tourist Information Bureau. 835 Avenue Wilfrid-Laurier, Quebec City, QC G1R 2L3; 418-641-6290; fax 418-522-0830; www.regiondequebec.com.

Language

Most Montrealers speak English, but when travelling through some areas of the province, you might as well be in France. But unlike speaking French in Paris, using a phrase or two en Français will most likely get a cheer of praise by most French-speaking Quebeckers.

Getting Around

Travelling in Montreal and Quebec City

Montreal is an island connected to the mainland by bridges to the north and south of the city. The city is served by the Ville-Marie Expressway, which leads to Highways 10, 15 and 20, travelling west and east. The Decarie Expressway leads to Hwy. 40, travelling north and west.

If you're a member of any recognized auto-club affiliates (AAA, CAA, etc.), the CAA-Québec will provide all club services. In Montreal, call 514-861-1313, and elsewhere in Quebec, call 1-800-222-4357. CAA-Québec also has a Web site: www.caaquebec.com

Public Transportation

Montreal

The Société de Transport de Montréal (STM) operates from 5:30 a.m. to 12:30 or 1:00 a.m., depending on the Métro line. Some bus lines run all night. The subway system consists of four Métro lines and covers 65 kilometres across 65 stations, with free transfers to the STM bus network of 163 daytime and 20 nighttime service routes. Exact fare is required. Free maps, discount tickets and day passes are available at all stations and in many convenience shops. At the time of publication, one adult ticket is $2.50 and six tickets are $11.25. The Tourist Card, which allows unlimited travel for one day for $8 or for three days for $16, is available year-round at the Berri-UQAM, Bonaventure and Peel Métro stations (and at various other stations in the summer months). Call 514-280-5507 for more details; call 514-786-4636 for bus lines, schedules and additional information; fax 514-280-5666; email: commentaires@stm.info; visit www.stcum.qc.ca.

Commuter Buses and Trains

Regular train service to Montreal's suburbs operates from Gare Centrale (Central Station) and Gare Windsor. Call 514-287-8726 for commuter-train schedules for both stations. Regular bus service on the South Shore runs from Métro Longueuil (450-463-0131) and in Laval from Métro Henri Bourassa (450-688-6520).

A ferry service offers rides to pedestrians and cyclists from the Old Port to Parc des Îles, Longueuil, Promenade Bellerive in East Montreal and Île Charron from mid-May to mid-October. Call 514-281-8000 for information.

Quebec City

The Société de Transport de la Communauté Urbaine de Québec operates bus lines throughout Quebec City. Fares at the time of publication are $2.50 for adults and free for children. Students and children over five need to present a valid student card for access at a reduced rate of $1.40. Day passes are available. Call 418-627-2511 for information.

A Winter Shuttle, the HiverExpress, operates daily from downtown Quebec City to Ste-Foy hotels and a number of outdoor activity sites. Call 418-525-5191 for reservations.

The Société des Traversiers du Québec operates year-round daily ferry services from Quebec City to Lévis, across the St. Lawrence River. For information call 418-644-3704; fax 418-643-5178; or visit www.traversiers.gouv.qc.ca.

Cars and Rentals

Most foreign driver's licences are valid in Quebec. Non-resident drivers and passengers of automobiles licensed in Quebec are entitled to the same compensation from the Société de l'Assurance Automobile du Québec as Quebec residents if they are injured in an accident in the province. Other non-resident accident victims, including pedestrians, cyclists and drivers of cars not licensed in Quebec, can be compensated in inverse proportion to their responsibility for any accidents. Owners of vehicles driven in Quebec must have at least $50,000 in liability coverage. For additional information, contact the Societé de l'Assurance Automobile du Québec at 514-873-7620 (in Montreal), 418-643-7620 (in Quebec City), or toll free at 1-800-361-7620, or visit www.saaq.gouv.qc.ca.

Distances are indicated in kilometres and speed limits in kilometres per hour. One kilometre equals about five-eighths of a mile. To convert from kilometres to miles, multiply kilometres by 0.6. To convert from miles to kilometres, multiply miles by 1.6. Metric measurements are used for motor fuel. One litre equals about one-quarter of an American gallon, or about one-fifth of an Imperial gallon.

Speed limits on highways and main roads are 100 km/h maximum and 60 km/h minimum. The provincial police prohibit possession of a radar detector, whether connected or not, and fines range from $500 to $1,000. Turning right on a red light is permitted throughout Quebec except on the island of Montreal and at intersections where road signs prohibit such turns. Seatbelt use by passengers and drivers is mandatory.

Montreal

- Alamo Rent-a-Car, Pierre Elliott Trudeau International Airport. 514-633-1222 or 1-800-327-9633; www.alamo.com.
- Avis Car and Truck Rental. Pierre Elliott Trudeau International Airport; 514-636-1902. Downtown, 1225 Rue Metcalfe; 514-866-2847; www.avis.com.
- Hertz Canada Ltée. 1073 Rue Drummond; 514-938-1717; www.hertz.com.
- Pelletier Car and Minibus Rental. 3585 Rue Berri; 514-281-5000; www.pelletierrentacar.com.
- Sako Location d'Autos Inc. 2350 Rue Manella; 514-735-3500; www.sako.com.

Consult the Yellow Pages for more agencies.

Quebec City

- Discount Location. 12 Rue Ste-Anne; 418-655-2206 or 1-800-263-2355; www.discountcar.com.
- Hertz Canada Ltée., Jean Lesage International Airport. 418-871-1571 or 1-800-263-0600; www.hertz.com.
- Via Route. 450 Rue de la Gare-du-Palais; 418-692-2660; www.viaroute.com.

Consult the Yellow Pages for more agencies.

Tours

Montreal

- Autocar Connaisseur Grayline. 1140 Rue Wellington; 514-934-1222; www.coachcanada.com. Sightseeing tours on board a replica of Montreal's streetcars of the past.
- Autocar Impérial. Infotouriste Centre, 1001 Square Dorchester; 514-871-4733; fax 514-871-9786; email: info@autocarimperial.com; www.autocarimperial.com. Bilingual city tours, some on double-decker buses.
- Aventure Boréale Inc. 514-271-1230 or 1-877-271-1230; fax 514-271-3153; email: info@borealtours.com; www.borealtours.com. Day trips to the countryside. Downtown departures for canoeing, fishing and hiking in the summer, and dogsledding, ice fishing, snowmobiling and snowshoeing in the winter. Transportation and meals included.

Getting Around

- La Balade du Vieux-Port. 514-496-7678. A bilingual guided tour of the Old Port's past, departing from the Quai Jacques-Cartier.
- Bateau-Mouche au Vieux-Port de Montréal. 514-849-9952 or 1-800-361-9952; fax 514-849-9851; email: info@bateau-mouche.com; www.bateau-mouche.com. Tour the city in a glass-roofed boat offering spectacular views. Five daytime excursions and a Parisian-style dinner cruise with gourmet menu and live entertainment leave daily from the Quai Jacques-Cartier.
- Delco Aviation Ltée. 450-663-4311 or 514-984-1208; fax 450-975-8965; www.delcoaviation.com. See Montreal from a seaplane in summer or try hydroskis in winter.
- Flowers Aviation Inc. 6324 3e Ave.; 514-727-6486. Cessna 206 seaplanes tour regions throughout the province.
- Guidatour. 514-844-4021 or 1-800-363-4021; email: info@guidatour.qc.ca; www.guidatour.qc.ca. Daily walking tours of Old Montreal from June through October. Tickets on sale at Basilique Notre-Dame. Private guided tours of Montreal and environs available in several languages.
- Montreal AML Cruises. 514-842-9300 or 1-800-563-4643; www.croisieresaml.com. Sail the St. Lawrence River on guided tour boats or dinner cruises. Bilingual guides.
- Montreal Guide Service. 514-342-8994; email: info@montrealguideservice.com; www.montrealguideservice.com. Multilingual guided tours tailored for individuals or groups.
- Old Montreal Ghost Trail. 514-868-0303 or 1-800-363-4021; email: fantom.montreal@videotron.net; www.phvm.qc.ca. Meet some of the city's most famous ghosts on an evening walking tour.
- Les Services des Calèches et Traîneaux Lucky Luc. 514-934-6105. Tour Montreal in your own horse-drawn carriage, sleigh or long coach. Door-to-door.
- Tour KPMG. Ste-Catherine W. (Attached to Promenades Cathedrale.)
- Vélo Aventure Montréal Inc. 514-847-0666; www.veloaventure.com. Rentals and sales of bicycles and in-line skates plus bicycle tours. Located at the Quai Convoyeurs in the Old Port.
- Vélo-Tour Montréal. 514-259-7272; www.velomontreal.com. Bicycle rentals and tours in English, French and Spanish.

Quebec City

- Pro Aviation Inc. 710 7e Ave., Ste-Foy; 418-872-0206; www.proaviation.net. See the city by seaplane.
- Calèches du Vieux-Québec. 418-683-9222. Horse-drawn-carriage tours of the Old Town.
- Corporation du Tourisme Religieux de Québec. 418-694-0665; www.patrimoine-religieux.com. Walking tours of religious sites.
- Gray Line and Dupont offer a variety of bus tours. 418-649-9226 or 1-888-558-7668; fax 418-525-3044; www.graylinequebec.com.
- Héli-Express. 418-877-5890; www.heliexpres.com. See Quebec City from above on a helicopter tour.
- Old Quebec Tours. 1-800-267-8687; www.oldquebectours.com. Bus tours of the city and environs for small groups. Whale watching tour available.
- Quebec Historical Society. 418-692-0556; www.societehistoriquedequebec.qc.ca. Walking tours to discover the city's past.
- Visites Historiques de Québec. 418-656-4245. Bus tours cover historical landmarks.
- Tours with the Compagnie des Six Associés. 21 Rue Ste-Angèle; 418-692-3033. Walking tours with broad themes, from medical practices in the 19th-century to the evolution of crime and punishment.

Accommodation

What follows is a good cross-section of the accommodation options Montreal and Quebec City offer.

Montreal has more than 23,000 rooms to suit every taste and every budget. The Greater Montreal area offers comfortable and convenient accommodations for groups of any size in hotels, motels, apartment-hotels, bed-and-breakfast homes, college dormitories, campgrounds and resorts. The major hotel chains are represented in the city, as well as a range of lesser-known but equally comfortable establishments.

The majority of these establishments are located in the downtown core, near the subway system. Many are within walking distance of the major convention sites and shopping areas.

The Quebec government is responsible for regulating and supervising hotel establishments and campgrounds, as well as issuing permits.

Non-Canadian residents can receive a cash rebate of the federal Goods and Services Tax (GST) and the Provincial Sales Tax (PST) on short-term accommodations and on some purchases.

Infotouriste offers a hotel reservation service for Montreal and Quebec City. Contact the office at 1001 Square Dorchester, Montreal, QC H3B 1G2; 1-800-363-7777 or 514-864-3838 or 1-877-266-5687 (North America); www.mytravelguide.com.

Approximate prices are indicated, based on the average cost, at time of publishing, for two persons staying in a double room (excluding taxes):
$ = $50–$90; $$ = $90–$180; $$$ = above $180.

For the locations of downtown hotels in Montreal, see the map on pages 8–9.

Montreal

Hotels: Pierre-Elliott Trudeau International Airport

- Day's Inn Montréal Aéroport. 4545 Chemin Côte-Vertu O., Ville St-Laurent, QC H4S 1C8; 514-332-2720; fax 514-332-4512; www.daysinn.com. Conference rooms, public transportation nearby. $$

- Econo Lodge Aéroport. 6755 Chemin Côte-de-Liesse, Ville St-Laurent, QC H4T 1E5; 514-735-5702 or 1-877-424-6423; fax 514-340-9278. Airport shuttle, conference room, outdoor swimming pool, nearby golf course. $$

- Four Points Hotel Dorval. 6600 Chemin Côte-de-Liesse, Ville St-Laurent, QC H4T 1E3; 514-344-1999 or 1-800-325-3535; fax 514-344-6720. Five minutes from airport. Family and corporate rooms. Indoor pool and waterslide, nearby golf course. $$

- Holiday Inn Aéroport-Montréal. 6500 Chemin Côte-de-Liesse, Ville St-Laurent, QC H4T 1E7; 514-739-3391 or 1-800-465-4329; fax 514-739-6591; email: holidayinnap@rosdevhotels.com; www.rosdevhotels.com. Free airport shuttle. Tropical garden, indoor and outdoor pools, sauna, whirlpool, nearby golf course. $$

- Hotel Ramada Aéroport Montréal. 7300 Chemin Côte-de-Liesse, Ville St-Laurent, QC H4T 1E7; 514-733-8818 or 1-800-318-8818; fax 514-733-9889. Airport shuttle, conference rooms, outdoor pool, nearby golf course. $$

- Montréal Aéroport Hilton. 12505 Chemin Côte-de-Liesse, Dorval, QC H9P 1B7; 514-631-2411 or 1-800-445-8667; fax 514-631-0192; www.hilton.com. Free airport shuttle, nearby golf course. $$$

- Quality Hotel Aéroport Montréal. 7700 Chemin Côte-de-Liesse, Ville St-Laurent, QC H4T 1E7; 514-731-7821 or 1-800-361-6243; fax 514-731-7267;

Accommodation - Hotels

email: info@qualityhoteldorval.com; www.qualityhoteldorval.com. Airport shuttle, babysitting, conference rooms, nearby golf course, spa and fitness centre, outdoor pool. $$

Hotels: Downtown

- Appartements Touristiques du Centre-Ville. 3463 Rue Ste-Famille, Suite 008, Montreal, QC H2X 2K7; 514-845-0431 or 1-877-845-0437; fax 514-845-0262; www.appartementstouristiques.com. Fitness centre, indoor pool, some rooms with cooking facilities, indoor parking, laundry room on main floor. $$, Map 1
- Auberge de la Fontaine. 1301 Rue Rachel E., Montreal, QC H2J 2K1; 514-597-0166 or 1-800-597-0597; fax 514-597-0496; www.aubergedelafontaine.com. Conference room, continental breakfast buffet, laundry service, Internet station. $$, Map 2
- Auberge le Jardin d'Antoine. 2024 Rue St-Denis, Montreal, QC H2X 3K7; 514-843-4506 or 1-800-361-4506; fax 514-281-1491; www.hotel-jardin-antoine.qc.ca. Airport shuttle. $$, Map 3
- Best Western Europa Centre-Ville. 1240 Rue Drummond, Montreal, QC H3G 1V7; 514-866-6492 or 1-800-361-3000; fax 514-861-4089; email: info@europahotelmtl.com; www.europahotelmtl.com. Airport shuttle, spa/fitness centre, conference rooms. $$, Map 4
- Best Western Ville-Marie Hôtel et Suites. 3407 Rue Peel, Montreal, QC H3A 1W7; 514-288-4141 or 1-800-361-7791; fax 514-288-3021; email: info@hotelvillemarie.com; www.hotelvillemarie.com. Conference rooms, some rooms with cooking facilities, fitness centre. $$, Map 5
- Le Centre Sheraton. 1201 Boul. René-Lévesque O., Montreal, QC H3B 2L7; 514-878-2000 or 1-800-325-3535; fax 514-878-2305; www.sheraton.com/lecentre. Business centre, Internet service in all rooms (charge), spa/fitness centre with indoor pool and lounge, non-smoking floors. $$$, Map 6
- Château Royal Hotel Suites. 1420 Rue Crescent, Montreal, QC H3G 2B7; 514-848-0999 or 1-800-363-0335; fax 514 848-1891; www.chateauroyal.com. Cooking facilities in all rooms, conference rooms, indoor parking. $$$, Map 7
- Days Inn Montreal Centre-Ville. 215 Boul. René-Lévesque E., Montreal, QC H2X 1N7; 514-393-3388 or 1-800-668-3872; fax 514-395-9999; www.daysinnmontreal.com. Conference rooms, free Internet access, non-smoking floors. $$, Map 8
- Delta Centre-Ville. 777 Rue University, Montreal, QC H3C 3Z7; 514 879-1370 or 1-877-814-7706; fax 514-879-1831; www.deltahotels.com. Indoor pool, fitness centre, near amenities. $$$, Map 9
- Fairmont La Reine Élizabeth Hotel. 900 Boul. René-Lévesque O., Montreal, QC H3B 4A5; 514-861-3511 or 1-800-257-7544; fax 514-954-2296; email: queenelizabeth.hotel@fairmont.com; www.fairmont.com/queenelizabeth. Conference rooms, airport shuttle, fitness centre, express check in/out, indoor pool, non-smoking and private concierge floors. The Beaver Club dining room. $$$, Map 10
- Four Points by Sheraton Hôtel & Suites Montréal Centre-Ville. 475 Rue Sherbrooke O., Montreal, QC H3A 2L9; 514-842-3961 or 1-888-625-5144; fax 514-842-0945; www.fourpoints.com. Conference rooms, business centre, fitness centre, pet policy. $$, Map 11
- Golden Square Mile. 2200 Mansfield Street; :514-844-1421, 1 866 844-2200 (Toll Free), www.goldensquaremile.com
- Hilton Montréal Bonaventure, Place Bonaventure. 900 de la Gauchetiere O., Montreal, QC H5A 1E4; 514-878-2332 or 1-800-445-8667; fax 514-878-3881; www.hiltonmontreal.com. Airport shuttle, conference rooms, rooftop

garden with indoor and outdoor pools. $$$, Map 12

- Holiday Inn Montréal-Midtown. 420 Rue Sherbrooke O., Montreal, QC H3A 1B4; 514-842-6111 or 1-866-655-4669; fax 514-842-9381; email: himidtown@rosdevhotels.com; www.rosdevhotels.com. Airport shuttle, indoor pool, conference rooms, fitness centre, Internet access, pet policy. $$$, Map 13
- Hôtel Château Versailles. 1659 Rue Sherbrooke O., Montreal, QC H3H 1E3; 514-933-8111 or 1-888-933-8111; fax 514-933-6867; www.versailleshotels.com. European charm, gym and sauna, babysitting, airport shuttle, near museums. $$$, Map 14
- Hôtel Courtyard Marriott Montréal. 410 Rue Sherbrooke O., Montreal, QC H3A 1B3; 514-844-8855 or 1-800-449-6654; fax 514-844-0912; www.courtyardmontreal.com. Airport shuttle, indoor pool, spa and fitness centre. $$$, Map 15
- Hôtel de la Couronne. 1029 Rue St-Denis, Montreal, QC H2X 3H9; 514-845-0901; fax 514-845-4165; www.hoteldelacouronne.ca. Airport shuttle, breakfast included, parking, some rooms with shared bath-rooms. $, Map 16
- Hotel Omni. 1050 Sherbrooke Street West; 514-284-1110; www.omnihotels.com. Map 17
- Hôtel Delta Montréal. 475 Ave. du Président-Kennedy, Montreal, QC H3A 1J7; 514-286-1986 or 1-877-286-1986; fax 514 284-4342; www.deltamontreal.com. Conference rooms, children's activity centre, indoor and outdoor pools, spa and fitness centre, underground parking. $$$, Map 18
- Hôtel de Paris. 901 Rue Sherbrooke E., Montreal, QC H2L 1L3; 514-522-6861 or 1-800-567-7217; fax 514-522-1387; www.hotel-montreal.com. Airport shuttle, youth hostel and apartment-hotel rates also available. $$, Map 19
- Hôtel des Gouverneurs Place Dupuis. 1415 Rue St-Hubert, Montreal, QC H2L 3Y9; 514-842-4881 or 1-888-910-1111; fax 514-842-1584; www.gouverneur.com. Airport shuttle, babysitting, conference rooms, indoor pool. $$$, Map 20
- Hôtel du Fort. 1390 Rue du Fort, Montreal, QC H3H 2R7; 514-938-8333 or 1-800-565-6333; fax 514-938-3123; email: reserve@hoteldufort.com; www.hoteldufort.com. Conference rooms, Internet access, fitness centre. $$$, Map 21
- Hôtel du Manoir Saint-Denis. 2006 Rue St-Denis, Montreal, QC H2X 3K7; 514-843-3670 or 1-888-567-7654; fax 514-844-2188; email: hotel@manoirstdenis.com; www.manoirstdenis.com. Restaurant on premises. $, Map 22
- Hôtel Dynastie. 1723 Rue St-Hubert, Montreal, QC H2L 3Z1; 514-529-5210 or 1-877-529-5210; fax 514-529-7170. Near amenities, bicycles at no charge (upon availability). $, Map 23
- Hôtel Inter-Continental Montreal. 360 Rue St-Antoine O., Montreal, QC H2Y 3X4; 514-987-9900 or 1-800-361-3600; fax 514-847-8730; www.montreal.intercontinental.com Conference rooms, babysitting, indoor pool, fitness centre. $$$, Map 24
- Hôtel Le St-Paul. 355 Rue McGill, Montreal, QC H2Y 2E8; 514-380-2222; fax 514-380-2200; www.hotelstpaul.com. Luxury boutique hotel in Old Montreal. $$$, Map 25
- Hôtel Lord Berri. 1199 Rue Berri, Montreal, QC H2L 4C6; 514-845-9236 or 1-888-363-0363; fax 514-849-9855; email: info@lordberri.com; www.lordberri.com. Airport shuttle, conference rooms, near bus terminal, fitness centre. $$, Map 26
- Hôtel Maritime Plaza. 1155 Rue Guy, Montreal, QC H3H 2K5; 514-932-1411 or 1-800-363-6255; fax 514-932-0446; email: info@hotelmaritime.com; www.hotelmaritime.com. Airport shuttle, conference rooms, indoor pool. $$$, Map 27

Accommodation - Bed & Breakfasts

- Hôtel de la Montagne. 1430 Rue de la Montagne, Montreal, QC H3G 1Z5; 514-288-5656 or 1-800-361-6262; fax 514-288-9658; www.hoteldelamontagne.com. Airport shuttle, conference rooms, outdoor pool, underground parking, swanky lobby bar. $$$, Map 28
- Hôtel Montréal Crescent. 1366 Boul. René-Lévesque O., Montreal, QC H3W 2R4; 514-938-9797; fax 514-938-9797. Conference room, near amenities. $$, Map 29
- Hyatt Regency Montréal. 1255 Rue Jeanne-Mance, P.O. Box 130, Montreal, QC H5B 1E5; 514-982-1234 or 1-800-361-8234; fax 514-285-1243; www.hyatt.com. Business centre, coffeemaker, Internet access. Iron and ironing board in every room. $$$, Map 30
- Loews Hôtel Vogue. 1425 Rue de la Montagne, Montreal, QC H3G 1Z3; 514-285-5555 or 1-800-235-6397; fax 514 849-8903; www.loewshotels.com. Two televisions, a fax machine and an oversized safe in every room. Conference rooms, babysitting, fitness centre. $$$, Map 31
- Montréal Marriott Château Champlain. 1050 Rue de la Gauchetière O., Montreal, QC H3B 4C9; 514-878-9000 or 1-800-200-5909; fax 514-878-6761; www.marriott.com. Airport shuttle, massage, hairdresser, sauna and fitness centre, indoor pool and babysitting. $$$, Map 32
- Novotel Montréal Centre. 1180 Rue de la Montagne, Montreal, QC H3G 1Z1; 514-861-6000 or 1-800-221-4542; fax 514-861-0992; www.novotelmontreal.com. Airport shuttle, conference rooms, babysitting, fitness centre. $$$, Map 33
- Quality Hotel. 3440 Ave. du Parc, Montreal, QC H2X 2H5; 514-849-1413 or 1-800-465-6116; fax 514-849-6564; wwww.choicehotels.ca. Pet policy, restaurant on premises. $$, Map 34
- Residence Inn by Marriott Montréal Westmount. 2170 Ave. Lincoln, Montreal, QC H3H 2N5; 514-935-9224 or 1-800-678-6323; fax 514-935-5049. Indoor pool, gym, free Internet access, fully equipped kitchens. $$$, Map 35
- Ritz-Carlton Montréal. 1228 Rue Sherbrooke O., Montreal, QC H3G 1H6; 514-842-4212 or 1-800-241-3333; fax 514-842-3383; www.ritzcarlton.com. Old-world elegance; shops, restaurant serving breakfast, lunch, dinner and afternoon tea. $$$, Map 36
- Sofitel Hotel. 1155 Sherbrooke West; 514-285-9000 or 514-289-1155; www.sofitel.com.

Bed & Breakfasts

Montreal has hundreds of bed-and-breakfast rooms available in many locations. There are also several services that cater to finding visitors accommodations that suit their needs. Stay in a loft in Old Montreal or a Victorian mansion in Westmount as an alternative to hotels.

- Angelica Blue Bed & Breakfast. 1213 Rue Ste-Élisabeth, Montreal, QC H2X 3C3; 514-844-5048 or 1-800-878-5048; fax 450-448-2114; email: info@angelicablue.com; www.angelicablue.com. Non-smoking, located in the heart of downtown Montreal. $$
- Auberge Bonsecours. 353 Rue St-Paul E., Montreal, QC H2Y 1H3; 514-396-2662; fax 514-871-9272. Located in Old Montreal, charming accomodation in renovated stables. $$
- B A Guest B&B. 2033 Rue St-Hubert, Montreal, QC H2L 3Z6; 514-738-9410 or 1-800-738-4338; fax 514-735-7493; email: info@bbmontreal.com; www.bbmontreal.com. The main guest home in a small network of B&Bs that range from downtown condominiums to Victorian mansions in tony Outremont and Westmount. $–$$
- Bed & Breakfast de Chez-Nous. 3717 Rue Ste-Famille, Montreal,

QC H2X 2L7; 514-845-7711; fax 514-845-8008; www.studios montreal.com. Near Rue Prince-Arthur. Studios and fully furnished apartments can accommodate as many as six people for short-term or longer visits. $$

- Bonheur d'Occasion. 846 Rue Agnès, Montreal, QC H4C 2P8; 514-935-5898; fax 514-935-5898; www.bbcanada.com/526.html. Meals, no credit cards. $

- Carole's Purrfect B&B. 3428 Rue Addington, Montreal, QC H4A 3G6; 514-486-3995; email: info@purrfectbnb.com; www.purrfectbnb.com. Vegetarian breakfast, ask ahead about pets, no credit cards, non-smoking rooms. $

- Chambres avec Vue/Bed and Banana. 1225 Rue de Bullion, Montreal, QC H2X 2Z3; 514-878-9843; fax 514-878-3813; email: bed@bedandbanana.com. Meals, no credit cards, non-smoking rooms. $

- Couette et Café Cherrier. 522 Rue Cherrier, Montreal, QC H2L 1H3; 514-982-6848 or 1-888440-6848; fax 514-982-3313; email: couette@sympatico.ca; www.bbcanada.com/2073.html. Meals and bistro on premises. $–$$

- Downtown Bed & Breakfast Network. 3458 Ave. Laval, Montreal, QC H2X 3C8; 514-289-9749 or 1-800-267-5180; fax 514-287-7386; email: mariko@bbmontreal.qc.ca; www.bbmontreal.qc.ca. Downtown, Old Montreal, Latin Quarter locations. Non-smoking rooms and handicapped facilities. 50 rooms. 6 suites. $

- Gîte Toujours Dimanche. 1131 Rue Rachel E., Montreal, QC H2J 2J6; 514-527-2394; fax 514-527-6129; email: info@toujoursdimanche.com; www.toujoursdimanche.com. Meals, non-smoking rooms. $$

- La Maison du Jardin. 3744 Rue St-André, Montreal, QC H2L 3V7; 514-598-8862; fax 514-598-0667; email: maisonjardin@yahoo.com; www.bbcanada.com/jardin. Meals, no credit cards. $

- A Montreal Oasis. 3000 Chemin de Breslay, Montreal, QC H2X 2G7; 514-935-2312; fax 514-881-7231; email: bb@aei.ca; www.bbcanada.com/694.html. Downtown, Old Montreal and Latin Quarter locations with or without private bath. Open fireplace, terrace and gourmet breakfast. 20 rooms. $

- Relais Montréal Hospitalité. 3977 Ave. Laval, Montreal, QC H2W 2H9; 514-287-9635 or 1-800-363-9635; fax 514-287-1007; email: b_b@martha-pearson.com; www.martha-pearson.com. Rooms near Old Montreal for smokers and non-smokers in furnished apartments rented on short- and long-term basis. $

- Welcome Bed & Breakfast. 3950 Ave. Laval, Montreal, QC H2W 2J2; 514-844-5897 or 1-800-227-5897; fax 514-844-5894; email: info@bienvuebb.com; www.welcomebnb.com. Country inn ambience, located downtown. $

Hostels and College Residences

Almost all the residences listed below are available in summer only, but they provide a safe, economical alternative to hotels. Make sure to book in advance.

- Auberge Alternative du Vieux-Montréal. 358 Rue St-Pierre, Montreal, QC H2Y 2M1; 514-282-8069; email: info@auberge-alternative.qc.ca; www.auberge-alternative.qc.ca. Open year-round. $

- Auberge de Jeunesse l'Hôtel de Paris. 901 Rue Sherbrooke E., Montreal, QC H2L 1L3; 514-522-6861 or 1-800-567-7217; fax 514-522-1387; email: questions@hotel-montreal.com; www.hotel-montreal.com. Open year-round, no curfew. $

- Auberge de Jeunesse de Montréal/Hostelling International. 1030 Rue Mackay, Montreal, QC H3G 2H1; 514-843-3317 or 1-866-83-3317; fax 514-934-3251; email: info@hostellingmontreal.com;

www.hostellingmontreal.com. Open year-round. $

- Chez Jean. 4136 Rue Henri-Julien, Montreal, QC H2W 2K3; 514-843-8279; www.aubergechezjean.com. Breakfast included, no credit cards, pet policy. $
- Collège Français. 5155 Rue de Gaspé, Montreal, QC H2T 2A1; 514-270-4459; fax 514-278-7508; email: vacancescanadamd@video tron.ca; www.montrealplus.ca/portalf/infosite/122548/1.html. Summer only, dormitory. $
- Concordia University. 7141 Rue Sherbrooke O., Montreal, QC H4B 1R6; 514-848-2424, x.4758; fax 514-848-4780; email: lcleduc@alcor.concordia.ca; www.residence.concordia.ca/summer.html. Summer only, dormitory, meals served daily. $
- Gîte du Parc Lafontaine. 1250 Rue Sherbrooke E., Montreal, QC H2L 1M1; 514-522-3910; fax 514-844-7356; email: info@hostelmontreal.com; www.hostelmontreal.com. Open year-round, meals. $
- McGill University Residences. 3935 Rue University, Montreal, QC H3A 2B4; 514-398-5200; fax 514-398-6770; email: reserve.residences@mcgill.ca; www.mcgill.ca/residences/summer. Summer only, dormitory. $
- Résidence Lallemand, Collège Brébeuf. 5625 Ave. Decelles, Montreal, QC H3T 1W4; 514-342-1320; fax 514-342-6607; email: residence@brebeuf.qc.ca; www.brebeuf.qc.ca. Summer only, dormitory. $
- Université de Montréal, Services des Résidences. 2350 Boul. Édouard-Montpetit, Montreal, QC H3T 1J4; 514-343-6531; fax 514-343-2353; email: residence@sea.umontreal.ca; www.resid.umontreal.ca. Summer only. $
- Université du Québec à Montréal. 303 Boul. René-Lévesque E., Montreal, QC H2X 3Y3; 514-987-6669 or 1-888-987-6669; fax 514-987-0344; www.residences-uqam.qc.ca. Summer only, cooking facilities, indoor pool, group rates. $
- Y.W.C.A. 1355 Boul. René-Lévesque O., Montreal, QC H3G 1T3; 514-866-9942; fax 514-861-1603; email: info@ydesfemmesmtl.org; www.ydesfemmesmtl.org. Recently renovated Y Hotel. $

Quebec City

Hotels: Downtown

- Delta Québec. 690 Boul. René-Lévesque E., Quebec, QC G1R 5A8; 418-647-1717 or 1-877-814-7706; fax 418-647-2146; www.deltahotels.com. Airport shuttle, conference rooms, non-smoking rooms, outdoor pool, spa and fitness centre. $$–$$$
- Fairmont Château Frontenac. 1 Rue des Carrières, Quebec, QC G1R 4P5; 418-692-3861 or 1-800-257-7544; fax 418-692-1751; email: chateaufrontenac@fairmont.com; www.fairmont.com/frontenac. The crème de la crème of old-world style. Airport shuttle, babysitting, conference rooms, non-smoking rooms, indoor pool, fitness centre. $$$
- Holiday Inn Select Quebec City-Downtown. 395 Rue de la Couronne, Quebec, QC G1K 7X4; 418-647-2611 or 1-800-267-2002; fax 418-640-0666; email: reservation@hiselect-quebec.com; www.holiday-inn.com. Airport shuttle, kids eat free, conference rooms, non-smoking rooms, indoor pool, fitness centre. $$
- Hôtel Château Bellevue. 16 Rue de la Porte, Quebec, QC G1R 4M9; 418-692-2573 or 1-800-463-2617; fax 418-692-4876; email: bellevue@vieuxquebec.com; www.vieux-quebec.com/bellevue. Mid-sized hotel, babysitting, near transportation. $$
- Hôtel Château Laurier. 1220 Place George V O., Quebec, QC G1R 5B8; 418-522-8108 or 1-800-463-4453; fax 418-524-8768; email:

laurier@vieuxquebec.com;
www.vieux-quebec.com/laurier.
Wireless Internet access, 9 deluxe
rooms with fireplace and therapeutic
bath, babysitting, non-smoking
rooms. $$

- Hôtel Clarendon. 57 Rue Ste-Anne,
Quebec, QC G1R 3X4; 418-692-
2480 or 1-888-222-3304; fax
418-692-4652;
www.hotelclarendon.com. Airport
shuttle, conference rooms, health
spa, near transportation. $$–$$$
- Hôtel Dominion 1912. 126 Rue St-
Pierre, Quebec, QC G1K 4A8;
418-692-2224 or 1-888-833-5253;
fax 418-692-4403; email:
reservations@hoteldominion.com;
www.hoteldominion.com. Mid-sized
hotel, conference rooms, non-
smoking rooms. $$$
- Hôtel du Capitole. 972 Rue St-Jean,
Quebec, QC G1R 1R5; 418-694-
4040 or 1-800-363-4040; fax
418-694-1916; email:
hotel@lecapitole.com;
www.lecapitole.com. Small but
luxurious hotel, babysitting,
conference rooms, non-smoking
rooms. $$$
- Hôtel Loews Le Concorde. 1225
Place Montcalm, Quebec, QC G1R
4W6; 418-647-2222 or 1-800-235-
6397; fax 418-647-4710; email:
loewsleconcorde@loewshotels.com;
www.loewshotels.com/leconcorde
home.html. Airport shuttle,
babysitting, conference rooms, non-
smoking rooms, outdoor pool,
fitness centre. $$–$$$
- Hôtel Manoir Victoria. 44 Côte du
Palais, Quebec, QC G1R 4H8; 418-
692-1030 or 1-800-463-6283; fax
418-692-3822; email:
admin@manoir-victoria.com;
www.manoir-victoria.com. Airport
shuttle, babysitting, conference
rooms, non-smoking rooms, indoor
pool, fitness centre. $$–$$$
- Hôtel Palace Royal. 775 Ave.
Honore-Mercier, Quebec, QC G1R
6A5; 418-694-2000 or 1-800-567-
5276; fax 418-380-2553;
www.hotelsjaro.com. Conference

rooms, indoor tropical garden with
pool, sauna and whirlpool bath,
fitness room, babysitting. $$$
- Québec Hilton. 1100 Boul. René-
Lévesque E., Quebec, QC G1R
4X3; 418-647-2411 or 1-800-445-
8667; fax 418-647-2986;
www.hilton.com. Babysitting,
conference rooms, non-smoking
rooms, outdoor pool, spa and fitness
centre. $$–$$$
- Terrasse Dufferin. 6, Pl. Terrasse
Dufferin; 418-694-9472

Hotels: Suburbs

- Days Inn, Québec Ouest. 3145 Ave.
des Hôtels, Quebec, QC G1W 3Z7;
418-653-9321 or 1-800-463-1867;
fax 418-653-2666; email:
dayssf@globetrotter.net;
www.daysinn.com. $$
- Hôtel Clarion Québec. 3125 Blvd.
Hochelaga, Ste-Foy, QC G1V 4A8;
418-653-4901 or 1-800-463-5241;
fax 418-653-1836; email:
hotel@clarionquebec.com. Indoor
pool, restaurant on premises, health
club. $$
- Hôtel Classique. 2815 Blvd.
Laurier, Ste-Foy, QC G1V 4H3;
418-658-2793 or 1-800-463-1885;
fax 418-658-6816; email:
info@hotelclassique.com;
www.hotelclassique.com. Indoor
pool, meeting rooms, free
parking. $$
- Hôtel Lindbergh. 2825 Blvd.
Laurier, Ste-Foy, QC G1V 2L9;
418-653-4975 or 1-800-567-4975;
fax 418-651-8805; email: hotel-
lindbergh@jaro.qc.ca;
www.hotelsjaro.com. Indoor and
outdoor pools, business centre,
conference rooms, babysitting. $$
- Hôtel Quality Suites. 1600 Rue
Bouvier, Quebec, QC G2K 1N8;
418-622-4244 or 1-800-267-3837;
fax 418-622-4067;
www.choicehotels.com. Babysitting,
conference rooms, free continental
breakfast, non-smoking rooms. $$

Bed & Breakfasts

- Acceuil B&B Bourgault Centre-
Ville. 653 Rue de la Reine, Quebec,

Accommodation - Bed & Breakfasts

QC G1K 2S1; 418-524-9254 or 1-866-524-9254; fax 418-524-9254; email: gbourgault@bnbbourgault.com; www.gites-classifies.qc.ca/accbou.htm. Meals, garden terrace. $$

- À la Maison Tudor. 1037 Rue Moncton, Quebec, QC G1S 2Y9; 418-686-1033; fax 418-686-6066; email: ckilfoil@lamaisontudor.com; www.lamaisontudor.com. Meals, apartments with cooking facilities for longer stays, non-smoking rooms. $$

- B&B Cafe Krieghoff. 1091 Ave. Cartier, Quebec, QC G1R 2S6; 418-522-3711; fax 418-647-1429; email: info@cafekrieghoff.qc.ca; www.cafekrieghoff.qc.ca. Meals, neighbourhood cafe on premises. $

- Chez Monsieur Gilles. 1720 Chemin de la Canardière, Quebec, QC G1J 2E3; 418-821-8778; fax 418-821-8776; email: mgilles@sympatico.ca; www.chezmonsieurgilles.com. Pool room, hot tub on rooftop terrace, near skiing and golf course. $$

- Hayden's Wexford House B&B. 450 Rue Champlain, Quebec, QC G1R 2E3; 418-524-0524; fax 418-648-8995; email: haydenwexfordhouse@videotron.net; www.haydenwexfordhouse.com. Meals, heritage home, non-smoking, near skiing. $$

- La Maison d'Élizabeth et Emma. 10 Rue Grande-Allée O., Quebec, QC G1R 2G6; 418-647-0880; www.bbcanada.com/699.html. Meals, non-smoking rooms. $

- La Maison Historique James Thompson. 47 Rue Ste-Ursule, Quebec, QC G1R 4E4; 418-694-9042; email: jamesthompson@canada.com; www.bedandbreakfastquebec.com. Meals, heritage building inside the walls of Old Quebec, no credit cards. $

Hostels and College Residences

- Association Y.W.C.A. de Québec. 855 Ave. Holland, Quebec, QC G1S 3S5; 418-683-2155; fax 418-683-5526; email: ydesfemmes@ywcaquebec.qc.ca. Sauna, pool, cooking facilities, near transportation. $

- Auberge de la Paix. 31 Rue Couillard, Quebec, QC G1R 3T4; 418-694-0735; email: alapaix@clic.net; www.aubergedelapaix.com. Breakfast included, no credit cards. $

- Auberge Internationale de Québec. 19 Rue Ste-Ursule, Quebec, QC G1R 4E1; 418-694-0755; fax 418-694-2278; email: reservation@hostellingquebec.com; www.cisq.org. Café serves meals in summer. Dorms or private rooms. $

- Résidence du Collège Mérici. 757, 759, 761 Rue St-Louis, Quebec, QC G1S 1C1; 418-683-1591; fax 418-682-8938; email: information@college-merici.qc.ca; www.college-merici.qc.ca. Open seasonally. Cooking facilities in all rooms. $

Dining

Montreal

Montreal boasts some of the finest restaurants in North America. With huge cultural diversity, there is something for everyone. The following is a select list of the restaurants available. The restaurants are listed alphabetically by ethnicity (e.g., French) and by general type (e.g., Brunch).

Approximate prices are indicated, based on the average cost, at time of publication, of dinner for two including wine (where available), taxes and gratuity: $ = under $45; $$ = $45–$80; $$$ = $80–$120; $$$$ = $120–$180; $$$$$ = over $180. Meals served are indicated as: B = breakfast; L = lunch; D = dinner; S = snacks; Late = open past midnight. Credit cards accepted are also indicated: AX = American Express; V = Visa; MC = MasterCard. Restaurants to which patrons may bring their own wine = BYOB.

American

- Hard Rock Café. 1458 Rue Crescent; 514-987-1420. Rock and roll–themed restaurant featuring classic American cuisine, memorabilia, music and really cool merchandise. L/D, Late, $, AX/MC/V.
- Nickels. 1384 Rue Ste-Catherine O.; 514-392-7771. Céline Dion's chain features burgers and smoked meat extraordinaire. B/L/D, Late, $, AX/MC/V.
- Upstairs Jazz Bar & Grill. 1254 Rue MacKay; 514-931-6808; www.upstairsjazz.com. One of Montreal's top live jazz venues. D, Late, $–$$, AX/MC/V.

Chinese

- Aux Délices de Szechuan. 1735 Rue St-Denis; 514-844-5542. Sumptuous décor, culinary artwork, efficient service. D, $, AX/MC/V.
- Chez Chine (Holiday Inn Select Montreal Centre-Ville). 99 Ave. Viger O.; 514-878-9888 or 1-888-878-9888; www.hiselect-yul.com. Authentic Chinese cuisine in a spectacular dining room. B/L/D, $–$$, AX/MC/V.
- Zen Restaurant. 1050 Sherbrooke West; 514-499-0801.

French

- Alexandre. 1454 Rue Peel; 514-288-5105. Twelve imported beers on tap. Regional cuisine. Typical Parisian brasserie. L/D, Late, $$, AX/MC/V. www.chezalexandre.com.
- Café de Paris/Le Jardin du Ritz (Ritz-Carlton Montréal Hotel). 1228 Rue Sherbrooke O.; 514-842-4212; www.ritzcarlton.com. Welcoming atmosphere and impeccable service, afternoon tea. B/L/D, $$, AX/MC/V.
- Claude Postel Restaurant. 443 Rue St-Vincent; 514-875-5067. Exquisite French cuisine and excellent crème brûlée. Located in Old Montreal. L/D, $$, AX/MC/V.
- La Colombe. 554 Rue Duluth E.; 514-849-8844. Elegant North African-influenced French cuisine in a cozy room. BYOB, D, $$, AX/MC/V.
- La Trattoria. 5563 Chemin Upper Lachine; 514-484-5303. Many inventive pizzas and pastas. BYOB, L/D, $, V/MC.
- Restaurant Le P'tit Plateau. 330 Rue Marie-Anne E.; 514-282-6342. Elegant but cozy spot where dishes from the south of France are served. BYOB, non-smoking, D, $, V/MC/No Interac.

Greek

- La Cabane Grecque, 102 Rue Prince-Arthur E.; 514-849-0122; fax 514-849-3879; www.lacabanegrecque.com. A family restaurant with steak and seafood specialities. BYOB, L/D, Late, $, AX/MC/V.
- Hermès (Himalaya). 1010 Rue Jean-Talon O.; 514-272-3880. Great Greek food, open late. L/D, $, MC/V.
- Restaurant Minerva. 17 Rue Prince-Arthur E.; 514-842-5451 or 514-842-5452. Steak, seafood, Italian and Greek cuisine. L/D, Late, $, AX/MC/V.

Indian

- Bombay Palace. 1172 Bishop St.; 514-932-7141; www.bombaypalacerestaurant.com. Culinary specialties from Bombay, including Tandoori Lamb Chops and Tiger Prawn Masala. Excellent buffet. L/D, $$, AX/MC/V.
- Punjab Palace. 920 Rue Jean-Talon O.; 514-495-4075; www.punjabpalace.ca. Inexpensive homestyle cooking with fantastic vegetarian and meat dishes. L/D, $, AX/MC/V.
- Maison Cari. 1433 Bishop & St. Catherine.
- Raga Buffet Indien. 3533 Chemin Queen-Mary; 514-344-2217; fax 514-845-8348. Vegetarian and tandoori cuisine. Worth the hike for the buffet. L/D, $, AX/MC/V.

Italian

- Bocca d'Oro. 1448 Rue St-Mathieu; 514-933-8414. Exotic menu,

Dining - Montreal

romantic atmosphere, great food. L/D, $, AX/MC/V.

- Brontë. 1800 Rue Sherbrooke O.; 514-934-1801 or 1-888-933-8111; www.versailleshotels.com. High-end Italian restaurant. Breakfast for guests of the Meridien/Chateau Versailles only. B/L/D, $$, AX/MC/V.
- Hostaria Romana. 2044 Rue Metcalfe; 514-849-1389. Serving continental cuisine, fish and seafood for the past 30 years. Features music nightly. L/D, $, AX/MC/V.
- Il Cavaliere (Hôtel Lord Berri). 1199 Rue Berri; 514-845-9236; fax 514-849-9855. Cozy atmosphere, exceptional Italian cuisine. B/L/D, $, AX/MC/V.
- Weinstein & Gavino's Pasta Bar Factory. 1434 Rue Crescent; 514-288-2231. A place to see and be seen, this bustling restaurant regularly accommodates up to 700 patrons. L/D, $–$$, AX/MC/V.

Japanese

- Higuma. 3807 Rue St-Denis; 514-842-1686. Simple place, great sushi. L/D, $, AX/MC/V.
- Kaizen Treehouse Sushi Bar & Restaurant. 4120 Rue Ste-Catherine O. (in Westmount); 514-932-5654; email: info@70sushi.com; www.kaizen-sushi-bar.com. Sushi and sashimi, with tasting menus for vegetarians and fish lovers alike. Live jazz from Sun. to Tues. L/D, $$, AX/MC/V.

Russian

- La Métropole. 1409 Rue St-Marc; 514-932-3403. Great food, excellent Russian tea and pastries, weekend music shows. L/D, $$, AX/MC/V.
- Troïka. 2171 Rue Crescent; 514-849-9333. Flavoured vodkas, Russian musicians. D, $$, AX/MC/V.

Spanish

- Casa Galicia. 2087 Rue St-Denis; 514-843-6698; fax 514-843-9159; www.casagaliciamontreal.com. Lively weekend flamenco shows

and tasty appetizers and main dishes. L/D, $$, AX/MC/V.
- Casa Tapas. 266 Rue Rachel E.; 514-848-1063. A friendly restaurant with rustic Spanish décor. Offers a new twist on tapas. D, $$, AX/MC/V.
- Casa del Popolo. 4873 St-Laurent; 514-284-3804; www.casadelpopolo.com.
- Cuisine Bangkok. 1616 Ste-Catherine W.; 514-935-2178

Brunch

- Beauty's. 93 Ave. du Mont-Royal O.; 514-849-8883. This hip hangout and Montreal breakfast institution serves up tasty diner fare. B/L, $, AX/MC/V.
- Café Santropol. 3990 Rue St-Urbain; 514-842-3110; fax 514-284-4256; www.santropol.com. Massive portions served in this urban oasis that opens a garden terrace in summer months. L/D, $, Interac only.
- Chez Cora Déjeuners. 1425 Rue Stanley; 514-286-6171; www.chezcora.com. One location of a chain serving hearty breakfasts with plenty of fresh fruit. B/L, $, AX/MC/V.
- Dusty's. 4510 Ave. du Parc; 514-276-8525. Diner specials, tasteful and simple, since 1950. B/L, $.
- Maison Kam Fung. 1111 Rue St-Urbain; 514-878-2888. Dim sum delights. B/L/D, $, AX/MC/V.
- Restaurant Lotte. 1115 Rue Clark; 514-393-3838. Known for its excellent dim sum. B/L/D, $$.

Cafés and Bistros

- Bistro Boris. 465 Rue McGill; 514-848-9575; www.borisbistro.com. Bistro fare on a huge, tree-shaded terrace. L/D, $$, AX/MC/V.
- Café Cherrier. 3635 Rue St-Denis; 514-843-4308; fax 514-844-3273. European-style brasserie serving Italian and Californian cuisine. B/L/D, Late, $, AX/MC/V.
- Café Santropol. 3990 St-Urbain (Corner Duluth), www.santropol.com.
- Ceramic Café Studio. 4201-B Rue

St-Denis; 514-848-1119. Paint-your-own-ceramics café. S, $, MC/V.

- Holder. 407 Rue McGill; 514-849-0333. French bistro fare, lively nightlife scene. L/D, $$, AX/MC/V.
- Le Jardin Nelson. 407 Place Jacques-Cartier; 514-861-5731; email: jardin.nelson@videotron.ca; www.jardinnelson.com. Outdoor courtyard in summer. Musicians serenade at this crêperie. L/D, Late, $, AX/MC/V.
- Shed Café. 3515 Boul. St-Laurent; 514-842-0220. Simple classics go well with drinks at this trendy spot on The Main. L/D, $–$$, AX/MC/V.

Family Fare

- Atwater Market. 138 Atwater St; 514-937-7754.
- Boustan. 2020 Cresent; 514-843-3576; www.boustan.ca
- Ganges Restaurant. 6079 Rue Sherbrooke O.; 514-488-8850. Good Indian food, sometimes with live music. L/D, $, AX/MC/V.
- La Capannina. 2022 Rue Stanley; 514-845-1852. Friendly family restaurant. Specialities: fresh pastas and seafood. L/D, $, AX/MC/V.
- Marché Jean-Talon. 7075 Ave. Casgrain; 514-277-1588
- Milano Fruiterie. 6862 St-Laurent; 514-273-8558
- Premiere Moisson. 1490 Sherbrooke W.; 514-931-6540; www.premieremoisson.com
- Chocolat Belge Elegant O & M, 1442 Sherbrooke W.; 514-849-7609
- Coco Rico. 3907 St-Laurent; 514-849-5554
- Euro Deli. 3619 St-Laurent; 514-843-7853
- La Vieille Europe. 3855 St-Laurent; 514-842-5773
- Maison de Cari. 1433 Rue Bishop; 514-845-0326. This hole in the wall serves up authentic, spicy Indian fare and cool British beers. L/D, $, AX/MC/V.
- Marché Mövenpick Restaurant. 1 Place Ville-Marie; 514-861-8181. A new dining experience: a dozen stands offer everything fresh, from

sushi and pasta to ice-cream sundaes and fresh juices. Available on one bill. B/L/D, Late, $, AX/MC/V.
- Pizza des Pins. 4520 Parc Avenue; 514-277-3178.
- Restaurant Daou. 519 Rue Faillon E.; 514-276-8310. Lebanese dishes made from family recipes are served in an informal dining room. L/D, $, AX/MC/V.
- Saint-Cinnamon. 1616 Ste-Catherine W., 514-846-9871

Fondues

- Fonduementale. 4325 Rue St-Denis; 514-499-1446. Ideal for group dining in a relaxed atmosphere. D, $–$$, AX/MC/V.
- La Fonderie. 964 Rue Rachel E.; 514-524-2100. Chinese and Swiss fondues. D, $, AX/MC/V.

Quick Eats

- Arahova Souvlaki. 256 St-Viateur O.; 514-274-7828. Serving succulent souvlaki with secret tzatziki sauce since 1972. L/D, $.
- Caribbean Curry House. 6892 Ave. Victoria; 514-733-0828. Caribbean-style jerk chicken, curried meat and potatoes and pina coladas. L/D, $, Interac only.
- Chez Claudette. 351 Laurier E.; 514-279-5173. Breakfast-all-day/late-night greasy spoon with excellent poutine and "Michigan" burger. B/L/D, $.
- Chez Lidia. 2205 Rosemont E.; 514-723-7772. For the topless breakfast experience. B/L/D, $.
- Frites Dorée. 1212 St-Laurent; 514-866-0790. Poutine with big curds in a 1950s-era setting. B/L/D, $.
- Jardin du Cari. 21 Rue St-Viateur O.; 514-495-0565. Excellent Jamaican favourites. L/D, $.
- Le Commensal McGill. 1204 Ave. McGill-College; 514-871-1480. Excellent view of Rue Ste-Catherine. Ongoing hot, cold and dessert buffet. Pay-by-weight concept. Other locations at 1720 and 5043 Rue St-Denis, 3715 Chemin Queen-Mary. L/D, $, AX/MC/V.
- Les Courtisanes. 2533 Ste-Catherine

E.; 514-523-3170. Truly retro all-day breakfast served by nude waitresses. B/L/D, $.

- The Main St. Lawrence Steak House Delicatessen. 3684 Boul. St-Laurent; 514-843-8126. Classic Montreal deli with smoked meat, applesauce, latkes and more. B/L/D, $, AX/MC/V.
- Pizza Pita. 6415 Boul. Décarie; 514-7313-7482. Natural, kosher foods with vegan options. Homemade soups, vegetarian pizza, falafel, shawarma sandwiches and spicy french fries. L/D, $.
- Rapido. 4494 Rue St-Denis; 514-284-2188. Excellent late-night poutine and all the standards. B/L/D, $.
- Schwartz's Montreal Hebrew Delicatessen. 3895 Boul. St-Laurent; 514-842-4813. Quintessential smoked meat sandwich joint. L/D, $.
- Slovenia. 6424 Rue Clark Street; 514-279-8845; www.sloveniameats.com

Four-Star Dining

- Ariel Bar a Vins Cuisine Locale, 2072 rue Drummond; Tel. 514-282-9790
- Au Tournant de la Rivière. 5070 Rue Salaberry, Carignan, QC; 450-658-7372. Call for directions (or check the dining chapter in this guide) to find this superb restaurant, located in converted barn. D, $$$$, AX/MC/V.
- Ristorante Bice. 1504 Sherbrooke W.; 514-937-6009; www.bicemontreal.com.
- The Beaver Club, Fairmont The Queen Elizabeth Hotel. 900 Boul. René-Lévesque O.; 514-861-3511; www.fairmont.com/queenelizabeth. Elegant atmosphere with open rotisserie and specialities including prime rib of beef and rack of lamb. L/D, $$$, AX/MC/V.
- Bofinger, 5667 Rue Sherbrooke O., tel. 514-315-5056
- Brasserie Brunoise, 1012 Rue de la Montagne; Tel. 514-933-3885
- Chez La Mère Michel. 1209 Rue Guy; 514-934-0473; fax 514-939-0709; www.chezlameremichel.com. A fine restaurant of long-standing reputation. The food is expensive but reliable. Seasonal dishes include bison and caribou. L/D, $$$, AX/MC/V.
- Joe Beef, 2491 Rue Notre-Dame O., tel. 514-935-6504
- La Trattoria, 1551 Rue Notre-Dame O., tel. 514-935-5050
- L'Express, 3927 Rue St. Denis; Tel. 514-845-5333
- Le Club Chasse et Peche, 423 Rue St. Claude; Tel. 514-861-1112
- Le Mitoyen. 652 Rue de la Place Publique, Ste-Dorothée, QC; 514-689-2977. A short drive north out of Montreal brings you to this charming restaurant. Try the rack of Quebec lamb. Hot bread and sweet butter accompany each meal. D, $$$, AX/MC/V.
- Le Muscadin. 639 Notre-Dame O.; 514-842-0588; www.lemuscadin.com. Old elegance in Old Montreal. Veal, lamb, beef and sole are all exceptional, and the wine list is arguably the best in the city. L/D, $$$, AX/MC/V.
- Les Halles. 1450 Rue Crescent; 514-844-2328. A great start for those who are new to Montreal, with a trustworthy (if pricey) à la carte menu. The menu douceur at lunchtime is a bargain. L/D, $$$$, AX/MC/V.
- Med Bar & Grill. 3500 Boul. St-Laurent; 514-844-0027. Great food served with panache. Try the seared tuna or the Arctic char. The wine list suits the fare perfectly. D, $$$, AX/MC/V.
- Milos. 5357 Ave. du Parc; 514-272-3522; fax 514-272-0178. Montreal's finest Greek cuisine, with the best fish in town. L/D, $$$, AX/MC/V.
- Psarotaverna Zante, 3449 Boulevard Saint-Laurent; Tel. 514-288-4777
- Restaurant Agora, 6544 Rue Somerled; Tel. 514-227-0505
- Restaurant Cube. 355 Rue McGill; 514-876-2823; www.restaurantvauvert.com (temporary). The latest in sleek,

urban dining. Prize-winning chef prepares unique menu, including fresh halibut served with Rose Finn Apple potatoes and duck prosciutto. L/D, $$$, AX/MC/V.

- Restaurant Le Globe. 3455 Boul. St-Laurent; 514-284-3823. Snazzy bistro with designer customers and Chef David McMillan's serious, modern cooking, which makes the best of local produce. D, $$$, AX/MC/V.
- Restaurant Renoir. 1155 Sherbrooke W.; 514-285-9000; www.restaurant-renoir.com.
- Sofia. 3600 Boul. St-Laurent; 514-284-0092; www.sofiagrill.com. Eclectic cuisine and DJ grooves in a hip, uniquely Montreal dining spot. L/D, $$, MC/V.
- Toqué! 900 Place Jean-Riopelle; 514-499-2084; fax 514-499-0292; www.restaurant-toque.com. Sultry décor, market cuisine, organic vegetables. Specialties include roasted leg of Quebec lamb, rare yellowfin tuna tempura and, for dessert, hazelnut biscuit with lemon cream. D, $$$, AX/MC/V.

Quebec City

Regional Flavour

- Auberge Baker. 8790 Ave. Royale, Château-Richer, QC; 418-824-4478 or 1-866-824-4478; www.auberge-baker.qc.ca. Game dishes served in a stone-walled room with a fireplace. Brunch/L/D, $$, AX/MC/V.
- Aux Anciens Canadiens. 34 Rue St-Louis; 418-692-1627; fax 418-692-5419; www.auxancienscanadiens.qc.ca. A menu including ham simmered in maple syrup, baked beans and blueberry pie is served in this 17th-century restaurant with five themed dining rooms. L/D, $$, AX/MC/V.
- Chez Ashton. 830 Boul. Charest E.; 418-694-0891. Québécois favourites, like poutine. L/D, $, AX/MC/V.

International

- Aviatic Club. 104–450 Rue de la Gare-du-Palais; 418-522-3555.

Enjoyable French, Asian and Tex-Mex food in a classy atmosphere. L/D, $$, AX/MC/V.

- Le Carthage. 399 Rue St-Jean; 418-529-0576. North-African food, with bellydancing some evenings. D, $$, AX/MC/V.
- L'Elysée Mandarin. 65 rue d'Auteuil; 418-692-0909
- Le Tokyo. 401 Rue St-Jean; 418-522-7571. Quebec's oldest Japanese restaurant, still serving excellent food. BYOB, non-smoking, D, $$, AX/MC/V.
- Nek8arre. 575 Rue Stanislas-Kosca, Village-des-Hurons (Wendake); 418-842-4308; www.huron-wendat.qc.ca. Interesting Huron food: buffalo, caribou, deer and clay-baked fish are served with corn and lentils. D, $$, MC/V.
- Restaurant Taj Mahal. 24 Boul. René-Lévesque West; 418-523-2007
- Sala Rossa. 4848 St-Laurent; 514.844.4227; www.casadelpopolo.com/salaresto.
- Yuzu Sushi Bar. 438 Rue de l'Église; 418-521-7253. Chic, expensive and recently nominated for having the nicest restrooms in Canada.

Italian

- Au Parmesan. 38 Rue St-Louis; 418-692-0341. One of the few restaurants along the touristy stretch of Rue St-Louis that provides excellent food. Extensive wine list. L/D, $$, AX/MC/V.
- Ciccio Café. 875 Rue de Claire-Fontaine; 418-525-6161. Excellent pasta and fish. L/D, $$, AX/MC/V.
- Le Graffiti. 1191 Rue Cartier; 418-529-4949. Italian and French dishes, and a wine list with over 400 bottles. L/D, $$, AX/MC/V.
- Le Michelangelo. 3111 Rue St-Louis; 418-651-6262. An exceptional place in Quebec City for Italian food. L/D, $$$, AC/MC/V.
- Les Frères de La Côte. 1190 Rue St-Jean; 418-692-5445. A

Mediterranean restaurant specializing in wood-fired pizzas. Run by two boisterous brothers from the south of France. L/D/Brunch Sundays, $–$$, AX/MC/V.

Cafés and Bistros

- Bistro Sous le Fort. 48 Rue Sous-le-Fort; 418-694-0852. Good and plentiful dishes with market-fresh produce. Non-smoking, L/D, $, AX/MC/V.
- Café de la Terrasse. 1 Rue des Carrières; 418-691-3763. Standard continental fare and afternoon tea. L/D, $, AX/MC/V.
- Café le Sultan. 467 Saint-Jean; 418-525-9449
- Chez Temporel. 25 Couillard; 418-694-1813
- Le Billig. 526 Saint-Jean; 418-524-8341
- Café au Bonnet. 298 St-Jean; 418-647-3031
- Le Café du Monde. 84 Rue Dalhousie; 418-692-4455. Quiches, moules-frites and pâtés. Parisian brasserie atmosphere. L/D/Brunch on weekends, $, AX/MC/V.
- Le Cochon Dingue. 46 Boul. Champlain; 418-684-2013; www.cochondingue.com. The name means "crazy pig" and the bistro fare includes steak and fries, burgers and mussels. B/L/D, $, AX/MC/V.
- Les Fréres de la Cote. 1190 Saint-Jean; 418-692-5445
- Le Hobbit. 700 Rue St-Jean; 418-647-2677. Great little neighborhood café. B/L/D, $, MC/V.
- Le Moine Echanson. 585 Saint-Jean; 418-525-7832
- Le Petit Coin Latin. 8 1/2 Rue Ste-Ursule; 418-692-2022. The specialty here is Swiss raclette: cheese and meats grilled on a small portable oven. L/D, $, MC/V.
- Pub Saint-Alexandre. 1087 Rue St-Jean; 418-694-0015. Excellent British pub grub in an authentic atmosphere. Good selection of sausages, the best Guinness in town. L/D, $, AX/MC/V.

Family Fare

- L'Astral (Hôtel Loews Le Concorde). 1225 Place Montcalm; 418-647-2222 or 1-800-463-5256; www.loewshotels.com. Great view in this revolving restaurant. International cuisine and Saturday night buffets. Brunch from 10 a.m. on Sundays. L/D, $, AX/MC/V.
- Le Buffet de LÀntiquaire. 95 Saint-Paul; 418-692-2661
- La Bastille Chez Bahüaud. 47 Ave. Ste-Geneviève; 418-692-2544. Great food at tables set in tree-filled garden. L/D, $$, AX/MC/V.
- Le Parlementaire: Restaurant de l'Assemblée Nationale. 418-643-6640. The dining room of the Quebec government is decorated in Beaux-Arts splendour. Reservations are recommended, as opening hours may vary according to the schedule of National Assembly business. Regional cuisine. B/L/D, $, AX/MC/V.
- Manoir Montmorency. 2490 Ave. Royale, Beauport, QC; 418-663-2877; fax 418-663-1666; www.chutemontmorency.qc.ca. Most romantic restaurant in Quebec City area. Overlooks falls from a rambling wooden building. Brunch/L/D, $$, AX/MC/V.

Four-Star Dining

- Aspara. 71 Rue d'Auteuil; 418-694-0232. First-prize winner at the Gala de la Restauration de Québec for exotic cuisine. Chef Beng an Khuong offers the best of Vietnamese, Thai and Cambodian cooking. L/D, $$$–$$$$, AX/MC/V.
- La Closerie. 1210 Place George-V O.; 418-523-9975. First-rate cuisine and intimate dining room. L/D, $$$, AX/MC/V.
- La Tanière. 2115 Rang Ste-Ange, Ste-Foy, QC; 418-872-4386; www.restaurantlataniere.com. A game restaurant with eight-course menu progressif; caribou, ostrich, venison and rabbit are all at home here. D, $$$$, AX/MC/V.
- Laurie Raphaël. 117 Rue Dalhousie; 418-692-4555; fax 418-692-4175; www.laurieraphael.com. Delicacies

from scallops to ostrich. L/D, $$$, AX/MC/V.

- Le Café du Clocher Penché. 203 Rue St-Joseph E.; 418-640-0597. Québécois haute cuisine at affordable prices. B/L/D, $, AX/MC/V.
- Le Champlain (Château Frontenac). 1 Rue des Carrières; 418-691-3763; www.fairmont.com/frontenac. Chef Jean Soulard, the first Canadian chef to receive the Master Chef of France award, serves classic French cuisine in a lavish dining room. B/L/D, $$$, AX/MC/V.
- Le Continental. 26 Rue St-Louis; 418-694-9995. Classic menu, service and 1950s-era uptown New York setting make this long-standing restaurant one of the best in the city. Try the rack of lamb, steak tartar or Dover sole; superb wine list. L/D, $$$, AX/MC/V.
- Le Saint-Amour. 48 Rue Ste-Ursule; 418-694-0667; www.saint-amour.com. Excellent food and romantic surroundings with glassed-in terrace. L/D, $$$, AX/MC/V.
- Restaurant Initiale. 54 Saint-Pierre; 418-694-1818. www.restaurantinitiale.com
- Michelangelo. 3111 Chemin St-Louis, Ste-Foy, QC; 418-651-6262; www.restomichelangelo.com. Salmon tartar or carpaccio with basil are hits at this new, expansive restaurant with a fabulous wine list. L/D, $$$, AX/MC/V.

Top Attractions

Montreal

- Basilique Notre-Dame-de-Montréal. 110 Rue Notre-Dame O., 514-842-2925 or 1-866-842-2925; fax 514-842-8275; www.basiliquenddm.org. Most celebrated church in Canada.
- Biodôme. 4777 Ave. Pierre-de-Courbertin; 514-868-3000; fax 514-868-3065; email: biodome@ville.montreal.qc.ca; www.biodome.qc.ca. Once the site of the 1976 Olympic track-cycling races, the building has been transformed into a re-creation of four natural habitats, including a rain forest, a polar landscape and the St. Lawrence marine ecosystem. A short walk from the Insectarium and the Jardin Botanique. Open daily 9–5, summer hours 9–6.
- Biosphère. 160 Chemin Tour-de-l'Île, Parc des Îles; 514-283-5000; www.biosphere.ec.gc.ca. An eco-museum inaugurated in 1995 as the first Ecowatch Centre in Canada. June to Sept. daily 10–6. Off-season closed Tues., open Mon., Wed. to Sat. 12–5, Sun. 10–5.
- Canadian Railway Museum. 110 rue Saint-Pierre (Saint-Constant), 450-632-2410.
- Casino Montréal. 1 Ave. du Casino, Île Notre-Dame; 514-392-2746 or 1-800-665-2274. Cabaret du Casino. 514-790-1245 or 1-800-361-4595; www.casino-de-montreal.com. Open 24 hours.
- Centaur Theatre. 453 St. Francois-Xavier; Box office: 514-288-3161; Administration: 514-288-1229; www.centaurtheatre.com.
- Centre de Commerce Mondiale. 747 Victoria Square; 514-982-9888; www.centredecommercemondial.com.
- École Nationale de Théatre. 5030 St-Denis Street; Tel.: 514.842.7954 or 1.866.547.7328 (Canada and U.S.A.), www.ent-nts.qc.ca.
- Ex-Centris. 3536 St-Laurent; 514-847-3536; www.ex-centris.com.
- Grand Prix. www.grandprix.ca
- Jardin Botanique de Montréal. 4101 Rue Sherbrooke E.; 514-872-1400; www2.ville.montreal.qc.ca/jardin. 150 acres of gardens, greenhouses and an insectarium. Open year-round 9–5, summer hours 9–6, Sept. 10 to Oct. 31 9–9.
- Shed 16 Labyrinth. Located at Clock Tower Pier Entrance of the Old Port of Montreal, near Berri Street. www.labyrintheduhangar16.com
- La Ronde. 22 Chemin Macdonald, Île Ste-Hélène; 514-397-2000; email: info@laronde.com;

www.laronde.com. Amusement-park rides and live entertainment all summer.
- Les Descentes (Rafting Montreal). 514-767-2230, 1-800-324-RAFT; www.raftingmontreal.com.
- Le Grand Seminaire de Mont. 2065, rue Sherbrooke W., 514-935-1169; www.gsdm.qc.ca.
- Maison des Cultures Amerindiennes. Place Jacques-Cartier Complex 320 St. Joseph Street East, Rm 400; (toll-free) 1-800-567-9604, TTY: (toll-free) 1-866-553-0554.
- Maison du Calvet. 401 rue Saint-Paul Est , 401rue de Bonsecours,
- Montréal International. 380, Saint-Antoine Street West Suite 8000; 514-987-8191; www.montrealinternational.com.
- Montreal Science Centre. Located on King Edward Pier, in the Old Port. The Pier is essentially the extension of Saint-Laurent Boulevard, south of de la Commune Street. www.centredessciences demotreal.com; 1-877-496-4724, 514-496-4724.
- Musée Missisquoi. www.museesmonteregie.com
- Olympic Stadium. 4141 Ave. Pierre-de-Coubertin; 514-252-8687.
- Oratoire Saint-Joseph du Mont-Royal. 3800 Chemin Queen-Mary; 514-733-8211 or 1-877-672-8647; www.saint-joseph.org. Thousands make pilgrimages to this site each year.
- Ofuro Spa. 777, chemin St-Adolphe (Morin-Heights), 450-226.2442; www.spaofuro.com.
- Palais de Justice. 1 Notre-Dame Est; 514-393-2721; www.justice.gouv.qc.ca.
- Parc Safari. 850, route 202 Hemmingford; 450-247-2727; www.parcsafari.com.
- Pepsi Forum. 2313 Saint Catherine Street West.
- Polar Bear's Club. 930 des Laurentides Bvld. (Piedmont), 450-227-4616; www.polarbearsclub.ca.
- IMAX, located in the Montreal Science Centre.

Quebec City
- Anglican Cathedral of the Holy Trinity. 31 Rue des Jardins; 418-692-2193; fax 418-692-3876; www.netministries.org/see/ churches.exe/ch15988. Modelled after London's Saint-Martin-in-the-Fields, the cathedral contains precious objects donated by King George III.
- Bibliotheque Gabrielle-Roy. 350 rue St-Joseph East.
- Compagnie des Six Associes. 418-692-3033; www.sixassocies.com.
- Celtic Cross. Grosse-Ile in Quebec; www.moytura.com/grosse-ile.htm.
- Centre d'Interpretation du Vieux-Port. 100 rue St-Andre; 418-648-3300; www.parkscanada.gc.ca/vieuxport
- Centre d'Interpretation de Place-Royale. 27, rue Notre-Dame; 418-646-9072.
- Chalmers-Wesley-United Church. 78, rue Ste-Ursule; 418-692-2640 (English), 418-692-3422 (French), www.chalmerswesley.org.
- Château Frontenac. 1 Rue des Carrières; 418-692-3861; www.fairmont.com/frontenac. Historic hotel built in 1893.
- Église Notre-Dame-des-Victoires. 12 Place Royale; 418-692-1650. Oldest church in North America.
- Église Saint-Jean-Baptiste. 480, rue Saint-Jean; 418-525-7188; www.saintjeanbaptiste.org.
- Ex Machina. 109 rue Dalhousie; 418-692-5323 ,www.lacaserne.net
- Francois-Xavier Garneau. 14 Saint-Flavien; 418-692-2240.
- Grand Séminaire de Québec. 1 rue des Remparts; 418-692-0645; www.gsdq.org.
- Grand Théatre de Québec. 269, boulevard René-Lévesque Est; Administration : 418-643-8111 Billetterie : 418-643-8131 ou 1 877 643-8131 (sans frais au Québec), www.grandtheatre.qc.ca.
- Hopital General de Québec. 260 Boul. Langelier; 418-529-0931
- Hotel Dieu de Québec. 11 Cote du Palais; 418-525-4444.

- Hôtel Dieu Hospital. 9 Rue McMAHON; 418-525-4444 extension 15281; www.crhdq.ulaval.ca.
- Hôtel du Parlement. 1045 Rue des Parlementaires; 418-643-7239 or 1-866-337-8837; www.assnat.qc.ca. Built between 1877 and 1886, the parliament is used today by the provincial government.
- Maison Henry Stuart. 82 Grand Allée West; 418-647-4347.
- Monastère des Ursulines. 12 Rue Donnacona; 418-694-0143. Oldest North American teaching institution for girls, with adjacent museum.
- Morrin Centre. 44 chaussée des Écossais; 418-694-9147; www.morrin.org.
- Musée de l'Amérique Francaise. 9 Rue de la Vieille-Université; 418-528-0157; www.mcq.org.
- Musée de Civilisation. 85 Rue Dalhousie; 418-643-2158, Toll free number 1 866 710-8031 (Canada and USA), www.mcq.org.
- National Assembly of Quebec. 1045, Rue des Parlementaires; 418-643-7239 Toll-free number: 1-866 députés (337-8837), www.assnat.qc.ca.
- Parks Canada Discovery Centre. www.pc.gc.ca; 418-233-4414 (in season), 418-235-4703 (off season).
- Parc d'Artillerie de Québec. 2 Rue d'Auteuil; 418-648-4205
- Parc Montmorency. Rue Port-Dauphin.
- Parc des Champs-de-Bataille. 390 Ave. de Bernieres; 418-648-4071.
- Plaines d'Abraham. 835 Ave. Wilfrid-Laurier; 418-648-4071.
- Sociéte des Ports Nationaux. 150 Dalhousie - C.P. 2268; Tel : 418-648-3640; www.portquebec.ca.
- Price Building. 65 rue St-Anne (Upper Town).
- Basilique Notre-Dame-de-Québec. 16 Rue Buade; 418-692-2533; fax 418-692-4382. Richly decorated with gifts from Louis XIV. Oldest parish north of Mexico.
- Ghost Tours of Quebec. www.ghosttoursofquebec.com.

- Place Royale. Information Centre: 27 Rue Notre-Dame; 418-646-3167; fax 418-646-9705. Among North America's oldest districts, with 400 years of Quebec history.
- Saint Andrew`s Presbyterian Church. 106 Ste. Anne Street; 418-694-1347.
- Saint-Matthew`s Anglican Church. 755 St-Jean Street.
- The Citadel. Guided tours in numerous languages. Côte de la Citadelle; 418-694-2815; fax 418-694-2853; www.lacitadelle.qc.ca. Star-shaped fortification built by the British, also known as the Gibraltar of America and still used by the military.
- Tours Martello (Towers). 418-648-4071; www.ccbn-nbc.gc.ca.
- Université Laval. 418-656-2131 or: 1-877-7-ULAVAL (1-877-785-2825).

Festivals & Events

Montreal

January–February
- Fête des Neiges. 514-872-6120; www.fetedesneiges.com. Month-long festival of outdoor activities, including skating, slides, snow sculpture and more on Île Ste-Hélène.
- Festival Montréal en Lumière. 514-288-9955 or 1-888-447-9955; www.montrealenlumiere.com. More than a week of concerts and outdoor activities at illuminated sites downtown towards the end of February.

March
- Montreal International Children's Film Festival. 514-848-0300. Presenting the finest film productions for young audiences, this competitive festival was a huge success during its debut season. Daily screenings at the historic Imperial Theatre. www.fifem.com.

Festivals & Events

April–May
- Vues d'Afriques. 514-284-3322; www.vuesdafrique.org. A multi disciplinary festival to showcase African and Caribbean cultural activities. Held at various locations.

May–June
- Cirque du Soleil. Old Montreal. www.cirquedusoleil.com.

June
- Grand Prix Air Canada. Gilles Villeneuve Circuit, Parc des Îles; www.grandprix.ca. The only Formula One race in North America.
- Le Mondial de la Bière. 514-722-9640; fax 514-722-8467; www.festivalmondialbiere.qc.ca. Montreal's annual five-day outdoor beer festival. Held at Gare Windsor.
- Le Tour de l'Île de Montréal. 514-521-8356; email: tour@velo.qc.ca. Annual 66-kilometre urban bicycle tour.
- Montreal Beer Festival. Old Port, Montreal. www.2camels.com/montreal-beer-festival.
- Montreal Chamber Music Festival. 514-489-7711; www.festival montreal.org. Ten days of outdoor concerts on Mont Royal by international musicians. Held at the Chalet de la Montagne and other locations.
- Montreal First Peoples' Festival. 514-278-4040; www.nativelynx.qc.ca. The visual arts, including screenings of films and videos, music and dance, highlight this celebration of the region's indigenous First Nations, Amerindians and Inuit.
- Montreal Bike Fest. 514-521-8356 (Montreal area) or 1-800-567-8356; www.velo.qc.ca.

June–July
- Montreal International Fireworks Competition. 514-397-2000; email: info@lemondialsaq.com; www.montrealfeux.com. Shows on Wednesdays and Saturdays, mid-June to late July. The Jacques Cartier Bridge is closed to cars during shows and offers excellent views. Seats also available for a charge at La Ronde, Île Ste-Hélène.
- Carifiesta. 514-735-2232. Annual Caribbean parade with costumes, food, music and dance held late June/early July annually. Downtown.

June–September
- International Flora Montreal. Lock Gardens, Quays of the Old Port; 1-866-55-FLORA, 514-33-FLORA; www.floramontreal.ca.

July
- FanTasia International Festival of Fantasy and Action Cinema. email: info@fantasiafestival.com; www.fantasiafest.com. The best Asian horror, sci-fi and fantasy films. Check the Web site for screening schedules and locations.
- Festival International de Jazz de Montréal. 514-871-1881 or 1-888-515-0515; www.montrealjazzfest.com. Ten days of concerts at outdoor and indoor venues downtown. Many free events.
- Festival International Nuits d'Afrique. 514-499-9239. www.festivalnuitsdafrique.com. A celebration of African and Creole film, dance and music. Various locations.
- Just for Laughs Comedy Festival. 514-845-3155 or 1-888-244-3155; www.hahaha.com. Two weeks of more than 1,300 shows indoors and out downtown.
- Les Francofolies de Montréal. 514-876-8989 or 1-888-444-9114; www.francofolies.com. A week of music at the Place des Arts complex involving 1,000 performers from the entire contemporary-music spectrum.
- Montreal Fringe Festival. 514-849-3378; www.montrealfringe.ca. Montreal's annual theatre festival celebrates art without limits. Various locations.
- Reggae Festival. Old Port; www.montrealreggaefestival.com.

August

- Festival de la Gibelotte. 450-746-0283 or 1-877-746-0283; www.festivalgibelotte.qc.ca. Participating venues serve up a robust stew made from catfish with locally-brewed beer at a giant street festival. Downtown Sorel (90 minutes downriver from Montreal).
- Festival des Montgolfières. 450-347-9555; www.montgolfieres.com. About 150 hot-air balloons participate in the event. St-Jean-du-Richelieu (30 minutes south of Montreal).
- International Expo Art Festival. Jacques-Cartier Pier (Old Montreal), 514-651-2855
- Tennis Masters Canada. 514-790-1245 or 1-800-361-4595; www.tenniscanada.com. Canada's International Tennis Championships. The tournament, held at Uniprix Stadium, alternates bewteen the male and female pros each year.

August–September

- World Film Festival. 514-848-3883; www.ffm-montreal.org. Various theatres.

Fall

- Montreal International Festival of Cinema and New Media. 514-847-9272; email: montrealfest@fcmm.com; www.fcmm.com. Unusual films at interesting venues.

September

- Veillées du Plateau. 514-273-0880; email: info@spdtq.qc.ca. Some of Quebec's finest folk musicians and callers perform traditional country hoedowns. Held on select Saturday nights between September and April.

October

- Black & Blue Festival. 514-875-7026; www.bbcm.org. Among the world's most popular gay weekend-long parties to benefit AIDS research.
- The Holocaust Education Series. 514-345-2605; www.mhmc.ca.

Lectures, films, survivor testimonies and art exhibits.
- Festival du Nouveau Cinema. Central Ticketing Office - Ex-Centris : 3536, boul. St-Laurent, 514-844-2172 or 1-866-844-2172; www.nouveaucinema.ca.

November

- Cinemania. 514-878-0082; email: info@cinemaniafilmfestival.com; www.cinemaniafilmfestival.com. A festival of French films with English subtitles, founded by an English-speaking fan of French cinema. Musée des Beaux-Arts de Montréal.

Quebec City

January–February

- Carnaval de Québec. 418-626-3716 or 1-866-422-7628; www.carnaval.qc.ca. The century-old annual carnival is known as the Mardi Gras of the north. Indoor and outdoor activities for the two weeks before Lent. Various locations.

June–July

- Expo-Québec. 418-691-7110 or 1-888-866-3976; www.expocite.com. The province's biggest agricultural fair, with highlights including the Carrefour Agro-Alimentaire, where culinary specialties of the region are showcased. Near Colisée de Québec.

July

- Festival d'Été de Québec. 418-523-4540 or 1-888-992-5200; www.infofestival.com. Largest North-American French-language festival of performing arts and street theatre. Various venues.
- St. Anne's Feast Day. 418-827-3781. On July 26, an annual pilgrimage attracts First Nations peoples, Gypsies and many others to the shrine of Sainte-Anne-de-Beaupré for a religious ceremony and festival.

July–August

- Grands Feux Loto-Québec. 418-523-3389 or 1-888-934-3473;

www.lesgrandsfeux.com. Fireworks displays at Montmorency Falls.

August

- Fêtes de la Nouvelle France. 418-694-3311 or 1-866-391-3383; www.nouvellefrance.qc.ca. Military displays, parades and historical re-enactments, plus a 10-day crafts exhibition. Various sites.
- Plein Art. 418-694-0260; www.salonpleinart.com. An outdoor sales exhibit for crafts of all kinds. Parc de la Francophonie, rue St-Amable.
- Festival International de Musiques Militaires de Québec. 418-694-4747; www.fimmq.com. A celebration of tradition in the earliest home of military music in Canada.

August–September

- Festival International du Film de Québec. 418-523-3456; www.fifq.org. A week-long event with screenings of Canadian and foreign films.

September

- Festival des Couleurs. 418-827-4561; www.mont-sainte-anne.com. Outdoor activities and cultural events mark the beginning of the fall and winter seasons. Mont Ste-Anne.
- Festival des Journées d'Afrique. 418-640-4213; www.festivaljourneedafrique.com. Traditional and modern music showcasing emerging musicians and renowned international performers.

October

- Concours Hippique de Québec. Expo Cité grounds. 418-659-2224, x. 222; www.hippiquequebec.com. Equestrian World Cup preliminary competition.
- Festival de l'Oie des Neiges de Saint-Joachim. 418-827-5914; www.festivaldeloiedesneiges.com. This celebration of snow geese consists of watching thousands of birds fly off each morning and return each night, with activities and craft displays in between. Côte-de-Beaupré area.

Museums & Galleries

Montreal

Museums

- Banque de Montreal. 119 St-Jacques St. W. (Near St-Sulpice), 514-877-6892 , www4.bmo.com.
- Centre Canadien d'Architecture. 1920 Rue Baile; Wed. to Sun. 10–5, Thurs. 10–9 (free admission after 5:30 on Thurs.); 514-939-7026; www.cca.qc.ca.
- Centre d'Histoire de Montréal. 335 Place d'Youville; Tues. to Sun. May to Sept. 10–5; off-season Wed. to Sun. 10–5; 514-872-3207; www.ville.montreal.qc.ca/chm.
- Lieu Historique National du Commerce-de-la-Fourrure-à-Lachine. 1255 Blvd. St-Joseph; 514-637-7433 or 514-283-6054 (winter); fax 514-637-5325 or 514-496-1263 (winter); email: lachine_cfl@pc.qc.ca.
- Marguerite-Bourgeoys Museum in the Notre-Dame de Bon Secours Chapel. 400 Saint Paul St. E., 514-282-8670; www.marguerite-bourgeoys.com.
- Musée Juste Pour Rire. 2111 Boul. St-Laurent; call for hours (exhibits are seasonal and sometimes require a group reservation); 514-845-4000; www.hahaha.com.
- Centre de l'Interpretation du Canal de Lachine. Corner 7th Ave. and Boul. St-Joseph, Lachine; 514-637-7433. Permanent exhibit illustrates the main phases of the canal's construction and its history.
- Le Monde de Maurice (Rocket) Richard. 2800 Rue Viau; Tues. to Sun. 12–6; 514-872-6666.
- Maison Saint-Gabriel. 2146 Place Dublin, Pointe-Saint-Charles; closed Mon. (call for hours); 514-935-8136; www.maisonsaint-gabriel.qc.ca.
- Lieu Historique National de Maison Sir George-Étienne Cartier. 458 Rue Notre-Dame E.; seasonal, 10–12 and 1–5; 514-283-2282.

Museums & Galleries

- Musée McCord of Canadian History. 690 Rue Sherbrooke O.; Tues. to Fri. 10–6, Sat. and Sun. 10–5, Mon. in the summer months 10–5; 514-398-7100; www.mccordmuseum.qc.ca.
- Musée d'Archéologie Pointe-à-Callière. 350 Place Royale; Mon. to Fri. 10–6, Sat. to Sun. 11–6, off-season Tues. to Fri. 10–5, Sat. and Sun, 11–5; 514-872-9150; www.pacmusee.qc.ca.
- Musée d'Art Contemporain de Montréal. 185 Rue Ste-Catherine O.; Tues. to Sun. 11–5, Wed. 11–9, closed Mon.; 514-847-6226; www.macm.org.
- Musée des Beaux-Arts de Montréal. 1379–80 Rue Sherbrooke O.; Tues. to Sun. 11–6, Wed. 11–9; 514-285-1600; www.mbam.qc.ca.
- Musée du Bienheureux Frère André, Oratoire Saint-Joseph du Mont-Royal. 3800 Chemin Queen-Mary; daily May to Sept. 7–9, off-season 7–5:30; 514-733-8211.
- Musée du Château Ramezay. 280 Rue Notre-Dame E.; daily June 1 to Sept. 30 10–6, off-season Tues. to Sun. 10–4:30; 514-861-3708; www.chateauramezay.qc.ca.
- Musée de Lachine.110 Chemin LaSalle; Wed. to Sun. 11:30–4:30; (call for hours in off-season); 514-634-3471.
- Musée des Hospitalières. 201 Ave. des Pins O.; Mon. to Fri. 9–5; 514-849-2919; www.museedeshospitalieres.qc.ca.
- Musée Marc-Aurèle Fortin. 118 Rue St-Pierre; Tues. to Sun. 11–5; 514-845-6108; www.museemafortin.org
- Musée Stewart. 20 Chemin Tour-de-l'Île, Île Ste-Hélène; daily May to Oct. 10–6, off-season Wed. to Mon. 10–5; 514-861-6701; www.stewartmuseum.org.

Galleries

- Dare-Dare Gallery. 460 Rue Ste-Catherine O.; 514-874-0049.
- Dominion Gallery. 1438 Rue Sherbrooke O.; Mon. to Fri. June to Sept. 10–5, off-season Tues. to Sat. 10–5; 514-845-7471.
- Edifice Belgo. 372 Rue Ste-Catherine O.; call for hours at the following galleries (most are open Tues. to Sat.): Galerie 303, Suite 305, 514-393-3771; Galerie René Blouin, Suite 501, 514-393-9969; Galerie Trois Pointes, Suite 520, 514-866-8008; Optica, Suite 508, 514-874-1666.
- Galerie de Bellefeuille. 1367 Ave. Greene; Mon. to Sat. 10–6, Sun. 12–5:30; 514-933-4406; www.debellefeuille.com.
- Galerie Le Chariot. 446 Place Jacques-Cartier; closed Jan., open Mon. to Sat. 10–6, Sun. 10–3, off-season Mon. to Sat. 10–4, Sun. 10–3; 514-875-4994.
- Gallery VOX. 1211 Boul. St-Laurent; Tues. to Sat. 11–5; 514-390-0382; email: vox@voxphoto.com.
- La Centrale. 4296 Boul. St-Laurent; Wed. 12–6, Thurs. and Fri. 12–9, Sat. and Sun. 12–5; 514-871-0268; email: galerie@lacentral.org.
- Leonard and Bina Ellen Gallery, Concordia University. 1400 Boul. de Maisonneuve O.; Tues. to Sat. 12–6; 514-848-2424, x. 4750; www.ellengallery.concordia.ca.
- Liane and Danny Taran Gallery, Saidye Bronfman Centre for the Arts. 5170 Côte-Ste-Catherine; Mon. to Thurs. 9–7, Fri. 9–4, closed Sat., Sun. 10–5, off-season Mon. to Thurs. 9–9, Fri. 9–2, closed Sat., Sun. 10–5; 514-734-2301.
- Musée d'Art Contemporain de Montréal. 185, Sainte-Catherine West (corner Jeanne-Mance), 514-847-6226; www.macm.org.
- Place des Arts. 514-842-2112; www.pda.qc.ca.
- Quartier Éphémere, Darling Foundry. 745 Rue Ottawa; Wed. to Sun. 12–8; 514-392-1554; www.quartierephemere.org.
- Walter Klinkhoff Gallery. 1200 Rue Sherbrooke O.; Mon. to Fri. June to Aug. 9–5, off-season Mon. to Fri. 9:30–5:30, Sat. 9:30–5; 514-288-7306.
- Zeke's Gallery. 3955 Blvd. St-Laurent; 514-288-2233.

Quebec City

Museums

- Centre d'Interprétation du Vieux-Port. 100 Quai St-André; May to Oct.; 418-648-3000 (call for schedule and rates). Information about Quebec's maritime history.
- Choco-Musée Érico. 634 Rue St-Jean; Mon. to Sat. 10–6, Sun. 11–5:30; 418-524-2122; www.chocomusee.com. A chocolate factory and free museum about the origins of cocoa.
- Citadel, Royal 22nd Regiment Museum. Open daily April 10–4, May and June 9–5, July to the first weekend in Sept. 9–6, Oct. 10–3, Nov. to April 1:30 P.M. bilingual tour (groups on reservation only); 418-694-2815; www.lacitadelle.qc.ca. Fortress built by the English and still an active military post. Guided tours of interior.
- François-Xavier Garneau House. 14 Rue St-Flavien; open Sun. for tours at 1, 2, 3 and 4 P.M.; 418-692-2240.
- Hôpital Générale. 260 Boul. Langelier; 418-529-0931. With advance notice, sisters from the Augustine order, which has run the hospital for 300 years, give guided tours of the grounds and the chapel.
- Literary and Historical Society of Quebec. Morrin Centre, 44 Chaussée des Écossais; 418-694-9147. Costumed interpreters showcase the cultural contribution and present-day faces of English-speaking communities in the Quebec City region.
- Maison Chevalier. 50 Rue du Marché-Champlain; Tues. to Sun. 9:30–5 (call for hours in off-season); 418-643-2158. Changing exhibits on Quebec history and civilization.
- Musée de l'Amerique Française. 92 Côte de la Fabrique; daily late June to Sept., 10–5, off-season Tues. to Sun. 10–5, closed Mon.; 418-692-2843; www.mcq.org. Four seminary buildings contain religious artifacts, trompe l'oeil ceilings and 18th- and 19th-century objects from England, France and Quebec.
- Musée des Augustines. 32 Rue Charlevoix; Tues. to Sat. 9:30–12 and 1:30–5, Sun. 1:30–5; 418-692-2492. Located inside the Hôtel Dieu hospital, this tiny museum contains 17th-century Louis XIII furniture and medical equipment from several centuries.
- Musée Bon-Pasteur. 14 Rue Couillard; 418-694-0243 or 1-888-710-8031 (call for schedule). Once a home for unwed mothers, nuns now run a guided tour of the grounds. Groups must reserve.
- Musée de la Civilisation. 85 Rue Dalhousie; daily June 24 to Sept. 7 9:30–6:30, Tues. to Sun. Sept. to June 10–5; 418-643-2158; www.mcq.org. Designed by Moshe Safdie, the museum contains three historic buildings and offers 10 theme-oriented exhibitions.
- Musée du Fort. 10 Rue Ste-Anne; daily April to Oct. 10–5, Dec. 26 to Jan. 4 12–4, Thurs. to Sun. Feb. to Mar. 11–4, rest of year by reservation only; 418-692-1759; www.museedufort.com. Chronicles Quebec's military battles.
- Musée National des Beaux-Arts du Québec. Parc des Champs-de-Bataille; daily June 1 to Labour Day 10–6, Wed. 10–9, off-season Tues. to Sun. 10–5; 418-643-2150 or 1-866-220-2150; www.mnba.qc.ca. Three buildings showing major Quebec art from 17th-century to present.
- Musée des Ursulines. 12 Rue Donnacona; May to Sept. Tues. to Sat. 10–12 and 1–5, Sun. 1–5, off-season Tues. to Sat. 1–4:30; 418-694-0694. Treasures include a parchment signed by Louis XIII, altar cloths and porcupine-quill baskets.
- Naval Museum of Quebec. 170 Rue Dalhousie; 418-694-5387 (call for schedule); www.mnq-nmq.org.
- Québec Expérience. 8 Rue du Trésor; daily May 15 to Oct. 15 10–10, off-season daily 10–5;

418-694-4000;
www.quebecexperience.com.
Special-effects exhibition details
life in Quebec from the first
explorers onward.

Galleries

- Complexe Méduse. #582–541 Rue
de St-Vallier E.; www.meduse.org.
New architectural explorations and
gallery space in Vieux-Québec.
- Galerie d'Art du Petit-Champlain.
88 Rue du Petit-Champlain; daily
(summer) 9–10, off-season 10–5:30;
418-692-5647; www.gald.ca/gapc.
Inuit art, lithographs and a vast
selection of ducks.
- Galerie d'Art Le Portal-Artour. 53
Rue du Petit-Champlain; daily 10–6;
418-692-0354. Artists from Quebec
and abroad.
- Galerie Linda Verge. 1049 Ave. des
Érables; Wed. to Fri. 11:30–5:30,
Sat. and Sun. 1–5; 418-525-8393;
www.galerielindaverge.ca.
Contemporary art.
- Galerie Madeleine Lacerte. 1 Côte
Dinan; Mon. to Fri. 9–5, Sat. and
Sun. 1–5; 418-692-1566;
www.galerielacerte.com.
Contemporary art.
- L'Héritage Contemporain. 634
Grande Allée E.; daily June to Sept.
11:30–10, Mon. to Fri. Oct. to May
11:30–5:30, Sat. and Sun. 12–5;
418-523-7337. Works of great
Canadian painters.
- Studio d'Art Georgette Pihay. 53
Rue du Petit-Champlain; daily June
24 to Sept. 30 10–9, off-season 9–5;
418-692-0297;
www.studiopihay.com. The late
painter-sculptor's workshop, with
permanent exhibitions.

Nature & Natural History

- Biodôme. (see listing p. 191)
- Biosphère. (see listing p. 191)
- Jardin Botanique de Montréal.(see
listing p. 191)
- Montreal Insectarium. Located on
Jardin Botanique grounds, 4581 Rue
Sherbrooke E.; daily year-round

9–5, summer 9–6, Sept. 10 to Oct.
31 9–9; 514-872-1400;
www.ville.montreal.qc.ca/
insectarium. Butterfly house and
other exhibits. Annual bug-eating
festival.
- Redpath Museum of Natural
History. 859 Rue Sherbrooke O.;
year-round Mon. to Fri. 9–5, Sun.
1–5, closed Fri. during summer
months; 514-398-4086;
www.mcgill.ca/redpath. Free
admission to one of Canada's oldest
museums.

Night Life

Montreal

This list will help guide you through
Montreal after dark. Refer to the Night
Life section for more details. For up-
to-date listings, consult the most recent
edition of *The Mirror* or *Hour* weekly
newspapers. Or try the French weekly,
Voir. All are available free of charge at
many bars, shops and restaurants
throughout Montreal.

- Aria. 1280 Rue St-Denis; 514-987-
6712. Weekend after-hours with
top DJs.
- Ballatu. 4372 Boul. St-Laurent; 514-
845-5447. World music, mainly
from Africa and the Caribbean.
- Barfly. 4062a bd. St-Laurent; 514-
284-6665
- Bifteck. 3702 Boul. St-Laurent;
514-844-6211. A raucous bar with
free popcorn.
- Bily Kun. 354 Mont-Royal east;
514-845 5392; www.bilykun.com.
- Blizzarts. 3956A Boul. St-Laurent;
514-843-4860. Sit in a booth, check
out the art, listen to electronic beats.
- Blue Dog. 3958 Boul. St-Laurent;
514-848-7006. Dark, loud, raw, this
bar attracts a younger crowd.
- Bourbon Complex. 1474 Rue Ste-
Catherine E.; 514-529-6969. Houses
favourite gay hangouts Le
Drugstore, Club Mississippi, La
Track and Bar Cajun and late-night
restaurant Club Sandwich.
- Brutopia. 1219 Rue Crescent; 514-
393-9277.

Nightlife

- B-Side. 3616,St.Laurent; 514-844-8883.
- Buonanotte. 3518 St. Laurent; 514-848-0644; www.buonanotte.com.
- Charlie's American Pub. 1204 Rue Bishop; 514-871-1709. Kick back and listen to some American Pie tunes.
- Chez Mado. 10181 Boul. Pie-IX; 514-325-0940. Best drag-show cabaret in town.
- Circus Afterhours. 915 St-Catherine Est; 514-844-0188.
- Club 1234. 1234 de la Montagne; 514-395-1111; www.1234montreal.com.
- Club 737. 1 Place Ville Marie; 514-397-0737.
- Club Soda. 1225 St-Laurent; 514-286-1010; www.clubsoda.ca.
- Club Tokyo. 3709 Saint-Laurent.
- Dominion Pub. 1243 Rue Metcalfe; 514-878-6354.
- Edgar Hypertaverne. 1562 Ave. du Mont-Royal E.; 514-521-4661. Many different beers and an excellent cheese platter.
- Frappé. 3900 Boul. St-Laurent; 514-289-9462. Known for its happy hour, its terrace and pool tables.
- Go-Go Lounge. 3682 Boul. St-Laurent; 514-286-0882. Psychedelic colours, kitschy-cool décor and over 25 different martinis.
- Grumpy's. 1242 Rue Bishop; 514-866-9010.
- Hard Rock Café. 1458 Rue Crescent; 514-987-1420. Rub elbows with the regulars and some surprise superstars while enjoying drinks, food and rock 'n' roll.
- House of Jazz (formerly Biddles). 2060 Rue Aylmer; 514-842-8656. A great place for live jazz and light eats.
- Hotel de la Montagne. 1430, Rue de la Montagne; 514-288-5656; www.hoteldelamontagne.com.
- Hurley's Irish Pub. 1225 Rue Crescent; 514-861-4111; www.hurleysirishpub.com. Celtic ambience with rowdy bar upstairs and mellow sitting room downstairs. Live music is almost always Irish.
- Jillian's. 2313 Ste-Catherine W., 514-228-3030; www.jillians.com.
- Laika. 4040 Boulevard St-Laurent; 514-842-8088; www.laikamontreal.com.
- L'Escogriffe. 4467A Rue St-Denis; 514-842-7244. Live shows some nights.
- Le Monkey. 1599 St-Denis; 514-285-1087.
- Le Parking. 1296 Rue Amherst; 514-282-1199. Popular gay dance club.
- Le Pistol. 3723 Boul. St-Laurent; 514-847-2222. Drinks, tasty salads and unusual sandwiches.
- Le Reservoir. 9 Duluth East; 514-849-7779.
- McKibbin's Irish Pub. 1426 Rue Bishop; 514-288-1580. Cozy traditional pub on three levels.
- McLean's. 1210 Peel; 514-392-7770; www.bar-resto.com/mclean.
- MED Bar & Grill. 3500 St. Laurent; 514-844-0027; www.medgrill.com. Millennium. 7500 Viau; 514-721-4949. Massive after-hours dance club. www.milmtl.com.
- Montréal Pool Room. 1200 Bvld. Saint-Laurent; 514-396-0460
- Newtown. 1476 Crescent; 514-284-6555; www.newtown.ca.
- O'Reagan's. 1224 Rue Bishop; 514-866-8464. Pub with frequent live music.
- Peel Pub. 1107 Rue Ste-Catherine O.; 514-844-6769; www.peelpub.com. A landmark drinking and eating hangout for regulars and college crowds with cheap beer and food. Open until midnight.
- Pub St. James. 3237 Boul. Des Sources; 514-683-4444; 380 St. Jacques. 514-849-6978. www.pubstjames.com.
- Shed Café. 3515 St. Laurent; 514-842-0220.
- Sir Winston Churchill Pub (Winnie's). 1459 Rue Crescent; 514-288-0623. Be seen on the terrace of this bar and dance hall.
- Sky Pub. 1474 Ste Catherine E; 514-529-6969.
- Stereo. 858 Rue Ste-Catherine E.; 514-286-0325. After-hours club with

amazing sound system. www.stereo-nightclub.com.

- St-Sulpice. 1680 Rue St-Denis; 514-844-9458. Huge old house with bars from the basement to the upstairs library. Large outdoor terrace in summer.
- Thursday's. 1449 Rue Crescent; 514-288-5656. Neighbourhood restaurant and bar with dancing.
- The Main Bar and Terrace.
- Time Café. 3509 Saint-Laurent; 514-842-2626.
- Tribe Hyperclub. 400 St. Jacques; 514-845-3066.
- Unity II. 1171, Ste-Catherine E., 514-523-2777.
- Vocalz Cafe. 7310 Maurice Duplessis 514-543-1566. Popular karaoke bar.
- Quai des Brûmes. 4481 Rue St-Denis; 514-499-0467. Bar often features live music.

Quebec City

For concerts, movies, theatre and nightlife, check local newspapers, especially the weekly Chronicle-Telegraph, an English-language paper which is available free of charge at tourist bureaus.

Shopping

Montreal

Antiques

- Antiques Hubert. 3680 Boul. St-Laurent; 514-288-3804. Vintage variety.
- Galerie Tansu. 1130 Boul. de Maisonneuve O.; 514-846-1039. This museum-like shop sells Japanese antiques and furniture. www.galerietansu.com.
- Grand Central. 2448 Rue Notre-Dame O.; 514-935-1467. Various antiques.
- Le Village des Antiquaries. 1708 Rue Notre-Dame O.; 514-931-5121. Several dealers under one roof.
- Milord. 1870 Rue Notre-Dame O., showroom at 1434 Rue Sherbrooke O.; 514-933-2433; www.milordantiques.com. Elegant European furniture and mirrors.
- Salvation Army. 1620 Rue Notre-Dame O.; 514-935-7425. Check out "As Is" section in thrift shop.
- Spazio. 8405 Boul. St-Laurent; 514-384-4343. Timeless collection of architectural antiques. www.Spazio.ca/fr/boutique.

Art

- Born-Neo Art Gallery. 404 Rue St-Sulpice; 514-840-1135. African carvings and textiles.
- Boutique du Musée des Beaux-Arts. 1390 Rue Sherbrooke O.; 514-285-1600. Shop reflects current exhibitions and offers posters, art books and more.
- Galerie Claude Lafitte. 2162 Rue Crescent; 514-842-1270; www.lafitte.com. Paintings by Canadian, European and American masters.
- Galerie d'Art Yves Laroche. 4 Rue St-Paul E.; 514-393-1999; www.yveslaroche.com. Canvasses and prints of established artists.
- Galerie Elena Lee Verre. 1460 Rue Sherbrooke O., Suite A; 514-844-6009; www.galerieelenalee.com. Unique glass art pieces.
- Galerie le Chariot. 446 Place Jacques-Cartier; 514-875-4994; www.galerielechariot.com. Gift shop sells Inuit art pieces.
- Galerie Laroche. 4 St-Paul east; 514-393-1999.
- Galerie Parchemine. 40 Rue St-Paul O.; 514-845-3368. Canvasses and prints for sale.
- Galerie Walter Klinkhoff. 1200 Rue Sherbrooke O.; 514-288-7306; www.klinkhoff.com. Work by established artists.

Books

- Anthologies Café Books. 1420 Rue Stanley; 514-287-9929. Specializes in art books and used books.
- Bibliomania. 460 Rue Ste-Catherine O.; 514-933-8156. Known for books, antiques and collectibles.
- Bibliophile. 5519 Chemin Queen-Mary; 514-486-7369. Specializes in Judaica.

Shopping - Montreal

- Chapters. 1171 Rue Ste-Catherine O.; 514-849-8825. Four floors, discount section and a Starbucks coffee counter.
- Cheap Thrills. 2044 Metcalfe; 514-844-8988; www.cheapthrills.ca. Good selection of used books.
- Diocesan Book Room. 625 Rue Ste-Catherine O. (Promenades de la Cathédrale); 514-843-9387 or 1-877-387-9387.Christian books and theology.
- Ethnic Origins Bookstore. 3173A Rue St-Jacques; 514-938-1188. Specializing in African and African-American culture.
- Ex Libris. 2159 Rue MacKay; 514-284-0350. Good selection of second-hand and out-of-print books.
- Indigo Books. 1500 Ave. McGill-College (Place Montreal Trust); 514-281-5549. Variety of books, cards, paper items and stationery. Chapters.indigobooks.ca.
- Nicholas Hoare. 1366 Ave. Greene, 514-933-4201; 1307 Rue Ste-Catherine O. (Ogilvy); 514-499-2005. Extensive selection.
- Paragraphe Books. 2220 Ave. McGill-College; 514-845-5811; www.paragraphbooks.com. Near McGill University, the shop contains a wide selection of titles plus a Second Cup coffee shop.
- Ulysses Bookstore. 560 Rue Président-Kennedy, 514-843-7222; 4176 Rue St-Denis, 514-843-9447. Travel and guide books and maps.
- Vortex Books. 1855 Rue Ste-Catherine O.; 514-935-7869. Specializes in literary works.
- Renaud-Bray. 5117 Parc Ave; 514-276-7651; 6925 Taschereau blvd; 450-443-5350; 7077, Newman blvd; 514-365-2587; 3050 Portland blvd; 819-569-9957; 1 Complexe Desjardins; 514-288-4844. www.renaud-bray.com.
- S.W. Welch. 3878 Boul. St-Laurent; 514-848-9358. Excellent selection of used books.
- Westcott Books. 2065 Rue Ste-Catherine O.; 514-846-4037. Shelves filled with second-hand books.
- The Word. 469 Rue Milton; 514-845-5640. A used-book haven in the McGill University ghetto.

Cameras

- Camtec Photo (Place Victoria Cameras). 495 Rue McGill; 514-842-4818; www.camtecphoto.com. Equipment, film supplies, repairs and processing.
- Image Point. 1344 Rue Ste-Catherine O.; 514-874-0824; www.imagepoint.ca. Photo and video equipment and repairs.
- Simon Cameras. 11 Rue St-Antoine O.; 514-861-5401. New and used equipment and film supplies.

Cigars

- La Casa del Habano. 1434 Rue Sherbrooke O.; 514-849-0037. Handles importation of Cuban cigars.
- Cigars Vasco. 1327 Rue Ste-Catherine O.; 514-284-0475. Vast array of cigars.

Clothing

- Addition-Elle and A/E Sport. 724 Rue Ste-Catherine O.; 514-954-0087. Fashions for women wearing size 14-plus.
- Banana Republic. 777 Sainte-Catherine Street West; 514-842-3509
- BCBG. 960 Rue Ste-Catherine O.; 514-868-9561. Also at 1300 Rue Ste-Catherine O., 514-398-9130. On top of the latest fashions.
- BEDO. 359 Rue Ste-Catherine O., 514-842-7839; 1256 Rue Ste-Catherine O., 514-866-4962; 3706 Boul. St-Laurent, 514-987-9940; 4903 Boul. St-Laurent, 514-287-9204; 4228 Rue St-Denis, 514-847-0323. Chain carries reasonably-priced basics and funkier pieces.
- Boutique Médiévale Excalibor. 4400 Rue St-Denis, 514-843-9993; 122 Rue St-Paul E., 514-393-7260. Exclusive handcrafted medieval-style clothing, jewellery, chain mail, gargoyles and banners.
- Bovet Complexe Desjardins. 150

Ste-Catherine O. 514-281-1611. Suits and sweaters for men of all sizes.

- Caban. 777 Rue Ste-Catherine O.; 514-844-9300. From pyjamas to party dresses, this store isn't just about housewares.
- Cache Cache. 1051 Rue Laurier O.; 514-273-9700. April Cornell's long, flower-print casual dresses, matching mother-child outfits (mainly dresses for girls aged 2–6), linens, accessories and housewares.
- City Styles. 1186 Rue Ste-Catherine O., 2nd floor; 514-499-9114. Urban styles by Sean John, Zoo York, Akademic, Lacoste, Timberland, G-Unit, Reebok and others.
- Club Monaco. 1455 Rue Peel; 514-499-0959. Canadian-owned company. Trendy professional and casual clothing for men and women.
- Concerto Pour Elle. 1216 Ave. Greene; 514-933-8817. Fashions and accessories for women.
- Cours Mont-Royal. 1455 Rue Peel. Many boutiques, including Space FB, DKNY, Face London, Giorgio Emporio, Harry Rosen, 3 Monkeys, American Apparel, Arithmetik.
- Diakoumakos. 415 Rue Mayor; 514-842-4846. Stylish fur coats.
- Eaton Centre. 705, Ste-Catherine West   514-288-3710; www.centreeaton.shopping.ca.
- Eva B. 2013 St-Laurent, 514-849-8246. Costume shop: 1604 St-Laurent. (Make an appointment first.)
- Fidel. 4340 Rue St-Denis, 514-845-6555. Stylish Montreal-based clothing line for men and women.
- FLY. 1970 Rue Ste-Catherine O.; 514-846-6888. A wide selection of urban attire from established labels and up-and-coming local designers.
- Fourreurs Maîtres. 401 Rue Mayor; 514-845-6838. Fur fashions.
- Friperie St-Laurent. 3976 Boul. St-Laurent; 514-842-3893. Cool clothes, new and used.
- Gap. 1255 Rue Ste-Catherine O.;

514-985-5311. Staples for a preppy wardrobe.
- Garnitures Dressmaker. 2186 Ste-Catherine W., 514-935-7421
- Grand'Heur. 4131 St-Denis; 514-284-5747. For women above 5'8".
- Guess. 1229A Rue Ste-Catherine O.; 514-499-9464. Chain selling jeans, casual wear and professional styles.
- Henri-Henri. 189 Rue Ste-Catherine E.; 514-288-0109. One of the best hat shops in town. From Borsalinos to berets, it attracts stars like Donald Sutherland and Charlie Sheen. www.HenriHenri.ca
- IMA. 24 Rue Prince-Arthur; 514-844-0303. High style from David Bitton, creator of Buffalo clothing line.
- InWear/Matinique. 1230 Rue Ste-Catherine W.; 514-866-1998. Casual and professional fashions for men and women.
- Jacob. 1220 Rue Ste-Catherine O.; 514-861-9346. Reasonably priced casual and professional fashions. Jacob.ca.
- Je L'ai. 159 Duluth Av. E; 514-284-5393; www.newearth.ca.
- Jeunes d'ici. 600 Rue Peel; 514-983-5864. Fashionable clothes for children.
- Le Château. 1310 Rue Ste-Catherine O. and other locations; 514-866-2481. Reasonably priced stylish clothes for youth and adults.
- Les Ailes de la Mode. 677 Ste-Catherine W., 514-282-4537; www.lesailes.com.
- Lululemon. 1394 Ave. Greene; 514-937-5151; 1232, Ste. Catherine st. West; 514-394-0770. Stylish Vancouver-based yoga clothing line for an active, stress-free life. www.Lululemon.com.
- Mango. 1000 Ste Catherine West; 514-397-2323.
- Mexx. 1125 Rue Ste-Catherine O.; 514-288-6399. Chain store with casual wear and professional styles.
- Montréal Fripe. 371 Ave du Mont-Royal E.; 514-842-7801. An enticing array of vintage and pre-worn clothing.

- MO851. 3981 Boul St-Laurent suite 444; 514-842-1221; www.m0851.com.
- Nevik. 240 St. Jacques West; 514-289-9449; www.nevik.com.
- Off the Hook. 1021A Rue Ste-Catherine O.; 514-499-1021. Hip hop–influenced urban fashion.
- Oink Oink. 1343 Greene Ave.; 514-939-2634; www.oinkoink.com. Cool newborn and children's clothes and some pricey designer wear, plus piles of games, toys and gadgets in this kid-friendly shop.
- Olam. 4339 Rue St-Denis; 514-282-9994. Stylish, colourful women's fashion.
- Old River. 705 Ste-Catherine W. 514-798-0520. Men's casual and formal wear.
- Parasuco. 1414 Rue Crescent; 514-284-2288. Centre for jeans.
- Pierre, Jean, Jacques. 158 Rue Laurier O.; 514-270-8392. Men's fashions.
- Promenades de la Cathédrale. 625 Ste-Catherine West; 514-845-8230.
- Puma. 2315 Rue Cohen; 514-339-2575, 514-738-9474.
- Requin Chagrin. 4430 Rue St-Denis; 514-286-4321. A renowned Montreal frippery full of vintage fashion finds.
- Roots. 1035 Rue Ste-Catherine O.; 514-845-7559. Sporty clothes, caps and jackets.
- Rudsak. 1400 Rue Ste-Catherine O.; 514-399-9925; www.rudsak.com. Beautiful soft-leather jackets and handbags in unexpected colours.
- Scarpa. 4901 Rue Sherbrooke Ouest; 514-484-0440; 4257 Rue Saint-Denis; 514-282-6363; 5133 Avenue Du Parc; 514-277-4529
- Scarlett. 254 Ave. du Mont-Royal E.; 514-844-9435; www.boutiquescarlett.com. Features daring clothing lines for men and women.
- Screaming Eagle. 1424 Boul. St-Laurent; 514-849-2843. Leather world.
- Soho Mtl. 3715 Boul. St-Laurent; 514-843-8201. Stylish clothing and shoes for the office or bar. Men's and women's styles.

- Space FB. 3632 Boul. St-Laurent, 514-282-1991; Les Cours Mont-Royal, 1455 Rue Peel, 514-848-6494. Simple staples and more in jersey, wool and cotton by hip Montreal based label.
- Tristan & America. 1001 Rue Ste-Catherine O.; 514-289-9609. Chain store with casual and formal clothes for men and women.
- U&I (Women) 3650 Blvd. St-Laurent; (Men) 3652 Boul. St-Laurent; 514-844-8788. Unique designs and upscale style.
- Urban Outfitters. 1250 Rue Ste-Catherine O.; 514-874-0063. Trendy urban wear.
- Zara. 1500 Ave. McGill College; 514-281-2001; 1200 Ave. McGill College; 514-868-1516; 2305 Chemin Rockland; 514-904-0771.

Surplus Stores
- Surplus International. 1431 Boul. St-Laurent; 514-499-9920. Cargo pants emporium.
- Army Surplus Canam. 1423 Boul. St-Laurent; 514-842-3465. Stylish surplus clothes.

Collectibles
- Antiques Lucie Favreau. 1904 Rue Notre–Dame O.; 514-989-5117. Like a visit to a sports hall of fame.
- Pause Retro. 2054 Rue St-Denis; 514-848-0333. Old toys, memorabilia and sports cards specialty.
- Retro-ville. 2652 Rue Notre-Dame O.; 514-939-2007. Coca-Cola items, old magazines, toys and neon signs.

Department Stores
- The Bay. 585 Rue Ste-Catherine O.; 514-281-4422. Fashions and more for the whole family.
- Holt Renfrew. 1300 Rue Sherbrooke O.; 514-842-5111. Top-of-the-line fashions for men and women.
- Ogilvy. 1307 Rue Ste-Catherine O.; 514-842-7711. Upscale women's fashions, fine jewellery, perfume, books.
- Simons. 977 Rue Ste-Catherine O.; 514-282-1840. Trendy women's

fashions and clothing for the whole family.

Electronics

- Alma Eléctronique. 1595 Boul. St-Laurent; 514-847-0366. Be prepared to haggle.
- Audiotronic. 368 Rue Ste-Catherine O. and 1622 Boul. St-Laurent; 514-861-5451. Decent prices on home items and camera equipment.
- Eléctronique Multi-Systèmes. 1593 Boul. St-Laurent; 514-845-0059. Reasonable prices, open to haggling.
- Future Shop. 460 Rue Ste-Catherine O.; 514-393-2600; www.futureshop.ca (check for other locations). Low-priced computer equipment, home electronics and CDs.

Games & Toys

- FrancJeu. 4152 Rue St-Denis; 514-849-9253. Educational toys and games for kids of all ages.
- La Grande Ourse. 129 Ave Duluth E.; 514-847-1207. Beautiful handmade wooden toys and games.
- Valet d'Coeur. 4408 Rue St-Denis; 514-499-9970. Gadgets and toys to stimulate creative exploration.
- Oink Oink. (see listing p. 204)

Housewares

- Atmosphère. 4349 Rue St-Denis; 514-527-1293. Furniture and art pieces.
- Caban. (see listing p. 197)
- Collage Tapis. 1480 Rue Sherbrooke O.; 514-933-3400. Imported Persian carpets.
- Côté Sud. 4338 Rue St-Denis; 514-289-9443. www.cotesud.ca Beautiful accents for bed, bath and beyond.
- Indiport Tapis Orientaux. 100 Rue St-Paul E.; 514-871-1664. Persian carpets.
- Morphée. 4394 Rue St-Denis; 514-282-0744; www.mmorphee.com. Striking furniture and domestic accessories.
- Senteurs de Provence. 4077 Rue St-Denis, 514-845-6867; 1061 Rue Laurier O., 514-276-7474. Blue-and-yellow-printed fabrics, scents and soaps.

Jewellery

- AmberLux. 625 Rue Ste-Catherine O. (Promenades de la Cathédrale); 514-844-1357. Amber set in pieces of all shapes and sizes.
- Bijouterie Elégant. 460 Rue Ste-Catherine O.; 514-876-3791. Gold objects and jewellery.
- Bijouterie Eliko. 698 Rue Ste-Catherine O.; 514-871-8528. Specializes in watches: Rolex, Swiss Army, Swatch, Tag Heuer and more.
- Bijoux Marsan. 462 Rue Ste-Catherine O.; 514-395-6007. Primarily gold.
- Birks. 1240 Square Phillips; 514-397-2511. Wide variety of fine-quality jewellery, silverware and china.

Music

- Archambault. 5005 Rue Ste-Catherine E.; 514-849-6201; 677 Rue Ste-Catherine O. (Complexe Les Ailes), 514-875-5975; www.archambault.ca. Large selection of CDs, sheet music and songbooks.
- Godin. www.godinguitars.com
- HMV. 1020 Rue Ste-Catherine O.; 514-875-0765. A three-floor megastore with thousands of CDs and DVDs.
- Inbeat. 3814 Boulevard Saint Laurent; 514-499-2063.
- Le Pop Shop. 3656 Boul. St-Laurent; 514 848-6300. New and used CDs and vinyl.
- Primitive. 3830 Rue St-Denis; 514-845-6017. Wide selection of used CDs and vinyl.

Shoes

- Boutique Courir. 4452 Rue St-Denis; 514-499-9600. An impressive selection of shoes and clothing for runners and lovers of the outdoors.
- Browns. 1191 Rue Ste-Catherine O.; 514-987-1206. Brand-name footwear for all occasions.

- La Godasse. 3686 Boul. St-Laurent, 514-286-8900; 4340 Rue St-Denis, 514-843-0909. An impressive selection of stylish, hard-to-find sneakers.
- Marie Modes. 469 Rue Ste-Catherine O.; 514-845-0497. Cowboy-boot specialists.
- Mona Moore. 1446 Rue Sherbrooke O.; 514-842-0662. Ultra-hip boutique with designer shoes for women.
- Sena. 4200 Rue St-Denis; 514-849-7243. Ecco, Birkenstock and other brands.
- Tony Shoe Shop. 1346 Ave. Greene; 514-935-2993. Stocks latest styles plus hard-to-find sizes and bargain annex.
- UN Iceland. 1378 Rue Ste-Catherine O.; 514-876-7877. A wide selection of footwear fashions.

Odds & Ends

- Au Papier Japonais. 24 Ave. Fairmount O.; 514-276-6863. Beautiful handmade paper and a delightful array of paper products, cards and gifts.
- Bell Centre Canadiens Boutique. 1260 Rue de la Gauchetière O. (Bell Centre); 514-989-2836. Jerseys, books, photos sold exclusively for the Habs.
- Boutique Médiévale Excalibor. (see listing p. 197)
- La Capoterie. 2061 Rue St-Denis; 514-845-0027. Condoms in 21 flavours and other gag gifts.
- Dix Milles Villages. 4182 Rue St-Denis; 514-848-0538. Fair-trade handcrafted goods from around the world.
- Dressmaker Garnitures Ltée. 2186 Rue Ste-Catherine O.; 514-935-7421. Open since the 1950s, this shop has an endless array of beads, feathers and ribbons.
- L'Echoppe du Dragon Rouge. 3804 Rue St-Denis; 514-840-9030. Medieval outfits, swords, jewellery and household items.
- Essence du Papier. 4160 Rue St-Denis; 514-288-9152; www.essencedupapier.com. Stationery, journals and writing implements.
- Espace Pepin. 350 St.-Paul West; 514-844-0114; www.pepinart.com.
- Grand Central. 2448 Rue Notre-Dame O.; 514-935-1467. Antiques.
- Jet-Setter. 66 Rue Laurier O.; 514-271-5058. Luggage plus loads of travel gadgets.
- Kamikaze Curiosités. 4156 Rue St-Denis; 514-848-0728. This store sells scarves, socks and accessories by day, but by night the space is transformed into a bar.
- Marché Almizan. 1695 Boul. de Maisonneuve O.; 514-938-4142. Sells imported spices and such Middle-Eastern specialties as fig marmalade and halvah.
- Mediaphile. 1901 Rue Ste-Catherine O.; 514-939-3676. Hundreds of magazines on display, with order forms for 10,000 more, plus top-notch inexpensive cigars from Cuba and Jamaica.
- Mélange Magique. 1928 Rue Ste-Catherine O.; 514-938-1458. New-Age and Pagan books, tarot decks and other items.
- Montreal Museum of Archaeology and History Pointe-à-Callière. 350 Place Royale; 514-872-9150. Stocks unique reproductions, jewellery, pottery and toys.
- Mortimer Snodgrass. 457 Victoria, St-Lambert and at 209 St-Paul West in Old Montreal; www.shop.mortimersnodgrass.com.
- Rubans, Boutons. 4818 Rue St-Denis; 514-847-3535. A store dedicated to ribbons and buttons.
- Tilley Endurables. 1050 Rue Laurier O.; 514-272-7791. Travel wear, well-known for hats.
- Noel Eternal. 461 St-Sulpice; 514-285-4944.

Environmental

- La Maison Verte. 5785 Sherbrooke west (corner Melrose), 514-489-8000; www.cooplamaisonverte.com.

Quebec City

Antiques

- Antiquités du Matelot. 137 Rue St-Paul; 418-694-9585. Specialties include engravings, old Canadian and Quebec prints and white ironstone.
- Décenie. 117 Rue St-Paul; 418-694-0403. Reupholstered vinyl furniture from the 1960s.
- Gérard Bourguet Antiquaire. 97 Rue St-Paul; 418-694-0896. Known for 18th- and 19th-century pine furniture.

Art

- Canadeau. 1124 Rue St-Jean; 418-692-4850. Reupholstered vinyl furniture and other finds from the 1960s.
- Lambert & Co. 1 Rue des Carrières; 418-694-0048. Features regional arts and crafts.
- Rue du Trésor, an open-air market near Notre-Dame Basilica showcasing locally produced prints and paintings. www.ruedutresor.qc.ca
- Sculpteur Flamand. 49 Rue du Petit-Champlain; 418-692-2813. Wood carvings.

Books

- Librairie du Nouveau Monde. 103 Rue St-Pierre; 418-694-9475. Features books by Quebec authors and publishers.
- Librairie Historia. 155 Rue St-Joseph E.; 418-525-9712. Volumes of used books.
- Librairie Pantoute. 1100 Rue St-Jean; 418-694-9748. Selection of English-language guidebooks for the region.

Clothing

- Autrefois Saïgon. 55 Boul. René-Lévesque; 418-649-1227. Quebec-made women's clothing with an Eastern touch.
- Bibi & Co. 42 Rue Garneau; 418-694-0045. Hats galore.
- Boutique Paris Cartier. 1180 Ave. Cartier; 418-529-6083. Fine women's fashions.
- La Corriveau. 24 Côte de la Fabrique; 418-694-0048. Handmade sweaters and moccasins.
- Laliberté. 595 Rue St-Joseph; 418-525-4841. Workshop and store famous for furs.
- Lambert & Co. 1 Rue des Carrières; 418-694-2151. Colourful wool socks.
- Logo Sport. 1047 Rue St-Jean; 418-692-1351. Sports gear.
- Magasin Latulippe. 637 Rue St-Vallier O.; 418-529-0024. Large selection of work wear and outdoor wear, including great warm hats.
- Mountain Equipment Co-op. 405 St-Joseph E.; 418-522-8884. The ultimate destination for outerwear and camping gear.
- Oclan. (Women) 52 Boul. Champlain; (Men) 67 1/2 Rue du Petit-Champlain; 418-692-1214; www.oclan.net. Designer clothes from Quebec and beyond.
- Peau sur Peau. 70 Boul. Champlain; 418-692-5132. Specializing in leather.
- Simons. 20 Côte de la Fabrique; 418-692-3630. Small branch of department store known for its own brand of men's and women's clothing, especially sweaters and hats.
- La Soierie Huo. 91 Rue du Petit-Champlain; 418-692-5920. Hand-painted silk scarves.
- X20. 200 Rue St-Joseph E.; 418-529-0174. Funky line of streetwear.

Jewellery

- Pierres Vives Joaillerie. 23 1/2 Rue du Petit-Champlain; 418-692-5566. specializing in exquisite cut gems and cultivated pearls, works of Quebec designers and more.
- Zimmermann. 46 Côte de la Fabrique; 418-692-2672. High-end jewellery.

Odds & Ends

- Baltazar Objets Urban. 461 Rue St-Joseph E.; 418-524-1991. Hip decorative objects.

Architecture

- Boutique Médiévale Excalibor. 1055 Rue St-Jean; 418-692-5959. Medieval madness.
- Comptoir Emmaus. 915 Rue St-Vallier E.; 418-692-0385. Thrift shop heaven! Four floors of second-hand clothes, books, furniture and housewares.
- Copiste du Faubourg. 545 Rue St-Jean; 418-525-5377. Handmade paper specialists.
- J.A. Moisan. 699 Rue St-Jean; 418-522-0685. Oldest grocery store in North America; stocks large selection of fine foods.
- J.E. Giguère. 59 & 61 Rue de Buade; 418-692-2296. Quebec-made pipes, Cuban cigars and other tobacco products.
- Mall Centre-Ville. Rue St-Joseph. Billed as the world's longest covered street, with dollar stores, bargain shops and restaurants.
- Maison de Thé Cammeilla Sinensis. 351 Emery (Opposite the Cinema Quartier Latin), 514-286-4002
- Paradis des Étampes Petra Werner. 603 Rue St-Jean; 418-523-6922. Huge choice of rubber stamps.
- Royaume de la Tarte. 402 Ave. des Oblats; 418-522-7605. Baked goods and decorated cupcakes.

Shopping Centres

- Halles le Petit Cartier. 1191 Ave. Cartier; 418-522-0201. A mini-mall of interest to gourmets.
- Place Québec. 900 Boul. René-Lévesque E.; 418-529-0551. Rather dreary, but useful, with post office, 40 stores and restaurants.
- Ailes de la Mode. 2450 Laurier, Ste-Foy; 418-652-4537 or 1-888-242-4537. This fashion plaza offers shuttle service to downtown hotels.
- Food & Flea Market. 936 Rue Roland Beaudin, Ste-Foy. Lively outdoor food and flea market.
- Galeries de la Capitale. 5401 Boul. des Galeries; 418-627-5800; www.galeriesdelacapitale.com. Enormous roller coaster in indoor playground amidst dozens of shops.
- Marché Vieux-Port. 160 Saint-André Quai; 418-692-2517.
- Place Laurier. 2700 Boul. Laurier, Ste-Foy; 418-651-5000; www.placelaurier.com. More than 350 stores under one roof is worth the trip.
- Place Ste-Foy. 2452 Boul. Laurier, Ste-Foy; 418-653-4184. Features 130 boutiques, including department stores such as Simons.
- Quartier du Petit-Champlain. 61, rue du Petit-Champlain; 418-692-2613; www.quartierpetitchamplain.com.
- Transparence. 61 Rue du Petit-Champlain; Tel. : 418-694-0669.

Toys

- Boutique L'Echelle. 1039 Rue Garneau; 418-694-9133. Jam-packed with toys of all kinds.
- Benjo. 543 Saint-Joseph Est; 418-640-0001.
- Club Jouet. 150–1100 Rue Bouvier; 418-624-9451. Popular and educational toys.

Architecture

Montreal

- Seminaire de Saint-Sulpice. 116 Notre-Dame West.
- Maison du Calvet. 401 Saint-Paul east, Old Montreal.
- Banque du Montreal. 119 St-Jacques St. W. (Near St-Sulpice); 514 877 6892. http://www4.bmo.com/
- Royal Victoria Hospital. 687 Pine Avenue West; 514-934-1934; www.muhc.ca.
- St. George's Church. 1101 Stanley Street. 514 866-7113.www.st-georges.org.
- St-Patrick's Basilica. 454 René Lévesque Blvd. West; 514-866-7379 Fax: 514-954-1218; www.stpatricksmtl.ca.
- Christ Church Cathedral. 1444 Union Avenue. 514-843-6577, 514-843-6577 (ext.371); www.montreal.anglican.org/cathedral.
- Cathedrale Marie-Reine-du-Monde. 1085 rue de la Cathédrale; 514-866-1661;

www.cathedralecatholiquedemontre
al.org.
- Église de la Visitation de la
Bienheureuse Vierge Marie. 1847
Blvd. Gouin Est; 514-388-4050.
- New York Life Insurance Co.
- Sunlife building. 1155, Metcalfe
street; 514-393-8820;
www.edificesunlife.ca.

- Place Ville Marie.
www.placevillemarie.com.
- Westmount Square. Westmount, QC;
514-932-0211.
- Dawson College. 3040 Sherbrooke
W., 514-931-8731;
www.dawsoncollege.qc.ca.

Photo Credits

T = top; C = centre; B = bottom.

Introduction
Théodore Lagloire: 12B, 13T, 15,16T; Julia Levine: 16B; Tourisme
Montréal 12T, 17, 18; Anne Whiteside: 1, 11T,13B, 14.

Montreal
Photographs by Phil Carpenter, except for those listed below.
Adam Korzekwa: 29T; Alain Chagnon: 91B; Alain LaForest: 41B; Anne Whiteside:
33B, 43B, 48B, 57, 63T, 75, 82T, 85, 88T, 91, 96, 89, 100B, 101, 102B, 105, 106B;
Anneclaire Le Royer: 27; Anton's Photo Express: 95B; Association Touristique des
Laurentides: 111, 115T; Beaver Club: 80T; Biosphère: 55; Caroline Hayeur: 47T;
Centre d'histoire de Montréal: 38; Château Ramezay Museum: 28T, 37; Cöpilia:
46B; Corporation de la Vieux-Port de Montréal/A.P.E.S.: 93B, 94B; Costin.ca: 11B,
18; Dan Moore: 17B, 22T; Daniel Dupuis: 97T; Dennis Farley: 88B, 90B; Festival
International de Jazz de Montréal/Caroline Guertin: 69T, 70T; Fort Chambly
National Historic Site: 112; Garth Gilker: 76B; Jardin Botanique de Montréal: 25T,
52, Jean-François Leblanc: 69B; Julia Levine: 73B, 77, 78T, 79T, 80B; Julie
d'Amour Léger: 49B, La Maison Simons: 58; Le Tour de l'Île de Montréal: Robert
Laberge: 72; Les Amis de la Montagne: 20B; Les Caprices de Nicholas: 78B&C;
Les Francofolies de Montréal: 71; Maison dul Calvet: 28B; Mathieu Thouvenin:
108C&B; Michel Tremblay: 25B, 26, 51, 53; Milos Restaurant: 79B; Montréal
Insectarium: 54; Mont-Tremblant Resort: 114, 116T&C; Musée d'Archéologie
Pointe-à-Callière: 36B; Musée des Beaux-Arts: 43, 44, 45; Musée McCord: 35, 36T;
Musée Missisquoi: 118B; Musée Stewart: 23B, 40C&B; Normand Rajotte: 39; Parc
des Îles de Montréal/Bernard Brault: 22B; Parks Canada: 113; Peter Spiro: 24B;
Pierre Pouliot: 115B; Place des Arts: 46T; René Limoges: 54C&B; Richard Bryant:
41T; Richard-Max Tremblay: 47C; Ritz Carlton Hotel: 108T; Robert Burley: 42T;
Roderick Chen: 92T; Sean O'Neill 50, 51T; Sebastien Cote: 20T; Seventy Nine
Images: 99T; Shelley MacDonald: 43C, 47B, 59C&B, 60, 61, 62T&C, 64B, 65,
67C&B, 82C, 83, 84T, 104B; Société des casinos du Québec Inc.: 23T; Srg666: 66;
Stéphane Poulin: 32T&B, 34, 73T, 86T, 87T&C, 89B; Tamara Scullion: 24T;
Timothy Hursley: 43T; Tony Tremblay: 19, 86B, Vladone: 10, 56; Tourisme
Cantons-de-l'Est: 117T&B, Peter Quine: 118T; Tourisme Montréal 17T, 21,
70C,71T, 94T, 95T.

Quebec City
Photographs by Théodore Lagloire, except those listed below.
Carnaval de Québec Kellogg's: 132; Patrick Donovan: 129T; ExpoCité: 133; Festival
d'été de Québec: 134B; Fondation Bagatelle: 163B; Laurie Raphaël: 140T; Mont
Sainte-Anne: Jean Sylvain: 167B, 168B; Musée de la Civilisation: 152C; Office du
tourisme et des congrès de la Communauté urbaine de Québec: 165B; François
Tremblay: 131, 134T; Alain Vinet: 119; Yuzu Sushi Bar: 139T, 142T.

Maps by Andrew Cameron and Peggy McCalla.

Index

Index

Index

212

Index

Index

Index